UNIVERSITY OF CALIFORNIA, SAN DIEGO

"They'd Sing and They'd Tell:"

Native American Song Cycles and Creation Stories in Southern California

A dissertation submitted in partial satisfaction of the
requirements for the degree of Doctor of Philosophy

in

Music

by

Steven Joel Elster

Committee in charge:

Professor Jane Stevens, Chair
Professor Jerry Balzano
Professor John Fonville
Professor Ross Frank
Professor Leanne Hinton
Professor John Koegel

2010

The Dissertation of Steven Joel Elster is approved, and it is acceptable

in quality and form for publication on microfilm and electronically:

Chair

University of California, San Diego

2010

iii

TABLE OF CONTENTS

LIST OF FIGURES

LIST OF ABBREVIATIONS

ESCR   Extended Southern California Region

Handbook   Alfred Louis Kroeber. *Handbook of the Indians of California*. Bureau of American Ethnology at the Smithsonian Institution. Bulletin 78 (Washington, D.C.: Government Printing Office, 1925; reprinted by New York: Dover Publications, Inc., 1976).

Listening   Don Laylander. *Listening to the Raven: The Southern California Ethnography of Constance Goddard DuBois*. Archives of California Prehistory no. 51 (Salinas, California: Coyote Press, 2004).

MHE   Alfred Louis Kroeber. *A Mohave Historical Epic*. Anthropological Records 11, no. 2 (Berkeley, California: University of California Press, 1951).

MIMS   Constance DuBois. "Mission Indian Myth and Song." DuBois Papers, Folder 27.

MMM   Alfred Louis Kroeber. *More Mohave Myths*. Anthropological Records 27 (Berkeley, California: University of California Press, 1972).

MOD   Constance DuBois. "The Mythology of the Diegueños." *Journal of American Folklore* 14 (1901): 181-5; reprinted in Laylander, *Listening*, p. 38-40.

SMM   Alfred Louis Kroeber. *Seven Mohave Myths*. Anthropological Records 11, no. 1 (Berkeley, California: University of California Press, 1948).

SOC   Constance DuBois. "The Story of Chaup: A Myth of the Diegueños." *Journal of American Folklore* 17 (1904): 217-42; reprinted in Laylander, *Listening*, p. 66-78.

Spirit Mountain   Leanne Hinton and Lucille Watahomigie, eds. *Spirit Mountain: An Anthology of Yuman Story and Song* (Tucson: University of Arizona Press, 1984).

YMM   Francis Densmore. *Yuman and Yaqui Music*. Smithsonian

Institution Bureau of American Ethnology 110 (Washington, D.C.: Government Printing Office, 1932).

YMS   George Herzog. "The Yuman Musical Style." *Journal of American Folklore* 41, no. 160 (1928): 183-231.

ACKNOWLEDGEMENTS

Many people helped me as I worked to complete this dissertation. I would like to thank Jane Stevens whose keen perceptions proved a balm as I gradually developed more and more understanding of the music and culture of the tribes of southern California. Ross Frank helped me to develop a broader understanding of the problems that have arisen when scholars have written about the history of a tribe or tribes. John Fonville, Gerald Balzano, and John Koegel provided me with invaluable assistance and support as I have worked on this and other projects. I am not a linguist. I want to thank Leanne Hinton for her insights into the interplay between music and words. Amy Miller's knowledge of Yuman languages made it possible for me to have at least an initial understanding of Kumeyaay, Quechan, and Mohave, and the way that these languages are used in songs. My friend Margaret Langdon provided similar support. Any errors of interpretation that I have made are, of course, mine alone.

A special debt of gratitude is due to the many tribal members who have supported my work. I will not attempt to mention the names of everyone. I do, however, want to thank Harry Paul Cuero, Jr. for his guidance, encouragement, and friendship. I also want to thank Wiley Elliot, Leroy Elliot, Mike Morales, Steve Benegas, and John Christman, and Sara Russell, Ione Dock's daughter.

Finally I would also like to thank my mother, Ernestine Elster; my wife, Esther; and my two children, Phillip and Rebecca!

VITA

1973	Bachelor of Arts, University of California, Los Angeles
1977	Master of Arts, California School of Professional Psychology, Los Angeles
1989	Master of Arts, University of California, San Diego
1989- 1995	Teaching Assistant, Department of Music, University of California, Los Angeles.
2010	Doctor of Philosophy, University of California, San Diego

PUBLICATION

"A Harmonic and Serial Analysis of Ben Johnston's String Quartet No. 6." *Perspectives of New Music* 29, no. 2 (Summer, 1991): 138-165.

Cynthia Schmidt and Steven Elster, editors. "The Guitar in Africa: The 1950s-1990s." The World of Music. Journal of the International Institute for Traditional Music 36, no. 2, 1994.

FIELDS OF STUDY

MAJOR FIELD: MUSIC

Studies in the Guitar during the Baroque
Professor Jane Stevens

Studies in Native American History
Professor Ross Frank

Studies in Microtonality
Professor John Fonville

Studies in Classical Guitar
Pepe Romero

ABSTRACT OF THE DISSERTATION

"They'd Sing and They'd Tell":

Native American Song Cycles and Creation Stories in Southern California

by

Steven Joel Elster

Doctor of Philosophy in Music

University of California, San Diego, 2010

Professor Jane Stevens, Chair

This study addresses music-making throughout a relatively large geographical region, one that extends beyond Southern California to include part of Northern Baja California in Mexico and also a portion of Arizona, an area designated here as the Extended Southern California Region (ESCR). Throughout the ESCR, singers from the various tribes perform "song cycles." A night-long performance of a song cycle generally involves the singing of a series of some 200 to 300 individual songs. In ESCR music, the melody of each song, its words, the rhythm of the percussion instruments used (most commonly hand-held gourd rattles), and the dance steps are closely integrated. The songs in a song cycle are divided into sets, each consisting of two or more songs.

During the first half of the 20th-century, a number of scholars, including Constance DuBois, Francis Densmore, Alfred Kroeber, Duncan Strong, and Ruth Underhill, studied the culture of one or more tribes. In the process, many of these researchers created transcriptions of songs and/or of the creation stories of a particular

tribe. With their transcriptions of creation stories, most scholars sought to create a record

of the narrative of each story, but they did not focus on the related question of

documenting how each singer-storyteller told his story. However, a survey of a selection

of these creation story-texts, taken from different parts of the region in question, shows

that they contain a number of clues regarding how they may have been told. Many

creation-story texts are divided into episodes, most of which are associated with a set of

songs. A rendition of some creation stories may have involved both

singing and telling, that is, spoken narration; furthermore, creation stories and song

cycles may be similar both in the manner of their performance and in their overall

structure.

INTRODUCTION

The study of the music of the tribes of Southern California and neighboring areas presents a number of challenges, one of which has to do with reconciling the traditions of the present with those of the past. On one hand, musical performance is alive and well today throughout the entire region. Most reservations have both young people who are eager to learn more about their culture and experienced tribal members who are willing to teach what they know. Throughout the year, master singers, along with anyone who is learning their songs, come together at inter-tribal gatherings, to sing and dance. On such occasions, singers perform song cycles, each of which consists of an extended sequence of songs. A performance of a song cycle may last for an entire night, usually ending sometime in the early morning. While each song cycle appears to be associated with a story, singers generally do not pause to speak about the meaning of the songs as they perform.

But hardships that the tribes of Southern California have faced over the last century and longer have taken a toll on each tribe. Many ceremonies and songs have been lost or set aside. The songs that performers sing today represent but a small portion of those of the past; nevertheless, at least some information concerning the past can be recovered by examining the publications and fieldnotes produced by scholars who studied these tribes during the first half of the twentieth century. These scholars generally spoke with elders whose knowledge of their respective tribal cultures was extensive. As part of the interview process, many of these scholars asked a singer or a storyteller to tell his or her tribe's creation story. Scholars wrote these stories down as they listened. In doing so, these scholars focused on recording the stories, but not on

1

documenting *how* or *when* or *for whom* these stories were told, despite the fact that they were speaking with singer/storytellers who apparently not only knew a creation story but also how the story was traditionally told. Still, each creation story text appears to contain bits and pieces of information concerning how it may have been narrated. While the data is fragmentary, it appears that singer/storytellers throughout Southern California may have employed a similar approach when narrating a creation story. And singing seems to have been an integral part of the narration of many creation stories.

There is a difference, however, between the kinds of information that can easily be known about the present day and about the past. It is, for example, not difficult to observe singers today. However, singers generally do not stop to discuss the meaning of their songs. In contrast, stories can be found in the creation-story texts that scholars have collected; but our knowledge of how these stories were told and whether they included songs is limited. The following study will attempt to bridge the gap between the past and the present, by focusing on the clues that are contained in a selection of creation story texts recorded between 1900 and World War II. When the clues are considered, a picture begins to emerge. It appears that singers from throughout the region approached the narration of creation stories in a similar manner, at least in certain respects. Ultimately any discussion of this music, past and present, must take into account the fact that the lives of tribal members and their communities were thrown into disarray upon the arrival of Europeans and Euro-Americans. Therefore, before discussing the music, I will consider some of the problems that the tribes of Southern California have faced.

Physical Hardships

Over the past five hundred years, the tribes of Southern California have faced a variety of hardships related to the arrival of Europeans and then later Euro-Americans. For these tribes, the first of these hardships may not have resulted from any direct or sustained contact with Europeans and Euro-Americans; rather, as Europeans and Euro-Americans began to travel to and settle in the Americas, they brought with them diseases. Once introduced, these diseases spread across the country, from community to community, but Native Americans lacked immunity to many of these diseases.[1] Some scholars have argued that many tribal members and their communities did not suffer, because they were located in relatively unpopulated areas. Others, such as historian Robert Jackson, have suggested that the spread of these epidemics was devastating. In a single epidemic, some tribes may have lost as many as one-third of their population. Jackson also argues that such epidemics led to a significant reduction in the population of the Native Americans in California long before Europeans or Euro-Americans began to arrive.

Once Europeans and Euro-Americans began to arrive, tribal members faced many other hardships. One had to do with how the land was managed. As they began to take control of the land, Europeans and Euro-Americans began to use the land management techniques that they were familiar with, while also suppressing some of the practices of local California tribes. For example, Native Americans utilized fire as a tool for maintaining the health and viability of a number of plants. When Native Americans were

---

[1] Robert Jackson, *Indian Population Decline: The Mission of Northwestern New Spain, 1687-1840* (Albuquerque: University of New Mexico Press, 1993), p. 3.

prevented from using fire as a land management technique, a number of changes began to

take place in the biome of California. Once-vast swaths of indigenous bunchgrasses

apparently shrank as tribal members lost the right to burn these fields as needed.[2] Fires

prevented debris or plants from accumulating and growing under oak trees, thereby

keeping these trees healthy. In turn, this ensured a steady supply of acorns, an important

food source.[3] While data concerning the songs that the tribes of Southern California sang

or the ceremonies they conducted as they managed their lands is limited; it is not hard to

imagine that the loss of traditional food supplies coupled with the loss of each tribe's

right to manage its lands had a significant impact.[4]

 As contact between the tribes of California and Europeans began to intensify, the

---

[2] Kat Anderson, "Burning for Increased Seed and Grain Production," in *Tending the Wild: Native American Knowledge and the Management of California's Natural Resources* (Berkeley: University of California Press, 2005), p. 262 ff. The introduction of certain domesticated animals probably had a profound impact on the biome of California. For a discussion that touches on how the introduction of cattle may have led to changes in at least one area, namely Owens Valley, California, see Robert Bettinger's discussion in "In the Shadow of White Mountain," DVD (UCSD-TV, 2004). For more information about this video, see: http://www.ucsd.tv/whitemountain/ (accessed on March 6, 2008.) Also see Bettinger's "Native Land Use: Archaeology and Anthropology," *Natural History of the White-Inyo Range: Eastern California,* Clarence A. Hall, Jr., ed. (Berkeley, The Regents of the University of California, 1991), p. 463-487. For an online version, see: http://content.cdlib.org/xtf/view?docId=ft3t1nb2 pn&chunk. id=d0e32991&toc.depth=1 &toc.id=d0e32991&brand=eschol (accessed on March 6, 2008.)

[3] See, for instance, "Managing Oak Stands with Fire" and "Ecological Effects of Burning Under Oaks," in Kat Anderson, *Tending the Wild*, p. 287-290. Also regarding the management of oaks, see Anderson, "An Ecological Critique" in *Forgotten Fires: Native Americans and the Transient Wilderness.* Henry T. Lewis and Kat Anderson, eds. (Norman: University of Oklahoma Press, 2002), p. 56.

[4] Deprived of their usual food sources, some tribal communities may have faced starvation. See Anderson's *Taming the Wild*. On the other hand, some (or many) tribes may have been able to take advantage of the food sources that Europeans or Euro-Americans began to cultivate. Bettinger suggests that this was the case for the Owens Valley Paiute. (Personal communication with Robert Bettinger, March 6, 2008.)

impact of contagious diseases grew more deadly. Starting in 1769 and continuing through 1823, Franciscan missionaries founded a chain of twenty-one missions in California. As each new mission was erected, the Native Americans who lived nearby joined (or were coerced or forced to join) that mission. Unfortunately, as tribal members moved into these missions; they found themselves living in close quarters, where contagious diseases spread quickly.[5]

While there is some evidence that the influence and impact of the Franciscan missionaries may have been limited to those tribes living near each mission, the changes that would occur as the U.S. government began to develop and then implement its policies with respect to Native Americans touched every tribal community, in every corner of the country. Such was the case as the government, beginning at the end of the nineteenth century, began to force Native American children to attend Indian boarding schools, where they were discouraged, sometimes by actual punishment, from remembering and/or celebrating their respective tribal cultures.[6] Artist and architect

---

[5] Jackson, *Indian Population Decline*, p. 134. Also see Robert H. Jackson's and Edward Castillo's *Indians, Franciscan, and Spanish Colonization: The Impact of the Mission System on California Indians* (Albuquerque: University of New Mexico Press, 1995).
[6] Many tribal members have discussed this subject with me, sometimes speaking about how they or members of their families were sent to Indian schools, both in California and in neighboring states.

Edward Davis wrote about in his journals.[7] Originally from the east coast, Davis moved

to San Diego in the 1880's, before settling in rural Mesa Grande, where he lived in close

proximity to the nearby Mesa Grande Band of Mission Indians.[8] In 1904, Davis wrote

that Native American youth were being sent to government-run Indian boarding schools

and that once there, they suffered from homesickness, tuberculosis, and other diseases.

> A high, a fearfully high percentage of the Indian youths sent away, carried away,
> and forced away from home, to be educated, are condemned to death just as
> surely as capital punishment has been pronounced from the bench. Some perhaps
> go with the seeds of consumption dormant in their systems but many more
> seemed to be taken down with the dread disease from no other apparent cause
> than homesickness. Intense homesickness, an unnatural way of living,
> unaccustomed food, too much indoor life, too much clothing and possibly too
> tight lacing may be inducing causes, but whatever it is, the facts speak for
> themselves. On the other hand, children attending the day schools, at home and
> where they can be with her parents, live on natural foods and ruffage [sic] and are
> generally seldom sick with consumption.[9]

At this same time, the tribes of Southern California were encountering still

another factor that eroded the viability of their tribal communities. In order to find work,

---

[7] Davis was also a photographer and he took numerous photographs of the Native
Americans from Southern California. The Edward Harvey Davis Papers, at the San
Diego Historical Society, contains a collection with a number of Davis's journals
including his handwritten notes and his drawings. For a brief biographical sketch of
Davis, see https://www.sandiegohistory.org/ bio/davised/davis.htm (Accessed on
February 29, 2008.) As part of its collection, the Society has articles concerning Davis's
career. See, for instance, Charles Quinn's *Edward H. Davis and the Indians of the
Southwest United States and Northwest Mexico: A Harvest of Photographs, Sketches, and
Unpublished Manuscripts of the Indefatigable Collector of Artifacts of These Border
Indians* (Downey, Calif: E. Quinn, 1965). Both the National Museum of the American
Indian and Huntington Free Library hold materials collected by Davis. Davis also
published articles, concerning the cultures of the tribes of southern California. Two of
these include: *The Diegueño Ceremony of the Death Images.* (New York: Museum of the
American Indian, Heye Foundation, 1919); and "Early Cremation Ceremonies of the
Luiseño and Diegueño Indians of Southern California," *Indian Notes and Monographs*, 7,
no. 3. (New York: Museum of the American Indian, Heye Foundation, 1921).
[8] Mesa Grande is located sixty miles northeast of the city of San Diego.
[9] Edward Harvey Davis Papers.

many adults were forced to leave their villages.[10] This, combined with the fact that many children were being sent to boarding schools, meant that the pool of young men and women who could accept leadership positions grew smaller each year. Ultimately, these changes and many others meant that the number of ceremonies that each tribe continued to perform was reduced with the passing of each year.

Survival

Despite this cultural loss, tribal members throughout the ESCR and beyond have preserved and passed on key aspects of their cultures, and they continue to do so today.[11] Knowledge of the song cycles is held and maintained by interested tribal members. Each experienced singer knows one or more song cycles, each of which consists of an extended sequence of some two to three hundred songs. Each song is relatively brief, perhaps three to five minutes in duration. (There is no fixed duration for a song.) Today, many performers sing a song cycle known as "*Bird*," and performers who sing "*Bird*" are often referred to as "*Bird* singers" here. Thus, someone might say that a particular performer is a *Bird singer* or that he sings *Bird.* Most singers are male. As each singer performs, he holds in one hand a single seed-filled gourd, the most commonly used percussion instrument. As he shakes this gourd, he generates a rhythmic accompaniment,

---

[10] Paul Apodaca discusses this subject in his dissertation on the Cahuilla and their music. See his "Tradition, Myth, and Performance of Cahuilla Bird Songs" (PhD diss., University of California, Los Angeles, 1999).

[11] Two scholars who have written about the continuity of the culture of the tribes of Southern California include: Paul Apodaca (see footnote 10). Ernest Siva, who is part Cahuilla and Serrano and who is both a tribal historian and a musician, has written about how he has reinstituted the playing of traditional songs on the flute. See his *Voices of the Flute: Songs of Three Southern California Indian Nations* (Banning, California: Ushkana Press, 2004).

sometimes referred to as "throwing gourd." As an experienced singer throws his gourd,

he is able to generate a variety of rhythmic patterns, which though they appear to be

straightforward are often highly complex.

A master singer[12] will sometimes perform alone; but more often other singers

will "help" him. Frequently a master singer and his helpers will sing together for years.

As a result, helpers are often mature, seasoned singers who are thoroughly familiar with a

master singer's song cycle. The lead singer's voice is always the loudest. Singing in

unison, the helpers' voices, however, are always softer, and they make every attempt to

blend their voices with that of the leader's. Their voices carefully conform to the timbre

and the dynamic of the lead singer's voice. In addition, the helpers throw their gourds in

synchrony with the leader's, not only matching his rhythmic patterns but also the physical

movements that he makes with his arm and wrist and hand as he throws his gourd.

Young men and/or boys will often ally themselves with a master singer, in order to study

and learn his song cycle or cycles. Although no set time may be specified, such

apprentices will often study with a master singer for several years or more. Today,

almost every tribe also has a group of girls and/or women who dance or who are learning

to dance. Wearing the appropriate regalia (usually ribbon blouses and camp skirts), they

accompany a singer by dancing. The singers generally stand side-by-side in a straight

line, all facing in one direction. There may be twenty or more singers in a line, or

perhaps as few as two or three. The dancers also stand side-by-side, but facing the

singers, whom they generally outnumber. Based on the size of the room or space,

dancers facing a given singer (and his helpers) often arrange themselves in parallel rows.

---

[12] For the sake of clarity, I will be referring to a lead sing as a master singer.

Because a performance may last all night, singers generally have chairs to rest on.

Without apparent effort, experienced singers and dancers are able to follow a master singer as he shifts from a straightforward duple pattern used in one song to the triple pattern used in another, or to the more complex "fancy steps" that are used in other songs. During a performance, the helper singers and dancers are able to stay with the master singer because of the extra-musical cues that he provides to the members of his musical team, with his voice, gourd, and non-verbal gestures. It is with these cues that the master singer indicates when the other singers should join him, when everyone should start to dance, or when the dancing should end. Generally, the dancing stops after the group has completed each song. In the company of his helpers and his less experienced students together with a group of dancers, a master singer will also travel to and perform at a variety of ceremonial events, often ones sponsored by neighboring tribes. At these events, it is not unusual to hear two or more master singers (each, perhaps, from a different tribe) performing simultaneously, each master singer accompanied by his helpers, a group of younger singer/students, and a group of dancers. Thus, the activities of singing and dancing often occur in an inter-tribal setting.

Today singers sometimes perform a portion of their song cycles at secular events such as at schools, and on the radio. More common are performances at the powwows held each year by reservations throughout the region. At a powwow, space is set aside so that powwow dancers and drummers can drum, sing, and dance. In addition, a separate area is set aside where singers and dancers gather to sing and dance to their song cycles.

Other tribal members simultaneously play the guessing game known as *"peon."*[13]
Singers also sing at night-long funerals. A catholic priest or deacon may conduct a
morning mass, but the singers and the dancers perform all night, providing support for all
of those who are expressing their grief.

The social and economic turmoil that tribal members have faced for more than a
century has presented each singer with a set of challenges, all the more so since many
ceremonies and song cycles appear to have been lost. From what I have discovered, the
typical singer of today usually begins his career with an incomplete knowledge of a song
cycle or cycles. In order to remedy this situation, each singer must in effect become an
historian. At inter-tribal gatherings, novice singers have the opportunity to speak with
more experienced singers, from whom they are able to gather information about the song
cycles that they are interested in. And a singer may hear songs at inter-tribal events that
he has not heard before.

Ethical Concerns

Master singers, along with their helpers, experienced students, and other
knowledgeable tribal members, appear to know the meaning of their song cycles and their
songs; but this seems to be part of the information that they generally prefer to share only
with each other or with students who may have decided to dedicate themselves to the
singing of one or more song cycles. Anyone else must respect the fact that singers will
likely not want to share or discuss the meaning of their songs or song cycles, at least not

---

[13] For a discussion of the game of *peon*, see Ralph Michelsen "Peon: A North American
Indian Game of Strategy" (PhD diss., University of California, Irvine, 1981). Also see
Apodaca, *Tradition*, p. 249-253.

in any detail. For this reason, I will not be providing a detailed exegesis of any creation story; and, in the following chapters, I provide translations for only a handful of songs.

My Experience

As a field, the study of the Native American music of southern California is still young. As one of the few people who have had the opportunity to research this music, I recognize that the experiences that I have had as I watched singers perform constitute an invaluable source of information. My introduction to this field of study came by way of introductions and the support that I received from other scholars who themselves had been working with the tribes of Southern California for many years. Eventually, I met and began to work with a small network of singers. My first introduction came from the late Florence Shipek, an anthropologist who began to work with local tribes in the 1950's.[14] She had interviewed Kumeyaay elders, and they had allowed her to record some of their songs, but with a wish in mind. They hoped that Shipek might someday return their songs to a younger group of dedicated, spiritual tribal leaders and singers. With this in mind, she introduced me to two Kumeyaay singers, Leroy Elliot, from Manzanita, and the late Tony Pinto, from Cuyapaipe. I met with Leroy Elliot and Tony Pinto and they promptly invited me to attend a funeral, where I would have the opportunity to hear them and other singers perform their song cycles. This was the start of my fieldwork, with a small group of tribal members from throughout southern

---

[14] See among other works by Shipek, *Pushed into the Rocks: Southern California Indian Land Tenure, 1769-1986* (Lincoln: University of Nebraska Press, 1988); and Delfina Cuero and Florence Shipek's *Delfina Cuero: Her Autobiography, an Account of Her Last Years, and Her Ethnobotanic Contributions* (Menlo Park, California: Ballena Press, 1991).

California. At a funeral, often two or more master singers arrive, and sometime before midnight, each singer begins to perform his song cycle. Each master singer is generally accompanied by a helper singer or singers, often very experienced singers in their own right. Each master singer sings a different song cycle. The performance of these song cycles is concurrent. The juxtaposition of the different song cycles produces a wall of sound that provides succor for those who are singing and dancing but also grieving.

My own introduction to the music of these tribes began in 1993. I discovered that musicians would attend the powwows that take place in the fall. As I attended more and more of these tribal gatherings, I realized these events were almost always attended by members of different tribes. At the Jamul Indian Village, in east San Diego County, I had the privilege of meeting and spending time with the late Mary Sanchez, an outstanding singer. Sanchez explained to me that her network of family members extended into Baja California. At Jamul, I also had the privilege of meeting with the late Helen Cuero, who had a keen appreciation for her culture. As a child, she and her sister would dance as their uncle sang *Lightning.* Cuero's network of family members also extended into Baja California as well as to the east, to include Campo. It was through hours of speaking with Mary Sanchez and Helen Cuero, as well as other singers, that I gradually became acquainted with their music and that of other singers. Other singers were supportive of my work and studies as well. I had the opportunity to spend time with the late Cahuilla singer Anthony Andreas. I have also had the privilege of hearing the music of and to become friends with singer Harry Paul Cuero, Jr. (not directly related to Helen Cuero), of Campo.

Organization of the Study

The music and the associated styles of performance that I discuss come from a relatively large geographical region that I refer to as the Extended Southern California Region (ESCR). After defining this region, Chapter 1 presents an initial introduction to ESCR music and music-making. Today musical performance typically centers around the performance of a song cycle, that is, the successive singing of some 200 to 300 individual songs. While scholars working in the first half of the twentieth century wrote down a number of ESCR creation stories, little is known about how these stories were told. Chapter 2 provides an introduction to the transcription of ESCR songs and creation stories. Chapter 3 examines a selection of creation-story texts taken from different parts of the ESCR. It appears, finally, that song cycles and creation stories appear to bear a number of commonalities, both in the manner of their performance and in their overall structure.

CHAPTER 1

MUSIC AND MUSIC-MAKING

The "Extended Southern California Region"

Native American singers approach the making of music in similar ways throughout the region that I call the Extended Southern California Region (ESCR), which includes tribes that are located within the southern part of Southern California;[1] the northern part of Baja California in Mexico;[2] and the area along the Colorado River roughly at the boundaries of California, Nevada, and Arizona, extending from there to the Gulf Of California. Map 1 in Figure 1.A-i shows the extent of the Extended Southern California Region.[3]

---

[1] The area extending south and east from the Oceanside/San Juan Capistrano to the California border.

[2] By Northern Baja, I mean the area extending from the U.S. border to a point just south of Cabo San Quintin, in Baja California, Mexico; this is approximately 100 miles south of Ensenada. For the location of Ensenada and of San Quintin, see Map 2.

[3] Except where noted, all figures were made by Steven Elster.

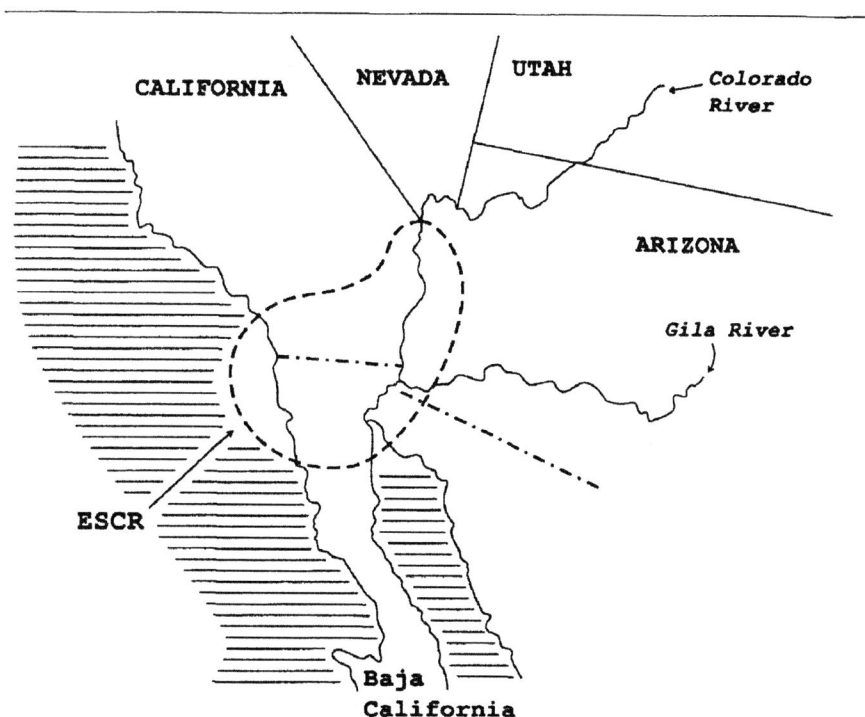

Figure 1.A-i. Map 1: The Extended Southern California Region (ESCR).

The approximately fifty tribes and tribal communities that inhabit this area all speak one of two language families: Yuman or Uto-Aztecan, which are completely unrelated. Despite these differences in language, Yuman- and Uto-Aztecan-speaking tribes in this area have similar types of music, and the way that they go about making music is similar. Map 2 (Figure 1.A-ii) provides a more precise outline of the ESCR, and also shows the extent of Uto-Aztecan and Yuman languages within the ESCR.

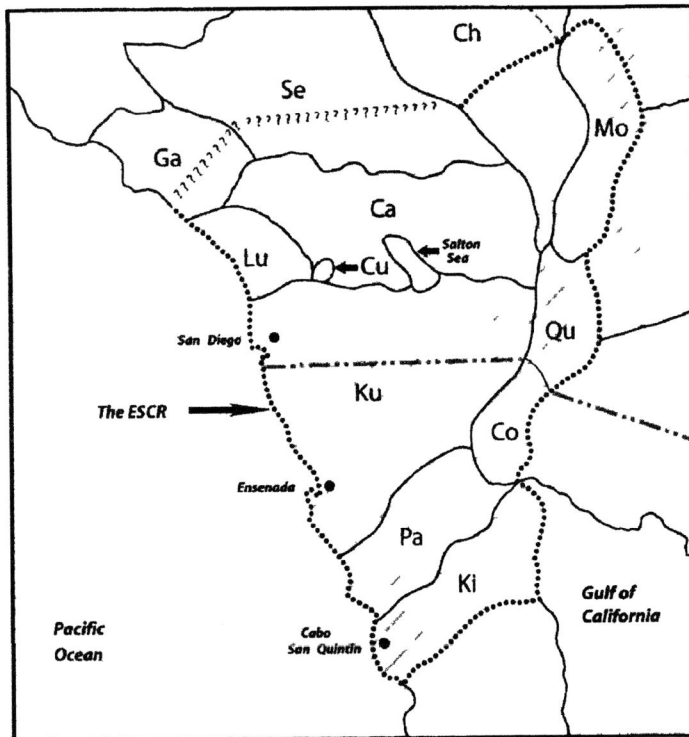

Figure 1.A-ii. Map 2: Yuman and Uto-Aztecan Language Families within the ESCR.
Ca=Cahuilla, Cu=Cupeño, Ch=Chemehuevi,[4] Co=Cocopa, Ga=Gabrielino,
Ki=Kiliwa, Ku=Kumeyaay, Lu=Luiseño, Mo=Mohave, Qu=Quechan, Pa=Paipai,
Se=Serrano

---

[4] I have included a portion of Chemehuevi territory as being within ESCR, as a way of acknowledging that in their most southern range the Chemehuevi are neighbors with the Mohave; furthermore, some Chemehuevi singers sing ESCR songs. At the same time, the Chemehuevi have songs that are not sung within the ESCR. For more on this, see "At the Boundary of the ESCR," starting on page 62.

The Yuman languages spoken within the ESCR include Cocopa, Kiliwa, Kumeyaay[5],

Quechan, Mohave, and Paipai; the Uto-Aztecan languages include Cahuilla,

Chemehuevi, Cupeño, Gabrielino, Luiseño, and Serrano.

The map of the ESCR is provisional and reflects the amount of information that

exists concerning the culture of each tribe. To a large degree, the information about the

musical traditions of any tribe seems to be inversely proportional to the speed at which

Euro-Americans settled in any particular area. Sustained development and expansion

started earlier in Los Angeles and its surrounding region than in San Diego County. As a

---

[5] I have not attempted to address the subject of the different Kumeyaay languages in Map 2 (Figure 1.A-ii). However, the linguist Amy Miller has offered the following comments: "There is a great deal of diversity among Kumeyaay languages. Languages in the U.S. include 'Iipay (spoken in such communities as Mesa Grande, Santa Ysabel, and Barona) and Tiipay (spoken in Jamul, among other southern communities). A third distinct language which Margaret Langdon (1991:188) calls Kumeyaay is said to be spoken in the area of Campo, Cuyapaipe and Manzanita. The extent of language variation in Baja California is not yet fully understood, but at least two Kumeyaay languages are spoken there, including Kumiai (which may include the varieties of La Huerta, San Jose de la Zorra, Neji, and Ha'a) and Ku'alh (spoken in Santa Catarina and heavily influenced by Paipai)." (Amy Miller, personal communication, October 8, 2009.) A number of people today do not recognize the existence of separate Kumeyaay languages; instead they recognize a Kumeyaay nation wherein different Kumeyaay dialects are spoken. See for instance Kalim Smith's "Language Ideology and Hegemony in the Kumeyaay Nation: Returning the Linguistic Gaze (master's thesis, University of California, San Diego, 2005).

result, much less seems to be known about the music of the Gabrielino[6] or the Serrano.[7] Therefore I represented the boundary of the ESCR within the Gabrielino and Serrano regions with a series of "'?'s." The establishment and the expansion of Euro-American cities proceeded at a slower pace in other parts of the ESCR. Reservations were established, where enclaves from each tribal community persisted. On tribal reservations throughout the ESCR, today, young and old alike continue to study and to revive their traditions.

---

[6] The Gabrielino have never been federally recognized. On the other hand, they have a list of members, belonging to four different groups/bands. See the website of the Gabrielino–Tongva Tribe, of Los Angeles , California, http://www.gabrielinotribe.org/ Members/Members.cfm (Accessed on October, 9, 2009); further, the tribe has posted a map, showing that their lands once included much of what is now Los Angeles and Orange counties. See: http://www.gabrielinotribe.org/maps/Tongva_assembly_051119 _lowres.pdf. The Serrano have a reservation called the San Manuel Band of Serrano Mission Indians. For one map that shows the lands of the Serrano and the Cahuilla, see: http://www.rims.k12.ca.us/serrano/cultural_region/pages/map1.html (Accessed on April 2, 2008)

[7] There are some sources regarding the music of the Gabrielino and the Serrano. The singer Ernest Siva is part Serrano and part Cahuilla. See his *Voices of the Flute: Songs of Three Southern California Indian Nations* (Banning, California: Ushkana Press, 2004). Also see Helen H. Roberts's *Form in Primitive Music An Analytical and Comparative Study of the Melodic Form of Some Ancient Southern California Indian Songs* (New York: American Library of Musicology, 1933). This study includes songs from the Catalineño (from Catalina Island, off the coast of Southern California), the Gabrielino, and the Luiseño.

Singing and Dancing

Three scholars have studied the music of the ESCR.[8] The earliest was the

ethnomusicologist George Herzog, who visited parts of the ESCR in 1927. The

following year, he published his article "The Yuman Musical Style," in which he

discussed the music of singers from Yuman-speaking tribes and provided his

transcriptions of thirty-nine songs.[9] In his 1966 dissertation on Luiseño music, Ralph

Heidsiek analyzed and discussed fifteen songs, and provided transcriptions for each.[10]

Barbara Kwiatkowska worked with and studied the music of some singers at Campo,

Manzanita, and Sycuan.[11] In her 1981 dissertation, she included her analyses of some

twenty songs, along with her transcriptions of each.

Before these three scholars began to study Native American music, they, like

myself, were trained in the canon of Euro-American music, where musicians learn to read

and perform from written scores. Musicians trained in this tradition are not necessarily

---

[8] In Chapters 2 and 3, I will be referring to still other scholars, some of whom were trained musicians. In the section, "Brother songs," starting on page 50, I refer to the work of the linguist Abraham Halpern who, while not a trained musicians, clearly grew to love ESCR music and frequently sang the songs that he had learned. (Margaret Langdon, personal communication).
[9] I discuss the topic of transcription in "Transcription of Songs: George Herzog," Chapter 2.
[10] Luiseño is one of the Uto-Aztecan languages. For Heidsiek's dissertation, see his: "Music of the Luiseño Indians of Southern California--A Study of Music in Indian Culture with Relation to a Program in Music Education" (PhD diss, University of California at Los Angeles, 1966).
[11] These tribes all speak a Yuman language. See Barbara Kwiatkowska's "The Present State of Musical Culture Among the Diegueño Indians from San Diego County" (PhD diss, University of California at Los Angeles, 1981). Her field tapes are at the Department of Ethnomusicology, University of California at Los Angeles.

prepared for what they hear in ESCR music, which is almost entirely vocal. In general,

the songs involve the repetition of relatively short phrases. In addition, ESCR singers are

known for their powerful, clear, strong voices. Not unexpectedly, Herzog, and even more

so, Heidsiek and Kwiatkowska, focused to a large extent on melody. In their

transcriptions, Heidsiek and Kwiatkowska wrote out each song, from start to finish,

showing every repetition of every phrase. As a result, their transcriptions demonstrate

that variations occur each time a singer repeats a given segment or phrase.

In placing so much emphasis on melody, these scholars deemphasized other

aspects of the music. ESCR music is more than vocal music, it is also dance music. In

addition, in order to understand ESCR music, the text to each song needs to be taken into

account. ESCR music-making also involves the generation of rhythmic patterns, using

percussion instruments (most often a shaken gourd filled with seeds). It would be

difficult to appreciate the close connection between the dance steps of a song, its melody,

text, and the accompanying percussion patterns without spending a considerable amount

of time watching the singers perform. However, neither Herzog nor Heidsiek seem to

have had this opportunity. Herzog's only chance to observe ESCR musicians firsthand

apparently occurred during a visit in the summer of 1927, when he made audio

recordings of many different singers.[12] It is likely that much of his analysis came from

listening to his field recordings. Heidsiek's work was also based primarily on listening to

audio recordings. He analyzed and transcribed fifteen songs that Josephine Cook

---

[12] Herzog, "The Yuman Musical Style," p. 183, 195. Herzog's fieldnotes along with the audio recordings that he made of singers on aluminum discs during the 1927 trip are at the Archives of Traditional Music, Indiana University.

recorded in 1934.[13]

In my own discussion of ESCR music, I focus on the interrelatedness of key musical elements: dance, melody, the text of a song, and the accompanying rhythmic pattern of the gourds. I am interested in the ways that these elements fit together like the dovetailed joints in a carefully engineered cabinet; each element is essential and supports the others. In order to show how connected these elements are, I have developed a particular style of transcription.[14]

Dance

The pulse of physical movement, generated through dance and other types of body motion is correlated with the rhythm of the music. The most fundamental dance step involves a shifting of weight from one foot to the other. Figure 1.B-i shows two of the most basic dance steps, one with an underlying triplet pattern and the other with a duple pattern. Both are common throughout the Extended Southern California Region (ESCR). Singers from Yuman-speaking tribes seem to use triplet patterns more often than duple ones.[15] In contrast, Cahuilla *Bird* singers appear to use duple patterns most frequently. In Figure 1.B-i, I indicate the movement from one foot to the other with the symbols *L,* for the left foot, and *R,* for the right.

---

[13] Heidsiek notes that the museum staff believed that Cook's aluminum discs were blank. He, on the other hand, found that they did contain audio recordings and that the sound was clear and therefore ideal for his study. Cook's recordings are part of the collection of the Southwest Museum of the American Indian that is now part of the Autry National Center, Los Angeles.

[14] In Chapter 2, I will be discussing transcription, as both a product and a process, one that reflects the particular research questions that each scholar has pursued.

[15] See Map 2, in Figure 1.A-ii.

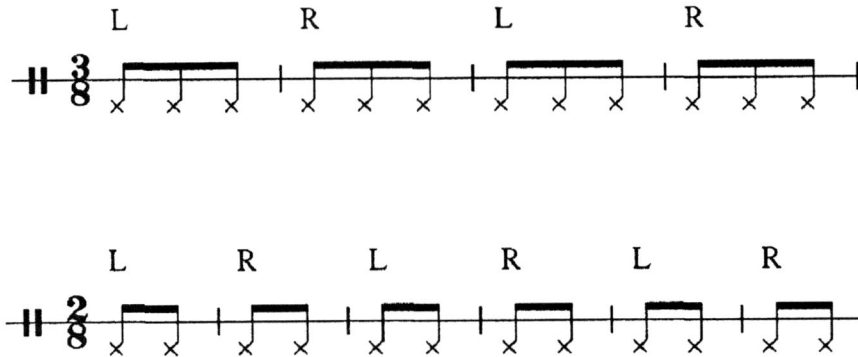

Figure 1.B-i. Basic dance motions.
Note: In this figure, the ♪ represents the basic tactus or pulse of each duple or triple measure. The dotted quarter note, for the triplet pattern, and the quarter note, for the duple pattern, equals approximately 76 beats per minute.

As they lean into each beat, singers and dancers may embellish this basic movement by slightly bending the knee of the leg that momentarily is not bearing weight, while lifting the heel of the foot. Singers and dancers may further embellish their dance steps by slightly pivoting their bodies to the left and then to the right, as they shift their weight from foot to foot. Singers and dancers also shake and nod their heads, while moving their arms and wrists. These movements are generally economical, since singers and dancers must be able to sing and dance throughout a night's performance. Like musicians and dancers everywhere, the movements of the most experienced singers and dancers are highly refined. For such performers, a subtle raising of their eyebrows or even the slightest movement of their shoulders or of one foot can seem to reflect the wealth of understanding and expression that these individuals have gained through a lifetime of singing and/or dancing.

Sometimes one, two, or more singers (or dancers) may step forward and engage in a more assertive form of dance. Then, the gentle shifting from the left foot to the right may, for instance, turn into a sequence of twist, jump, and land. Facing to the right and with knees deeply bent, a dancer jumps, sending his or her body pivoting through the air to the left. The dancer then lands with both feet on the ground, knees deeply bent. He or she is now ready to reverse the procedure, to jump and pivot to the right. As they continue to pivot and jump, dancers and singers may issue loud staccato shouts or grunts. Often these vocalizations occur on the downbeat, as they land on the ground. Other dancers may shout or grunt on an upbeat, literally as they pivot through the air. These shouts and pivoting motions create an impressive counterpoint to less vigorous movements of the other singers and dancers. Figure 1.B-ii indicates how the motions and shouts of such dancers might correspond to a basic underlying triple pulse.

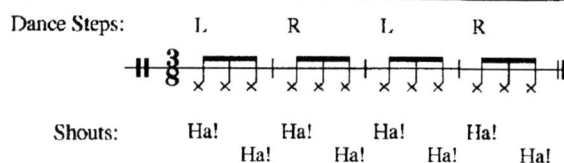

Figure 1.B-ii. Dance steps with shouts.

Rhythm

Another basic element of music making throughout the ESCR is the act of generating a rhythmic pulse, using percussion instruments. Each singer holds a percussion instrument in one hand, most frequently a rattle, made from a dry and hollowed-out gourd filled with some seeds.[16] Such rattles may vary in diameter from

several inches to as much as five or six inches. Including the length of the handle, a

gourd rattle may be as much as a foot in length.

Figure 1.B-iii reproduces photographs of two gourd rattles taken by Frances

Densmore, a researcher who traveled throughout the United States speaking with and

recording singers from different tribes. In 1922, she traveled to Yuma, Arizona.[17]

During her visit, she interviewed singers from the following ESCR tribes: Cocopa,

Kumeyaay,[18] Mohave, and Quechan.[19] The photographs included in Figure 1.B-iii show

two gourds: one Cocopa (the larger of the two) and the other Mohave. Densmore wrote

that the Cocopa gourd was painted red and that:

> A smaller gourd rattle was used by the Mohave when singing the Bird songs. The
> Mohave rattle was decorated with a pattern of diagonal lines which was said to
> have no meaning. Inside this rattle were about thirty tiny balls of pottery made
> especially for this purpose and baked in the fire. The handle was of ironwood,
> fastened in place with gum made by masking and cooking arrow weed stalks and
> adding red paint.[20]

Although Densmore does not provide the measurements for these gourds, their size can

estimated be based on the size of today's gourds. The gourd rattles in Densmore's

---

[16] Other percussion instruments were used as well, one of these being a tortoise shell
rattle. For a drawing by Ed Davis, of this kind of rattle, see the Davis Papers. The image
is online at: https://www.sandiegohistory.org/collections/davis/images/ rattle.jpg
(accessed on May 31, 2010).

[17] See Chapter 3 for a more detailed discuss of Densmore's work.

[18] Densmore interviewed singers at Campo and perhaps from other Kumeyaay-speaking
tribes as well.

[19] See Figure 1.A-ii, for the location of the Mohave, the Quechan, or other tribes.
Densmore also interviewed a Yaqui singer or singers. In Densmore's *Yuman and Yaqui
Music*, Smithsonian Institution Bureau of American Ethnology, 110 (Washington, D.C.:
Government Printing Office, 1932).

[20] This pattern is not discernable in Densmore's black and white photograph. Ibid., p. 25.

photographs are similar to those used today.

Cocopa   Mohave

Figure 1.B-iii. Two gourd rattles.

During a performance, a master or lead singer stands in the line with the other singers. As he performs, the others follow him closely. As he raises his gourd, they raise theirs. As he lowers his gourd, they lower theirs. Their movements are synchronized and are essentially a part of the choreography.[21] Some singers use the term "throwing gourd" when referring to the act of creating a rhythmic pattern with a gourd rattle. For most singers, "throwing gourd" involves more than moving their gourds in a simple up and down motion. Starting with the lower arm at a 90-degree angle to the body and with the wrist close to the torso, a singer raises and lowers the arm/wrist/gourd, circumscribing a path that is something on the order of a vertical ellipsis. This motion sends the seeds crashing and sliding against the inside walls of the gourd. Through years of practice, singers learn to generate a variety of sounds and rhythmic patterns by using different motions. I refer to the various motions that singers use as "strokes." In addition, I refer to the rhythmic patterns that singers generate on their gourd as "gourd patterns."

In their transcriptions of the songs they analyzed, Herzog, Heidsiek, and Kwiatkowska each made at least some mention of the rhythmic patterns singers produced with gourd rattles. Herzog's notation and discussion of gourd patterns suggests that he perceived them as consisting of straightforward divisions of the beat. For example, he wrote that,

> In a few song-series, the rattle produces continuous beats or figures such as ♩ ♩ ♩ etc., or ♫ ♫ ♫ or ♪♪♪ ♪♪♪ ♪♪♪ etc., and the like.[22]

Often Heidsiek notated the rhythmic accompaniment that singers created with their

---

[21] Herzog, YMS, p. 195.

[22] Ibid. In Herzog's article, the first eighth of triplet (♪♪♪) is accented.

gourds.[23] Kwiatkowska took note of a broad variety of rhythmic patterns used in the vocal melodies and a much smaller variety of rhythmic patterns, produced by the gourd.[24] Some of the latter include: ♫. or ♫♩ or ♩♫ or ♫♩ .[25]

While it may also seem as if gourd patterns consist of little more than straightforward divisions of a beat, they are complex. For one thing, singers use a variety of "strokes," as they generate different rhythmic patterns. Herzog thought this might be the case. He reported that a singer generates sound with his gourd when raising or lowering it:

> The figure ♪♩ often results from the reverberation of pebbles, shaken backwards preparatory to the forward movement of the next beat.

Nevertheless, Herzog concluded that this effect was not entirely intentional, and asserted that the gourd technique of ESCR singers was in a formative stage.

> The figure might not always be intentional. In a similar way, a double beat occurs in a series of single beats: ♩ ♩ ♫ ♩ ♩ etc. Sometimes the use of this figure is clearly intentional, since it occurs consistently at the same places in the repetitions of the song. (See No. 15.) Both practices are in a stage in which standardization and wholly intentional, controlled use have not been reached.[26]

In fact, the gourd technique of ESCR singers is advanced. It seems likely that Herzog's failure to grasp this probably reflected his relative unfamiliarity with this music.

---

[23] His transcriptions were based on listening to tapes. In some of the songs the percussion accompaniment was not generated by a rattle but tapping or stomping with a foot.

[24] In her dissertation, Kwiatkowska takes note of at least nineteen different rhythmic patterns in melodies of songs. *Musical Culture*, 126-127.

[25] Kwiatkowska, *Musical Culture.* Her transcriptions of songs are on page 222-333.

[26] "No. 15," refers to Herzog's fifteenth transcription. Herzog, YMS, 93.

This lack of experience sometimes resulted in errors or at least misconceptions.[27] Each experienced singer appears to have developed a unique repertoire of strokes used to generate a variety of different rhythmic patterns. For instance, the Kumeyaay singer Harry Paul Cuero, Jr., a member of the Campo tribe, uses at least two types of strokes as he sings *Bird*. Wiley Elliot, a member of the neighboring Manzanita tribe who has spent many years studying and performing alongside Cuero, offered me a fruitful perspective on gourd patterns. Today, Cuero and Elliot perform along with other singers at ceremonies and at other events throughout the ESCR.[28] In order to learn the 200-300 songs contained in a song cycle, each singer must spend long hours singing with both experienced and novice singers. Despite the norm of group participation that centers around spending long hours repeating and singing songs, Elliot's experience suggests that novice singers may be learning by other than rote means. Each novice singer may develop and employ a unique strategy to make sense of and remember hundreds of songs.

When he first learned to sing *Bird*, Elliot explained that he did not begin by memorizing the words; instead he focused on learning the gourd patterns for each song. As he pursued this path, Elliot found that each gourd pattern could be described as a sequence of two different kinds of strokes that he refers to as "down" and "swish." No other singer with whom I have spoken uses this terminology. Elliot explained that a "down" stroke involved a preliminary raising of the gourd (during which little or no sound was produced) followed by a downward driving motion. This latter movement

---

[27] See Chapter 2, where I discuss Herzog's transcriptions in more detail.
[28] Like other ESCR musicians, Cuero and Elliot also receive invitations to perform outside of the ESCR.

causes the seeds to crash against the bottom wall of the gourd, making a sound that was of relatively short duration. With a "swish" stroke, the time that the seeds spend sliding along the walls of the gourd is increased. Whereas the down stroke produces a shorter, staccato sound, the sound produced by a swish stroke might be described as more of a shushing, swishing sound. While a down stroke involves more of an up-and-down movement, and probably involves more arm motion, a swish stroke involves a much tighter, circular motion, generated primarily by rotating the wrist. Figure 1.B-iv shows the motion that the seeds traverse for both types of strokes as they move inside of the gourd. The illustration on the left depicts the seeds at the bottom of a down stroke, just as they are about to collide with the bottom of the gourd. The figure on the right illustrates the swish stroke. Here the seeds are shown sliding down one side of the gourd but before they reach the bottom. In the following discussion, I use Elliot's terminology of down and swish strokes when describing ESCR gourd patterns.[29]

As they sing *Bird,* Cuero and Elliot use gourds with a relatively large diameter, close to the diameter of the Cocopa gourd shown in Figure 1.B-iii. This larger diameter gives the seeds more time to slide against the walls of the gourd during a swish stroke. To study the strokes that Cuero uses as he sings *Bird,* I slowed down a recording that he made of the *Bird* song *Xwaynaamia wey,* which has an underlying triplet pattern. Cuero uses a "down" stroke on the first and third beats of this pattern and a sliding or "swish" stroke on the second beat. In Figure 1.B-v, each down stroke is represented with the

---

[29] Wiley Elliot, personal communications, June-November, 2009. Although I am adopting Elliot's terminology for gourd strokes, any errors in interpretation that I make are of course my own.

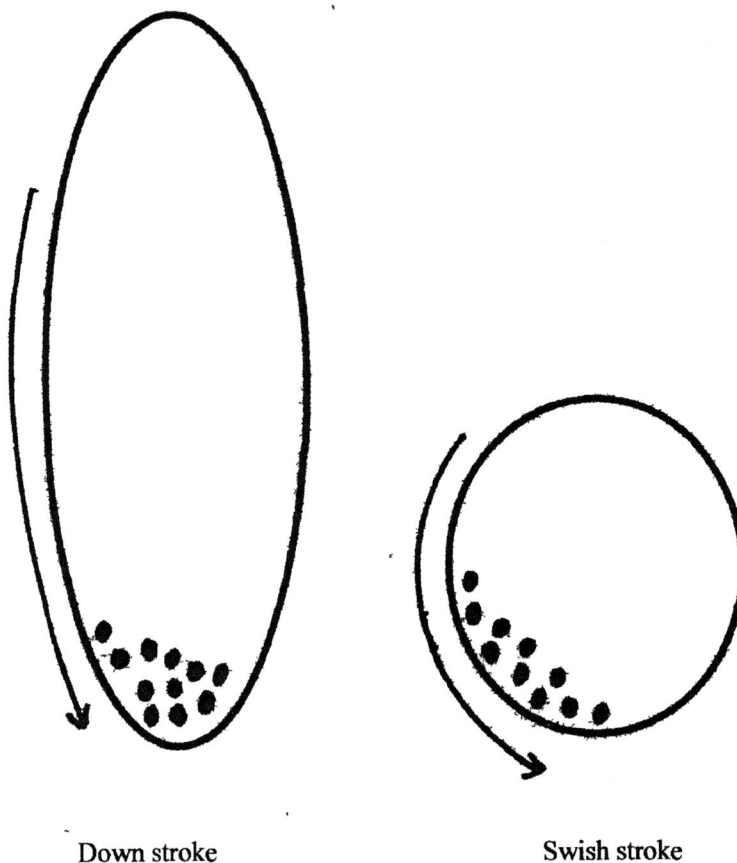

Down stroke   Swish stroke

Figure 1.B-iv. Two possible strokes used when "throwing gourd."

letter D, the swish stroke is represented with the letter S. During both strokes, the sounds

of multiple seeds striking the insides of the gourd begin slightly before each beat and end

slightly after it. This is more exaggerated in the swish stroke, however. For both strokes,

the precise moment at which the seeds begin to slide (or cease to slide) is difficult to

pinpoint. In the swish stroke, the seeds seem to begin their slide somewhere between a

sixteenth and a thirty-second note before the downbeat. (See 1. in Figure 1.B-v.) The shush of the beads crashing against the insides of the gourd then crescendos as the seeds

arrive at the bottom-most part of the gourd. (See 2. In Figure 1.B-v.) The sound

continues even after the beat, for a brief moment. (See 3. in Figure 1.B-v.)

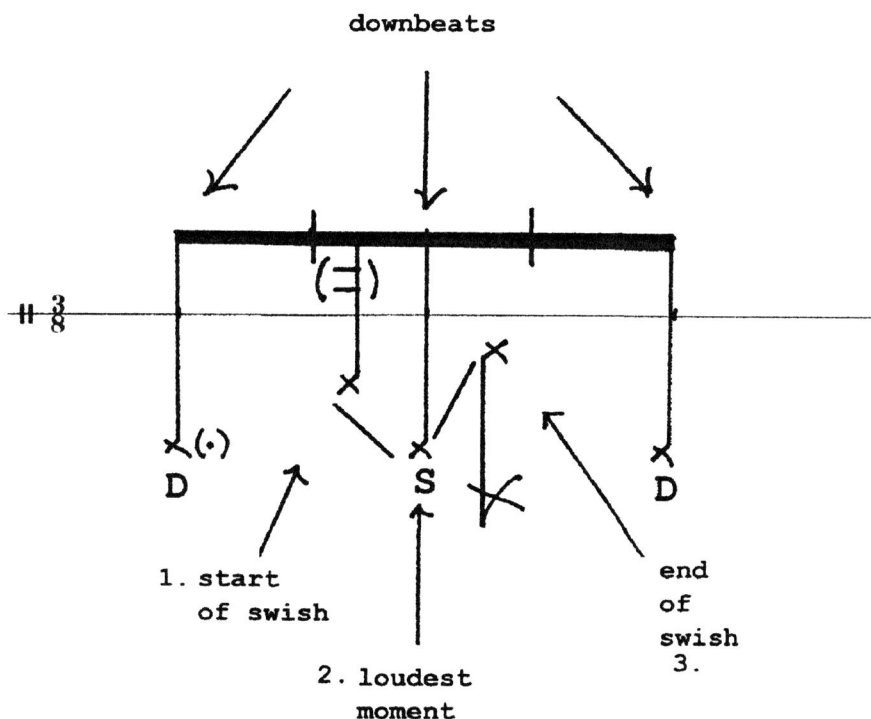

downbeats

1. start
   of swish

2. loudest
   moment

end
of
swish
3.

D   S   D

Figure 1.B-v. Harry Paul Cuero, Jr.'s gourd pattern.
(Note: for songs with an underlying rhythmic pattern of three beats. The figure shows
both "down" and "swish" strokes.[30])

In the following notated examples, I indicate gourd patterns using standard rhythmic

notation in combination with the symbols *D* and *S*, for down and swish strokes,

---

[30] In this figure, the start and the end of the swish appear to be at higher pitches than the
sound that occurs on the downbeat. This is not accurate. I used what appears to be
different pitch levels, as a means of indicating the motion of the seeds.

respectively. Figure 1.B-vi shows how I notate Cuero's pattern of gourd strokes, in a song with a steady triplet pattern.

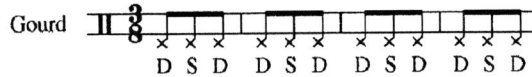

Figure 1.B-vi. Cuero's gourd pattern.

The idea that gourd patterns can be described as a succession of down and/or swish strokes can help to provide more definition to the gourd patterns that Herzog and Kwiatkowska indicate. The quality of Herzog's recordings is poor. It is much easier to hear the voice than the percussion instruments, whether rattle or rubbed box or basket. I listened to the recording that corresponds to Herzog's transcription 15 in his "The Yuman Musical Style."[31] The swish strokes are of relatively short duration and it sounds as if the singer might be using a gourd with a small diameter.[32] Regarding the rhythmic patterns of the gourd, I found that ♫ sounded as if it might have been produced by a sequence of two down strokes (DD). In contrast, the ♫♩ pattern sounded as if it might be down-swish-down (DSD). It seems possible that the rhythmic pattern that Herzog notated as ♫ may have also consisted of down-swish-down (DSD). As indicated earlier, Kwiatkowska reported a wide variety of rhythmic patterns in the vocal lines. Her transcriptions show a much smaller variety of gourd patterns, including, for instance, ♫. and ♫♩ and ♩♫ and ♫♩. Kwiatkowska does

---

[31] Herzog, YMS, 212. See footnote 26. For Herzog's recordings, see footnote 12.
[32] See the text that footnote20 refers to.

not consider which gourd strokes might have been used to generate these different

gourd patterns. [33]   On the other hand, she is sensitive to the differences in gourd patterns.

In the first of her transcriptions, Kwiatkowska shows, for instance, that the

singer introduced the song with nine repetitions of the following rhythmic pattern:

♫♩ . As he began to sing, the singer switched his gourd pattern to ♫♩.♩ . It seems

possible that in both cases, the sequence of strokes may have been down-swish-down

(DSD).

Song texts

Each song contains words, usually no more than six, though the number of words

is not set. In general, some words in a song are ones that can be translated or that at least

may resemble spoken words. Others, however, will be vocables, that is, they consist of

words or syllables that cannot be directly translated such as "fa-la-la" or "tra-la-la-la-la."

On the other hand, this does not mean that vocables lack meaning. Vocables such as "fa-

la-la" may be associated with a particular song, one that is sung in a particular context,

and with certain feelings in mind. All may be part of the meaning for a vocable or set of

---

[33] For these, see Kwiatkowska's dissertation. Her transcriptions of songs are on p. 222-333.

vocables.[34]

Consider, for instance, the *Bird* song *Xwaynaamiia wey*, as sung by Cuero. As is apparently often the case for songs from the ESCR, the text for the song *Xwaynaamiia wey* is based on a small number of words, in this case just two: *xwaynaamiia wey*, neither of which can be translated. According to Cuero, the sung word *xwaynaamiia* is based on the spoken word *kwiinám*.[35] In the song, *kwinám* appears to have been transformed, as suggested in Figure 1.B-vii. It appears that *kwii* has become xway and that *nám* has turned into *naa-mii-a*.

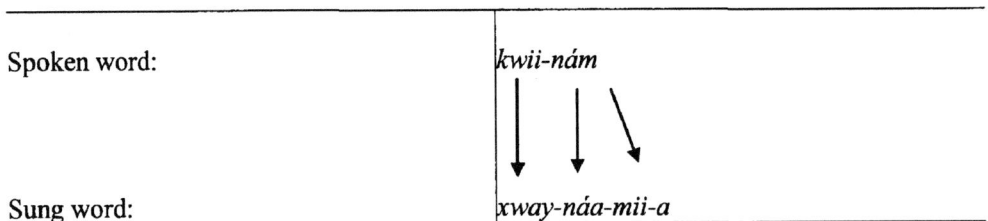

Spoken word:	*kwii-nám*
Sung word:	*xway-náa-mii-a*

Figure 1.B-vii. Possible relationship between *kwiinám* and *xwaynaamiia*.

The word *xwaynaamiia* can be divided into four short syllables: *xway + naa + mii + a*. With the addition of *wey*, this makes for a sequence of five syllables, as shown in Figure 1.B-viii.

---

[34] For one author who argues, I believe correctly, that the words in ESCR songs have meaning, whether or not they can be translated, see Kalim Smith's *Language*. For a discussion of vocables in songs, see Leanne Hinton's chapter "Songs Without Words," in her book *Flutes of Fire: Essays on California Indian Languages* (Berkeley: Heyday Books, 1994), 145-151. See also Hinton's articles, "Vocables in Havasupai Songs," in Charlotte Frisbie's: *Southwestern Indian Ritual Drama* (Albuquerque: University of New Mexico Press, 1980), 275-305, and "When Sounds Go Wild: Phonological Change and Syntactic Re-Analysis in Havasupai," *Language*, Vol. 56, no. 2 (1980): 320-344.
[35] Regarding the long vowel, *"ii,"* in the word *kwiinam,* "ii" sounds like the *i* in *petite*. Regarding the word *xwaynaamiia*. The first syllable, *xway*, sounds like the English word *"whey."* See Appendix 1: Pronunciation guides.

Syllables				
1	2	3	4	5
xway-	*naa-*	*mii-*	*a*	*wey*

Figure 1.B-viii. The words *xwaynaamiia wey* divided into five syllables.

While singers do not generally identify themselves as composers, ESCR song texts contain at least some features that facilitate their being set to music.[36] The words *xwaynaamiia wey* contain two repeated sounds.[37] When sung, *xway* and *wey* sound alike; that is, the beginning of the text sounds like its end, a feature that is often seen in ESCR song texts.

Another key feature of ESCR songs has to do with the way the text is parsed across the underlying rhythmic pattern. When spoken, the second syllable of *kwii nám* receives the accent.[38] In this song, the pattern of accented and unaccented syllables generally follows this pattern. *Naa,* the second syllable of *xwaynaamiia,* always occurs on a downbeat. The syllables *mii* and *a* usually follow on consecutive eighth note pulses.[39] Like *naa, wey* also always occurs on a downbeat. *Xway,* the first syllable of *xwaynaamiia,* often takes the upbeat. Figure 1.B-ix shows an excerpt from the song, where "xway" takes the upbeat. To emphasize the idea that this phrase can generate its own internal momentum, I modified this excerpt by adding repeat signs, even though no phrase in this song is repeated outright. However, phrases like the one shown in Figure 1.B-ix do occur in many ESCR songs, in short repeated phrases that are repeated. The

---

[36] Some performers today do compose some songs but probably not entire song cycles. For some discussion of dreaming as composing, see my Chapters 2 and 3, on Kroeber.

[37] This is another common characteristic of ESCR songs.

[38] In most cases, the last syllable of a Yuman word is stressed. This can be indicated with an accent mark, as in Quechán or Cocopá or Kumeyáay.

[39] I want to thank the linguist Leanne Hinton, for this insight.

xway, on the upbeat, is followed immediately by *naa,* on the downbeat. In turn, *na* is followed by *mi* and *a,* on consecutive eighth notes. The *wey* follows on the next downbeat. As *xway* is sung on the following upbeat, it seems to hocket or mimic the sound of *wey.* In this example, ♩.≈76.

Figure 1.B-ix. *Xway* on the upbeat.

As suggested in Figure 1.B-x, and discussed below, the words *xwaynaamiia wey* always occur in this order. When all five syllables of the text are used, they occur over the space of three measures. Thus, these syllables can be divided into three parts, corresponding to the measure in which they appear. See Figure 1.B-x.

Parts/Measures:	A	B			C
	xway-	naa-	mii-	a	wey
Syllables:	1	2	3	4	5
	Syllables				

Figure 1.B-x. The words *xwaynaamiia wey.*

In the following discussion, I refer to the text as containing parts **A**, **B**, and **C**, where **A**=*xway,* **B**=*naa+mii+a,* and **C**=*wey.* In the song, the syllable *wem* is sometimes used in the place of *wey.* When referring to the *wem,* I use the symbol **C'**. I will be referring to each repetition of these parts as being a "line."

Figure 1.B-xi shows the four lines of text that make up the first section of this song. As can be seen, each line is slightly different; moreover, the variation in these four lines seems almost systematic. Each line contains **B** (the syllables *naa-mii-a*). Line 2 contains all three parts, **ABC**. Lines 1 and 3, on the other hand, each contain only two parts. Line 3 contains **AB** but **C** is omitted. Line 1 contains **BC** but is missing **A**. The variation in Line 4 is of a different type. Whereas line 2 contains **ABC**, line 4 contains **ABC'** (**C'**=*wem*).

There is still another aspect to the variation of the text in section 1. The lines appear in pairs. The first line of each pair contains two parts (**AB** or **BC**). In contrast, the second and fourth lines contain three parts (**ABC** or **ABC'**). It is almost as if each partial statement of the words (**AB** or **BC**) sets up an expectation that is resolved in the next line that contains three parts (**ABC** or **ABC'**). Such subtle variation and structural organization is typical in ESCR song texts.

Line #'s	Parts						Pairs of the lines
	1	2			3		
1		**B** mii-		a-	**C** wey		**B C**
2	**A** xway-	naa-	**B** mii-	a-	**C** wey		**A B C**
3	**A** xway-	naa-	**B** mii-	a			**B C**
4	**A** xway-	naa-	**B** mii-	a-	**C'** wem		**A B C'**

Figure 1.B-xi. The text of section 1.

As Herzog listened to the audio recordings that he had made, "melodic units" would have been one of the musical attributes that he could readily identify.[40]   Herzog used the symbol *"a"* to represent the first melodic unit in a song and the symbol *"r"* to represent to section that contained the rise. Thus, he wrote that some songs had the form: *"a a . . . . r a."*[41]

While Herzog's analysis of the structure of songs seem accurate to a point, they are based primarily on the melody. However, I make a point of showing that song texts provide an important key to understanding the form of a song. I will show that a still finer sense of the structure of a song (its lines and its sections) can be developed by considering the melody along with the text and the dance steps and a song's gourd patterns.

---

[40] I think Herzog may have used his audio recordings as his primary source material as he made his transcriptions. See footnote 12.
[41] YMS, 196.

The song *Xwaynaamiia wey* does in fact contain two sections. I refer to these as sections 1 and 2. In section 2, a section of the melody does rise to a higher pitch level. In *Xwaynaamiia wey,* all of the words and syllables in section 2 are found in section 1. With the exception of three additional lines, section 2 is identical to section 1. (see Figure 1.B-xii). Lines 1 and 2 of section 2 are identical to the first two lines of section 1. Similarly lines 6 and 7 are the same as the last two lines of section 1. Lines 3-5, of section 2, are the added lines. In these lines, line 3 (**AB)** is followed by two lines of **ABC** instead of one , as in lines 1-2 or in lines 6-7. As can be seen in Figure 1.B-xi and Figure 1.B-xii, sections 1 and 2 both end with the **C'** that is the syllable *"wem."*

Line #'s	Parts 1	2	3	Seq.	Comment
1		**B** *naa- mii- a-*	**C** *wey*	**B C**	First two
2	**A** *xway-*	**B** *naa- mii- a-*	**C** *wey*	A B C	lines of section 1
3	**A** *xway-*	**B** *naa- mii- a*		A B	
4	**A** *xway-*	**B** *naa- mii- a-*	**C** *wey*	A B C	Inserted Lines
5	**A** *xway-*	**B** *naa- mii- a-*	**C** *wey*	A B C	
6	**A** *xway-*	**B** *naa- mii- a*		**B C**	Last two
7	**A** *xway-*	**B** *naa- mii- a-*	**C'** *wem*	A B C'	lines of section 1

Figure 1.B-xii. Section 2 of *Xwaynaamiia wey.*

Combining text, melody, and dance

When this song text is considered along with its accompanying melody and rhythm and dance steps, a still better idea of the skill and art that is involved in the creation and/or the modification of these songs begins to emerge. I say creation and/or modification because for the most part there does not seem to be any way to know when a song cycle or any of its songs were first composed. Some singers are composing songs today but probably not entire song cycles. The song cycles that singers perform today appear to be ones that they have learned from other singers.[42] Even so, it seems likely that each singer will to some extent modify the songs that he performs, throughout his lifetime.[43]

Referring to Figure 1.B-ix, where the syllable *xway* occurred on an upbeat, one might also anticipate that this syllable *xway* might also sometimes take the downbeat. In fact this does sometimes occur. Figure 1.B-xiii contains a hypothetical example of such an occurrence, one that does not occur in the song. The example shown in Figure 1.B-ix has an underlying triplet rhythm.

---

[42] See footnote 36.

[43] Here I am thinking of George Devereux and his combined interests in anthropology and Freudian psychology. Devereux spent time with and studied the Mohave. Devereux wrote that through dreams, the Mohave polished and recycled their collective unconscious thoughts, feelings, and impulses. While this statement seems rather abstract, it seems likely that generations of singers have in fact polished and/or modified their shared repertoire of songs and song cycles. See George Devereux's "Mohave Coyote Tales," *The Journal of American Folklore* 61, no. 241 (Jul. - Sep., 1948): 233-255.

Figure 1.B-xiii. A hypothetical example, where "*xway*" hypothetically takes the downbeat.

Xwaynaamiia wey is, however, a type of song that some singers refer to as being "fancy." Some of its phrases have a steady underlying triplet rhythm. In contrast, other phrases contain passages during which the rhythm temporarily shifts to a duple rhythm, before returning to the triple rhythm. The rhythmic shifts can be hard to anticipate. Only experienced singers and dancers are able to anticipate the rapid metric shifts that are present in fancy dances. "Non-fancy" songs, in contrast, are songs that employ a single rhythmic pattern throughout. Sometimes singers refer to these as being "single-step" songs. As shown in Figure 1.B-vii, in normal speech, the syllable *kwii* is not accented. The next and final syllable *nám* receives the accent. A phrase, such as the one shown in Figure 1.B-xiv, where *xway* takes the downbeat, thus goes against the normal rules of everyday speech. Possibly reflecting this fact, every time *xway* takes the downbeat, it occurs in a fancy phrase, a phrase wherein the meter vacillates suddenly between duple and triple. It is during these moments that the rhythmic surprises in *Xwaynaamiia wey* are presented.

Having discussed the text of this song, we can now take into account the elements of dance and text and melody and the rhythm of the percussion accompaniment. Section 1 begins in a "non-fancy" manner. In the first two lines, the repetition of the pitch G establishes this pitch as a tonal center. The text **BC** (*mii-a wey*) in line 1 is answered in line 2 with **ABC** (*xway-naa-mii-a wey*). (See Figure 1.B-xv, on page 46) The underlying rhythmic pattern is triplet.

With these two lines, now set to music, we can consider a phenomenon that linguist Leanne Hinton refers to as "vowel insertion." In discussing Havasupai music,[44] Hinton wrote:

> It is in the matter of vowel-insertion that many more vowels are inserted in songs than in speech. And the rules determining where vowels will be inserted are not so much linguistics rules as they are metric rules--or rules that correlate meter with syllabicity.

To consider whether vowel insertion might help to explain the text that is used in lines 1 and 2, I reproduce here the figure showing the relationship between the spoken word *kwii-nám* and the sung word *xwaynaamiia.* (See Figure 1.B-xiv).

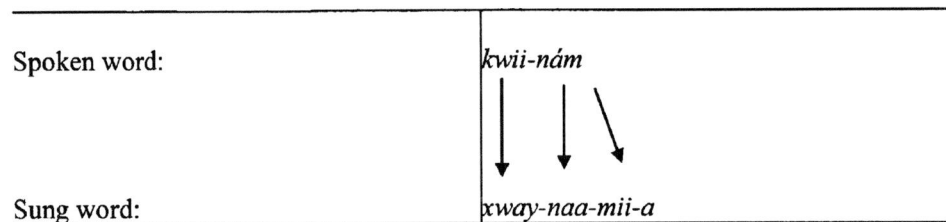

Spoken word:	*kwii-nám*
Sung word:	*xway-naa-mii-a*

Figure 1.B-xiv. Possible relationship between *kwiinám* and *xwaynaamiia.*

This figure shows how the extra vowels that turn *nám* into *naa-mii-a* can be thought of as having been inserted, for the purpose of filling out the beat. In lines 1 and 2, *xway* occurs on the upbeat. (See Figure 1.B-xv, p. 46.) It is immediately followed by *naa,* on the downbeat. The syllables *mii* and *a* can be thought of as being strung over the next two eight notes, before the appearance of *wey,* on the next downbeat.

---

[44] Havasupai is one of the Yuman languages. See Map 3, Figure 1.D-i. See Leanne Hinton's *Havasupai Songs: A Linguistic Perspective* (PhD diss., University of California, San Diego, 1977), p. 90. Her dissertation was also published as: *Havasupai Songs: A Linguistic Perspective.* Ars Linguistica 6 (Tuebingen: G. Narr, 1984.)

As singers and dancers begin dance to lines 1 and 2, a pattern of movements is established along with the expectation that this pattern will continue. The singers begin to shift from one foot to the next, together with the arrival of each downbeat. Just based on these two opening lines, it seems likely that at least some singers and dancers may expect this motion to continue for the remainder of the song.

The rhythmic surprise begins to take shape in line 3. In the first measure of line 3, the syllable *xway* takes the downbeat instead of an upbeat. This signals a possible disruption in the way the syllables of *xwaynaamiia* will appear, in the measures that follow. In fact, in this song, whenever *xway* takes the downbeat, the steady triple rhythmic pattern is about to be interrupted. In measure 2, *naa* takes the downbeat. The surprise continues to take shape, when *naa* is not immediately followed my *mii* and *a*, on consecutive eighth notes; instead *naa* occurs by itself, in a measure with two eighth notes rather than three. In measure 3, an additional surprise arrives when the syllable *mii* also falls on the downbeat. In order to ascertain that *mii* is in fact sung on a downbeat, one must listen to Cuero's percussion accompaniment, on his audio recording. In this line, Cuero uses a down stroke on syllables *xway, naa,* and now on *mii.* Because *naa* is only held for two eighth notes, anyone unfamiliar with this song will likely be caught flat-footed. The steady pattern of three beats per measure has been interrupted. Experienced singers and dancers, on the other hand, will have no trouble anticipating what is about to happen.

The text for line 3 consists of **AB** (*xway* + *naa-mii-a*). **C** (*wey)* is not included. The omission of this word in combination with the single measure of $\frac{2}{8}$ results in a sense of incompleteness. In turn, this is resolved, in line 4, when the triple meter returns. In addition, the text for line 4 consists of all three parts of the text, **ABC'** (*xway-naa-mii-a wem*). This brief discussion of section 1 provides some understanding of the ways that the dance steps and the words along with the melody (and its rhythm) *and* the rhythm of the gourd are all joined together to form an integrated whole, in this song. Figure 1.B-xv (p. 46) shows all of these elements, taken together. The shift from one foot to the next is indicated with the symbols "L," for the left foot, and "R," for the right. The rhythmic pattern of the gourd and the strokes that Cuero uses are indicated with the symbols "D," for a down stroke, and "S," for a swish or sliding stroke.

Section 2 of *Xwaynaamiia wey* is shown in Figure 1.B-xvi (p. 47). I have already shown how the text in section 2 is derived from the text of section 1. Now, I consider the relationship between the melody and the text in sections 1 and 2. The first lines of sections 1 and 2 are the same. The second lines of both sections are also similar. Lines 2 of sections 1 and 2 are similar in some respects. The text is the same in both lines. The rhythm of the melody in both lines is nearly the same. Their melodies are, however, different. The melody of line 2 in section 1 initially rises up to B, before descending a major third (from B to G). In line 2 of section 2, the melody rises higher, up to D, and then descends a perfect fourth (from D down to A). Thus, the melodic contour of both lines are similar, but line 2 of section 2 rises up higher. This is a good example of the rise, in an ESCR song today. The relationship between the third lines of sections 1 and two follow a similar pattern. The text is the same. Both lines contain the text **AB** (*xway + naa-mii-a*) The rhythm of the melodies is similar, except that in line 3 of section 2 some additional eight notes have been added, to fill in the melodic line. The melodic contours of both lines are similar, in that they both descend. In performance, as the melody rises in pitch level, in lines 2 and 3, the intensity of the singer's gestures and the volume of their voices generally increase. Singers and dancers dancing to the fancy steps in line 3 may emphasize their movements. Line 3 of section two is followed by lines 4-5 that both contain all three parts of the text **ABC** (*xway- naa-mii-a wey*). In these two lines, the pitch level of the melody descends and again is centered around the pitch G, as used in section 1. The contour traces a descending major third, from B to G. Lines 6 and 7 of section 2 are the same as the last two lines of section 1.

Thus, section 2 consists of an artful variation on section 1. However, the variation is subtle, not overstated. Figure 1.B-xvii (p. 48) shows all of the elements mentioned thus far: the rhythmic pattern of the gourd, the melody, and the words (as organized into Sections 1 and 2). The performance begins with a short introduction, played on the gourd. During a performance, Cuero repeats Sections 1 and 2 a number of times.

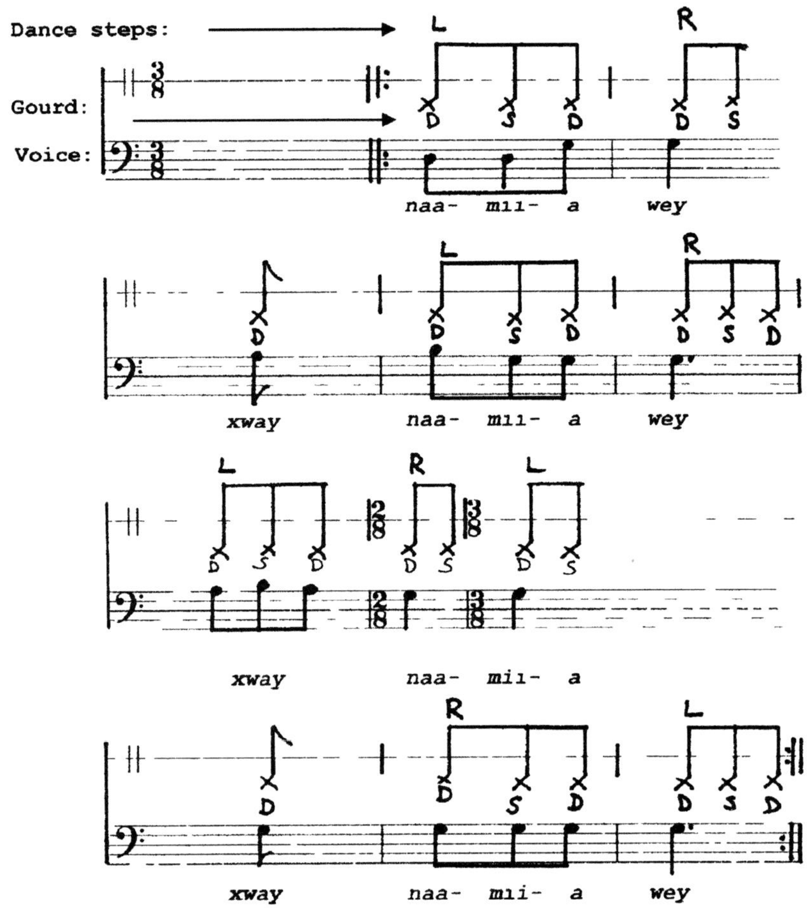

Figure 1.B-xv. Section 1 of song *Xwaynaamiia wey,* showing the songs text along with its melody and gourd pattern.

Figure 1.B-xvi. Section 2 of *Xwaynaamiia wey.*

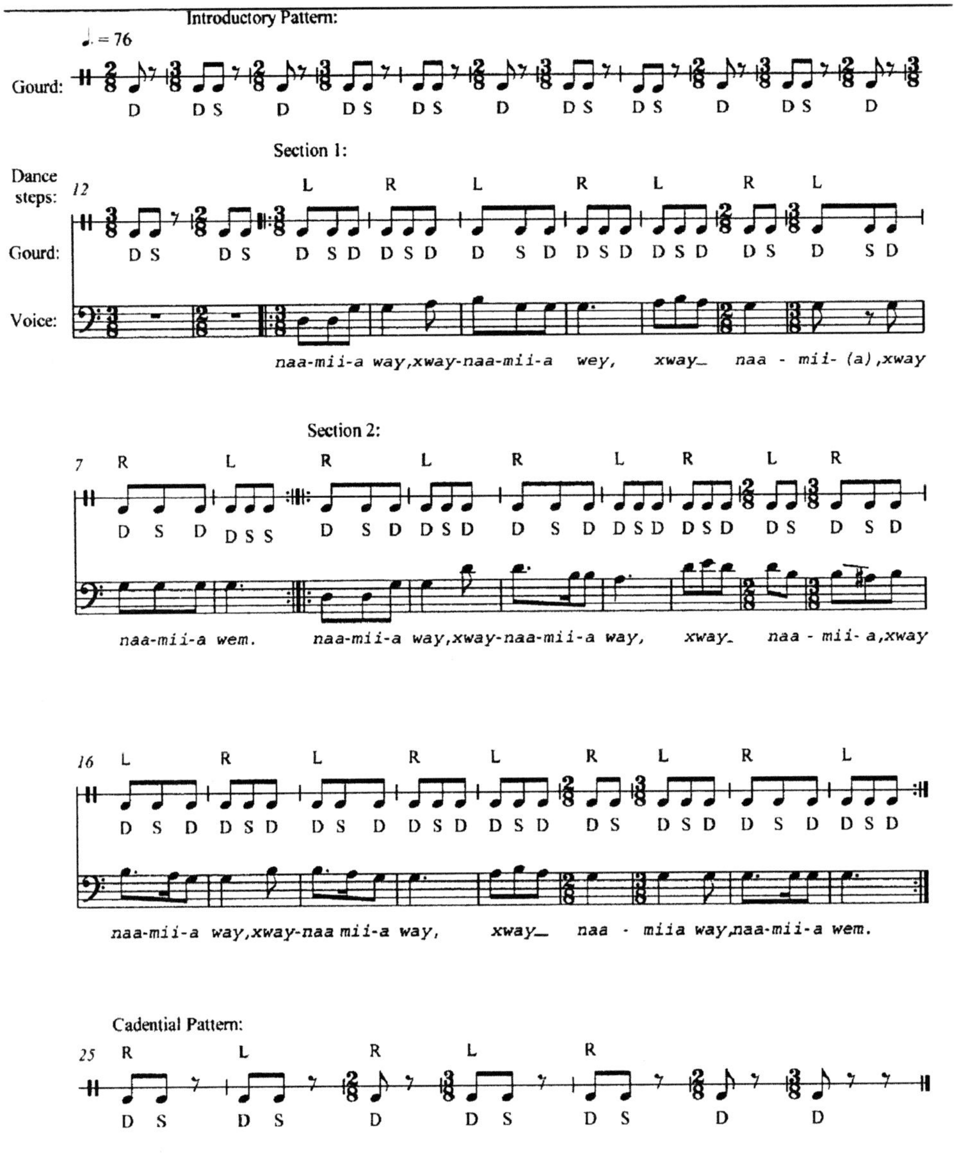

Figure 1.B-xvii. *Xwaynaamiia wey:* Singing, dancing, and gourd.

Brother Songs

In the previous section, I considered music-making by considering an example song and by then focusing on some of its key dimensions: dance, the melody and rhythm of the example song, the accompanying gourd pattern, and the text of the song. In this section, I shift the focus and look at groups of songs. The night-long performance of a song cycle consists of the singing of two- to three-hundred songs, but these songs are almost always presented in sets. Thus a performance can also be described as the singing of sets of songs, one set after the other. The songs in a set are sometimes referred to as brothers (a term I use here).

Brother songs usually share a number of characteristics, yet each brother song is unique. One method that is often used to differentiate one from another is rhythmic variation. Brother songs are also almost always linked through the use of shared sounds, that is, the use of similar song texts; and for a listener it is not difficult to hear that the songs in each set contain similar words and/or vocables. The songs in a set may also focus on the same subject matter, but for many reasons this may be difficult if not impossible to discern. Knowledge of the meaning of the words may be lost over time as songs are passed from singer to singer. At the same time, at least some singers know the meaning of many of the songs that they sing; but this is part of the knowledge that master singers generally only share with a devoted student, perhaps one who has decided to commit to singing a song cycle for his life. While members of the public are invited to attend powwows where they can hear *Bird* or song cycles being performed, singers are likely to be reluctant to discuss the meaning of their songs.

In the 1930's, the linguist Abraham Halpern began his study of the Quechan language. With the help of the Quechan singer William Wilson and others, Halpern made a transcription of *Lighting,* excerpts of which were included in *Spirit Mountain: An Anthology of Yuman Story and Song*, published in 1984.[45] Referring to the excerpts that he included in *Spirit Mountain,* Halpern seemed to suggest that a performance of *Lightning* involved singing as well as spoken narration, "In this narration, the singer as a rule first described the actions of the protagonist and then sang a series of songs relating to the same actions."[46] In *Spirit Mountain,* Halpern included twenty-nine episodes from *Lightning.*[47] Each of these twenty-nine episodes consists of a segment of the story that the singer narrated by *speaking*. Of these, twenty-seven are followed by a set of brother songs, meaning that a performance of these episodes probably involved both *speaking* and *singing*. Halpern wrote out the words for each episode, in both English and in Quechan, thus making it possible to consider the sound of the words in each song as well as the subject matter of each song.

Today's performances of a song cycle almost always involve singing, without spoken narration. In what follows, I consider a selection of creation story texts that were

---

[45] See Leanne Hinton and Lucille Watahomigie, editors. *Spirit Mountain: An Anthology of Yuman Story and Song* (Tucson: University of Arizona Press, 1984), 335-344. "Episodes" is my terminology.

[46] *Spirit Mountain,* 335.

[47] In the 1930's and in New York, George Herzog recorded Halpern singing a selection of *Lighting* songs. See George Herzog "United States, New York, ca. 1937-1938." The Archives of Traditional Music, Indiana University), Accession number, 87-043-F. The contemporary Quechan singer Preston Arrowweed performs *Lightning*. Arrowweed tells the story of *Lighting* in the new film by Daniel Golding. See Golding, director, videography, and film editor, *Journey from Spirit Mountain.* DVD. Produced by the Ah-Mut Foundation in association with the Hokan Media Productions, 2007.

gathered 50 to 100 years ago. Most if not all of these texts contain hints in the form of remarks or brief notes that provide some information concerning how the creation story was narrated. I show that the act of performing a creation story may have involved the narration of a long sequence of episodes, and that many of these episodes may have included both a spoken part (a part in which the singer conveyed a segment of the story through the medium of speech) and a set of songs (wherein the singer touches on the same subject matter but now by singing a set of brother songs). None of the other creation story texts that I consider provides as much detail about the songs and the spoken sections as does Halpern's excerpts of *Lightning*. As will be seen in the following discussion, a set of brother songs can convey a great deal of information; further the information conveyed in a set of songs seems designed to approach a topic in a way that complements the spoken segment.

Consider a single episode from *Lightning*, one that focuses on the stars as they move through the skies (See Figure 1.C-i).[48] *Lightning* describes the journey of a super human being known as Wonder Boy who exists at what I refer to as the time of creation.[49] As he travels, Wonder Boy describes what he sees. In the spoken section of the episode in question, the narrator begins by saying: "Thus, it became light, and the stars which have emerged and come this way dwindle." Next, the narrator refers to Wonder Boy, who has been "going along heading west." At this point, the narrator, now

---

[48] Shown in Figure 1.C-i. This is the 28th of the 29 episodes that Halpern included in his excerpts from *Lightning,* in *Spirit Mountain,* 343.

[49] I discuss the time of creation and other related concepts in more depth in Chapters 2 and 3. However, I must emphasize that I am not principally concerned with the exegesis of creation stories per se; instead I focus on the larger question of how creation stories may once have been performed, and their possible relationship to song cycles today.

taking on the voice of Wonder Boy, looks up at the stars and says, "I will describe you." With these words, Wonder Boy refers to the five songs that he is about to sing. Next the narrator watches Wonder Boy as he begins to sing. The narrator says that Wonder Boy "stood describing it again. He is telling of the morning star."

(Quechan)	(English)
'aíim vaàíim nyam 'anyáayem xamshé kwacuupáac viikwadíivec mataavíirek 'anyaaxáap tadóm petek viiyáam ayúuk, nyakanáavxa kanáaventi viiváwk.	Thus, it became light, and the stars which have emerged and come this way dwindle and going along heading west, he sees it and saying, "I will describe you," he stood describing it again. He is telling of the morning star.
1 xamuushíits aamay nuuwaamk	Stars pass overhead
2 xamuushíits aamay vuuxwiirk	Stars wandering overhead
3 xamuushíits aamay nuuyiivk	Stars pass overhead
4 xamuushíits aamaym uunyayk	Stars trail across the sky
5 xamuushíits aamaym nyaavaak	Stars trail across the sky
nyakaanaavk aanyemuuvany	He describes stars sitting in the sky.

Figure 1.C-i. An episode from Halpern's transcription of *Lightning.*[50]
Source: *Spirit Mountain,* p. 343.
(Note: See Appendix 1: Pronunciation guides.)

Similar sounds

Figure 1.C-i shows that the majority of these five brother songs contain similar

---

[50]Halpern did not use the writing system that I am employing. For instance, for the first songs, he did not write xamuushíits aamay nuuwaamk; instead, he wrote xamu:šíːc aːmay nuːwaːmk, as can be seen in Figure 1.C-ii. In Halpern's writing system, "ː" indicates the preceding vowel is extended; furthermore "š" sounds much like "sh." "C" sounds something like an English "ts." Believing that many of the people, like myself, will not be linguists, I decided to write out the words to these songs, without using any special symbols. I do the however use accents marks to indicate which syllable is stressed in speech. Therefore I wrote "xamu:šíːc aːmay nuːwaːmk" as "xamuushíits aamay nuuwaamk." Amy Miller kindly assisted with the writing of these words. She also provided the alphabets that I use in Appendix 1: Pronunciation Guides.

sounds. Halpern placed the fifth song on two separate lines (Figure 1.C-ii). For the purposes of analysis, I label the two lines of song 5 as lines 5a and 5b. As can be seen in Figure 1.C-iii, songs 1-4 and line 5a, all contain common words and sounds. The first shared sound is *xamuushiits.* The second is either *aamay,* or the similarly sounding *aamaym.* Thus the sounds for songs 1-4 and line 5a can be represented as: $a + b$ (or b') + x^{1-5}. As I will show, line 5b is similar to songs 1-4 to and line 5a because it focuses on the same subject, the stars. However, because the words for lines 5b sound nothing like those that came before, I represent the text for line 5b with the symbols $c + d$.

1	xamu:ši:c a:may nu:wa:mk	Stars pass overhead
2	xamu:ši:c a:may vu:xwi:rk	Stars wandering overhead
3	xamu:ši:c a:may nu:yi:vk	Stars pass overhead
4	xamu:ši:c a:may u:nyayk	Stars trail across the sky
5a	xamu:ši:c a:may nya:va:k	Stars trail across the sky
5b	nyaka:na:vk a:nyemu:vany	He describes stars sitting in the sky

Figure 1.C-ii. The five songs, from *Spirit Mountain.*

The difference between songs 1-5a is found in the third words of each these song; but the sounds of these third words are not entirely unique. The shared sounds that exist between some of them constitute still another unifying element.[51] As shown in Figure 1.C-iv, the first syllable of the third words of songs 1-4 each contain a long *"uu"* vowel, a unifying element.

---

[51] Here, I refer to only some of the differences and similarities in these third words.

Words:	1st	2nd	3rd
1	a *xamuushiits*	b *aamay*	x^1 *nuuwaamk*
2	a *xamuushiits*	b *aamay*	x^2 *vuuxwiirk*
3	a *xamuushiits*	b *aamay*	x^3 *nuuyiivk*
4	a *xamuushiits*	b' *aamaym*	x^4 *uunyayk*
5a	a *xamuushiits*	b' *aamaym*	x^5 *nyaavaak*
5b	c nyakaanaavk	d *aanyemuuvany*	

Figure 1.C-iii. Shared sounds.

Third words		syllables		Final *"k"*
		1st	2nd	
1	*nuuwaamk*	*nuu*	*waamk*	*k*
2	*vuuxwiirk*	*vuu*	*xwiirk*	*k*
3	*nuuyiivk*	*nuu*	*yiivk*	*k*
4	*uunyayk*	*uun*	*yayk*	*k*
5a	*nyaavaak*	*nyaa*	*vaak*	*k*

Figure 1.C-iv. The last words of songs 1-5a.

These repeated *uu*'s would register in the minds of both singers and audience members, as these songs were performed, one after another. In addition, song 1-4 and the first line of song 5 all end with a final *k* sound, adding still another unifying element. In contrast, the sounds of the second syllables of songs 1-4 and of the first line of song 5a are unique. The pattern seems far from random. The variation seems subtle yet striking.

Similar subject matters

From the English translation that Halpern provided for each of these songs, there seems to be no doubt that all of these songs focus on the same subject matter, namely the stars in the sky. At the same time, each song focuses on some different aspect of the stars, so that each song is unique. As will be seen, the resulting variation is subtle. The differences are apparent yet not overstated.

The fact that each song focuses on the stars can be seen first of all in the words that they have in common. We have seen that in songs 1-4 and in the first line of song 5, the first words are the same, namely *xamuushiits*. *Xamuushiits* contains two parts: *xamuushii + ts*. *Xamuushii* seems to correspond to the spoken word *xamshé*, meaning "star." The *ts* is the subject marker, meaning that *xamshe* (star) is the subject of songs 1-4 and also of the first line of song 5. In the song, *xamshé-ts* has been altered. As shown in Figure 1.C-v, a vocable, in the form of the long vowel *uu*, has been inserted into this word, transforming it from a spoken word to a sung word:

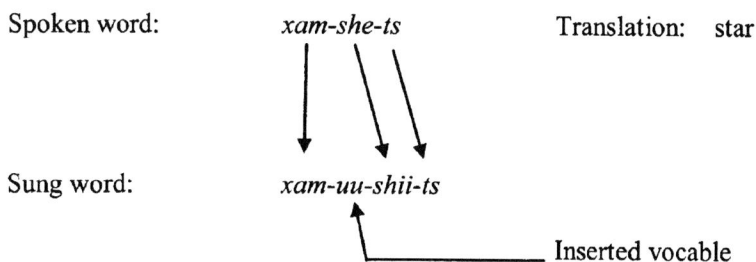

Spoken word: *xam-she-ts*   Translation: star

Sung word: *xam-uu-shii-ts*

                Inserted vocable

Figure 1.C-v. *Xamshé-ts* and *xamuushiits*.

Songs 1-4 and line 5a are also similar in that the second word of each of these songs is either *aamay* or *aamaym. Aamay* corresponds to the spoken word *'amay,* meaning "area above, high place, top summit, sky." Thus for songs 1 and 2, the first two words, *xamuushiits aamay,* mean something on the order of "stars, up above." The second word for 3-4, and 5a is *aamaym* (with the added suffix *m*). This suffix can mean "through" or "from." *Aamaym* can be translated as "through or from the sky above." The first two words of these three songs, *xamuushiits aamaym,* thus mean "stars, up through the sky." This is very similar to the meaning of the first two words of songs 1 and 2: "stars, up above, in the sky."

Thus, the first two words in brother songs 1-5a portray similar meanings. The real differences between songs 1-4 and the first line of song 5 are expressed in the last word of these songs. In the first brother song, the third word is *nuuwaamk.* This word probably corresponds to the spoken word *náam-k.* The suffix *"k"* indicates that this word is a verb. *Naam* means, "they go away from a reference point." As can be seen in Figure 1.C-vi, the spoken word, *naamk,* has been transformed into a sung word through the addition of the long vowel *uu.* This is followed by the consonant *w,* also inserted as a vocable. The *w* may have been added to separate the long *uu* from the long *aa* that directly follows.[52]

---

[52] Amy Miller, personal communication.

Spoken word: *náam-k*   Translation: a group of somethings is
                                               going

Sung word: *n-uu-w-aam-k*

                                ————— Inserted vocables

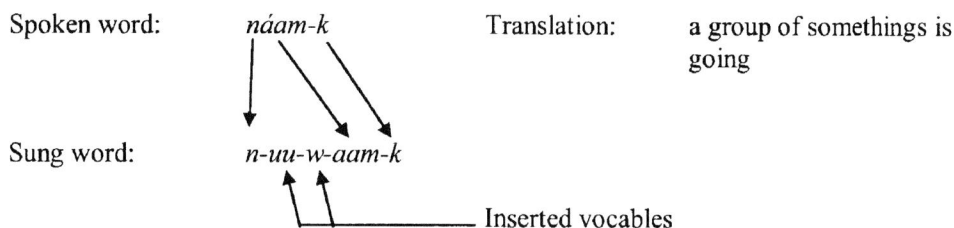

Figure 1.C-vi. *Náam-k* and *nuuwaamk.*

Halpern's translation for this song is as follows:

	(Quechan)	(English)
1	*xamuushíits áamay nuuwaamk*	Stars pass overhead[53]

The first song sets the stage for subject matter that Wonder Boy will be describing with
this set of brother songs, namely the stars, as they move across the skies. Each
subsequent brother song describes the stars but in some slightly different fashion.
Halpern's translations of songs 1 and 2 begin to show the subtle differences in the way
that each of these songs approaches the act of looking at the stars. Halpern's translation
of song 1 depicts Wonder Boy describing the stars, as they *pass* overhead. In subtle
contrast, with his translation of song 2, Halpern shows Wonder Boy as describing the
stars, as they *wander* overhead. Here is Halpern's translation of song 2:

	(Quechan)	(English)
2	*xamuushíits áamay vuuxwiirk*	Stars wandering overhead

Halpern's translation for the third song presents still another method used for establishing
unity between a set of songs, while still allowing each song to be unique. Here is
Halpern's translation for the third song:

---

[53] It appears that Halpern's translation for *nuuwaamk* is "to pass."

	(Quechan)	(English)
3	*xamuushíits aamay nuuyiivk*	Stars pass overhead

As can be seen, Halpern's translation for song 3 is identical to his translation of song 1,

suggesting that the last words for song 1 (*nuuwaamk*) and for song 3 (*nuuyiivk*) carry the

same meaning. Halpern translated the fourth brother song as:

	(Quechan)	(English)
4	*xamuushíits aamay uunyayk*	Stars trail across the sky

Thus song 4 presents still another method for describing the motion of the stars in the

skies. Here is Halpern's translation for the first line of the fifth song.

	(Quechan)	(English)
5a	*xamuushíits aamay nyaavaak*	Stars trail across the sky

As can be seen, Halpern's translation for song 5a is identical to the one that he provided

for song 4, suggesting that the third words of song 4 (*uunyayk*) and the first line of song 5

(*nyaavaak)* mean the same thing.

The situation may not be so obvious, however. Finding the spoken word that

corresponds to *nyaavaak* is not so straightforward. In attempting to find a spoken word

or words that might correspond to *nyaavaak*, Miller[54] has suggested three possibilities:

uuváa (to be present and moving about), *uuvá* (to sit), and *aváa* (to arrive). In thinking

about how *nyaavaak* may be related to a spoken word, I will consider just one of these

words, *aváa* (to arrive). See Figure 1.C-vii.

---

[54] Again, based on personal communications.

Spoken word: *avá-k*   Translation: to be situated

Sung word: *ny-aa-vaa-k*

Inserted consonant and lengthened vowels[55]

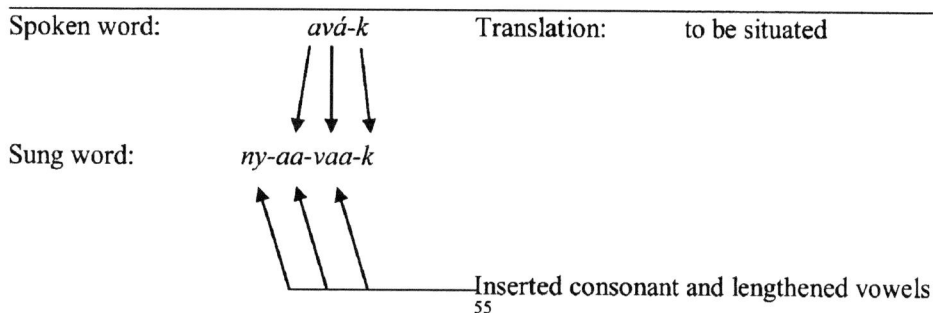

Figure 1.C-vii. Possible relationship between *avá-k* (a spoken word) and *nyaavaak*.

Whereas the third words for song 4 and the first line of 5 probably do not carry the same meaning, these two songs still provide two subtly different ways of describing the motion of the stars. The second line of song 5 contains only two words. The translation provided by Halpern is:

	(Quechan)	(English)
5b	*nyakaanaavk aanyemuuvany*	He describes stars sitting in the sky

Thus, the second line of song 5b presents still another viewpoint, from which to describe the motion of the stars in the skies.

As seen in this example, when combined with a segment of the narrative that is spoken, this set of songs offers a complementary method of describing the same subject matter. As seen in Figure 1.C-i, the spoken segment contains a number of details. For instance, in the spoken section, the narrator refers to Wonder Boy. The narrator tells us that Wonder Boy has been traveling. With the onset of night, Wonder Boy pauses to sing about the stars. Whereas each song contains relatively few words, when taken together

---

[55] The consonant "*n*" is added to the start of the sung word. In the sung word, the vowel "*a*" is lengthened. It becomes "*aa.*" I thank Leanne Hinton, for this insight.

this set of songs enables Wonder Boy to describe the stars from a number of different points of view.

While the above discussion is based both on the similar sounds of the texts and the meanings of the words, listeners can still easily distinguish the progression of sounds as they listen to sets of songs. It is not difficult to hear when a singer has finished singing one set of songs and begins to sing the next, for the words and the vocables in each subsequent set will be different enough so as to be unique. This then provides a much better sense of what it means to perform and to listen to a song cycle. Throughout the ESCR, singers can be heard performing song cycles. Like *Bird* and *Lightning,* many of these song cycles contain an underlying rhythmic pattern that is relatively rapid and therefore easily danced to.[56] Other song cycles contain songs that are performed at much slower tempos, but can still be danced to.[57] Regardless of the tempo, the overall structure of song cycles today is relatively straightforward. They consist of the performance of one set of songs after another.

At the Boundary of the ESCR

When describing a style of music as performed within a given region, it is always helpful to consider the styles performed outside that region. As one moves from the ESCR to the boundary region outside it, the transition may not be abrupt, however. ESCR song cycles are performed outside of the ESCR, but so are other styles of music, ones that apparently cannot be heard within the ESCR. Figure 1.D-i (p. 66) provides a

---

[56] See the *Bird* song, in "Singing and Dancing," Chapter 1.

[57] For example, consider the Mohave *Deer* song.

map of the ESCR with some of the areas that extend beyond it. In particular, it shows the areas to the north and to the northeast of this Extended Southern Californian Region. In these bordering areas, some singers perform ESCR song cycles. Others seem to have adopted ESCR songs and then transformed them. This seems to have been the case, for example, for the Walapai and the Havasupai. Both are Yuman-speaking tribes; and both are located upstream of the Mohave along the Colorado River. Walapai singer Keith Mahone, for instance, has released a commercial recording of himself singing *Bird*,[58] suggesting that at least some ESCR song cycles have been adopted by at least some Walapai singers. This is also true for the Havasupai.

In the previous section, I focused on an episode from Halpern's published excerpts of *Lightning*. By focusing on the texts of the songs, the sounds of their words and their meaning, I demonstrated how a topic can be illuminated by considering it from many different points of view, as expressed in one song after another. Here, I briefly first touch on an example of a Havasupai song and the contrasting manner in which this song is used to convey a story, and then on the idea that Southern Paiute tribes adopted some ESCR song cycles. In her dissertation on Havasupai music, Leanne Hinton discusses a number of the different styles of performance that the Havasupai use. The Havasupai as well as other tribes outside of the ESCR have songs that seem to be designed to tell a story, through the medium of song. Consider, for example, Hinton's translation of *Matathwidita*, a Havasupai song that begins with a description of the actions of an old lady as she attempts to shoo away some children who are teasing her. With each line of

---

[58] See Keith Mahone's *Bird songs of the Hualapai.* CD (Phoenix, Arizona: Canyon Records, 1996).

the song, the singer adds to the story, progressing through the narrative, from start to finish. The words to the song tell the story, with no need for the singer to pause and speak in order to clarify what is happening. Figure 1.D-ii (p. 67) shows an excerpt from this story, as translated by Hinton in her line-by-line translation of the song, together with her running summaries that focus on conveying the gist of each line or of several lines.

Like the Havasupai, the Southern Paiute, whose tribes are located to the north of the Havasupai and the Walapai, have styles of music that are distinct from the ESCR style of performance and some styles that are similar.[59] At the same time, the Southern Paiute sing songs that are related to some ESCR cycles. Sometime in the late nineteenth century, the Southern Paiute tribes are said to have adopted four ESCR song cycles. In 1910, linguist Edward Sapir, on the basis of his interviews with the Paiute singer, Tony Tillohash, reported that the Southern Paiute had adopted four ESCR song cycles *(Salt, Coyote, Bird,* and *Mountain Sheep)* as well as aspects or facets of the funeral/mourning

---

[59] William Bright writes that the term "Southern Paiute" refers to "some sixteen Numic bands or subgroups which share a geographical center in Southern Utah." He also states that Uto-Aztecan languages, specifically those classified as belonging to the Numic branch, were spoken throughout the Great Basin. See Edward Sapir's *Southern Paiute and Ute Linguistics and Ethnography,* ed. William Bright. The Collected Works of Edward Sapir. Vol. 10 (Hawthorne, New York: Mouton de Gruyter, 1992), p. 13.

ceremony as practiced by ESCR tribes.[60]

In the process of adopting these four ESCR song cycles and aspects of ESCR ceremonies, the Southern Paiute apparently changed them, at least to some degree. On one hand, some songs were (or are) performed in sets. Referring to the "Cry," or funeral ceremony, Sapir stated: "Some of the 'cry' songs belonged together in a set of two or three and were sung together. Such were called 'brothers.'"[61] Sapir suggested that Paiute musicians had retained some aspect of the songs they had adopted. At the same time, Sapir wrote that the Paiute were adapting, changing the songs, employing them, for instance, in contexts that may have been foreign to an ESCR musician of the time. Whereas today ESCR musicians perform *Bird* at funerals and wakes, in the nineteenth and during the first quarter of the twentieth centuries, this may not have been the case. At that time, ESCR musicians probably still performed song cycles specifically reserved

---

[60] Sapir met Tony Tillohash, at the Carlisle Indian School, in 1910. Tillohash then moved to Philadelphia, for three months, where Sapir was able to interview him. See Sapir, Collected Works, Vol. 10, p. 789. Regarding the adoption of ESCR song cycles, see Sapir's "The Mourning Ceremony of the Southern Paiutes (Abstract)," as published in *Science* 35, 673 (1912); in *American Anthropologist* 14, 169 (1912); and reprinted in Edward, Sapir's *Culture*, Edited by Darnell, Regna, Judith Irvine, and Richard Handler. The Collected Works of Edward Sapir. Vol. 3 (Berlin: Mouton de Gruyter, 1999). For a more detailed treatment of the same, see "Kaibab Paiute and Northern Ute Ethnographic Field Notes," Sapir, Collected Works, Vol. 10, 780.
[61] Sapir, Collected Works, Vol. 10, 836.

for wakes and funerals.[62]   Concerning the Southern Paiute, however, Sapir wrote that

Salt and *Coyote* and *Bird* and *Mountain Sheep* were, however, sung at their Cry (funeral)

ceremonies. Tillohash reported that the Paiute had conducted ten different Cry

ceremonies, from 1894-1909, suggesting that these ceremonies were held on an

approximately annual basis.

As further evidence that the Southern Paiute had changed the ESCR songs that

they had adopted, Sapir noted that these songs appeared to be in a Yuman language.

Since Paiute is a Uto-Aztecan language, Paiute singers would probably have not been

able to understand these songs. Sapir writes that the Southern Paiute were responding to

this problem by transforming the songs, by gradually replacing the Yuman words and

vocables with Paiute vocables. Or, as explained by the editors of *Culture: The Collected*

Works of Edward Sapir,

> Sapir's interview notes and his annotations to several Cry song texts make it clear
> that Southern Paiute singers, specifically song leaders from Moapa and St.
> George, were actively involved in composing new roan/salt and bird songs and in
> transforming the language and music of older ones, effectively reducing the
> original Yuman texts to vocables. Thus it is not surprising that overall the non-
> Paiute Cry song texts are no longer recognizable as Yuman, although the sound
> may be. [63]

---

[62] For a description of some of the music that would have been heard at a funeral of a
Yuman-speaking tribe, see T.T. Waterman, *The Religious Practices of the Diegueño.*
University of California Publications in American Archaeology and Ethnology 8, no.6
(Berkeley, University of California Press, 1910). This is reprinted in *The Early
Ethnography of the Kumeyaay.* Classics in California Anthropology, edited by Steven
Shackley (Berkeley: Phoebe Hearst Museum of Anthropology, University of California,
Berkeley, 2004).   For a more detailed discussion, see Abraham Halpern's *Kar?uk:
Native Accounts of the Quechan Mourning Ceremony.* Edited by Amy Miller, and
Margaret Langdon. University of California Publications in Linguistics 128 (Berkeley,
Calif: University of California Press, 1997).

[63] See Sapir, Collected Works, Vol. 3, p. 565.

So there are musicians outside the ESCR who sing cycles such as *Bird* that are also sung within the ESCR today. In one case, the Southern Paiute apparently adopted some ESCR song cycles perhaps a century or so ago, during which time they may have changed, as the Paiute gradually assimilated them. In addition, the excerpt from the Havasupai song *Matathwidita* (Figure 1.D-ii) shows that the idea of songs that tell stories extends well beyond the ESCR. As part of their winter stories, the Paiute were known to have stories in which the spoken narrative was interspersed with songs. It seems likely that story/songs, as a genre, are widespread. The approach that ESCR singers have developed may be unique, however, in that no one song is expected by itself to convey a segment of the story. It is rather a set of songs that used to illuminate a subject from a variety of perspectives.

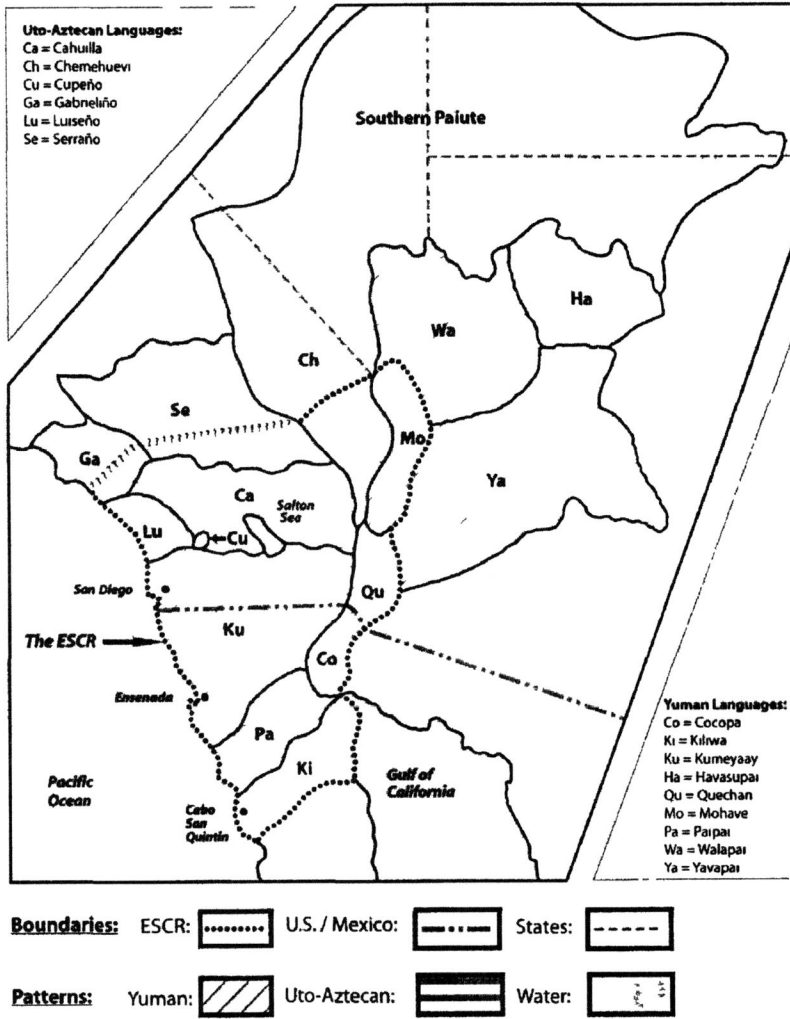

Figure 1.D-i. Map 2: Showing the ESCR, the Pai-Speaking tribes of the Colorado, and the Southern Paiute.

Line-by-line translation:[64]	Running summary:[65]
Matathwidita (place name)	*Matathwidita* was our warm home.
Warm house	Children were playing there.
Clay (Voices) ringing, ringing There they were doing it Using a slingshot	Voices ringing, they were using slingshots and shooting clay balls.
There they were doing it, until The boy who cries easy "Tay,tay!"	The-Boy-Who-Cried-Easy cried out, "Tay,Tay!"
That's what he said Old Lady The one who loses her temper easy	The-Old-Lady-Who-Loses-Her-Temper-Easy got up and picked up her cane, thinking the other kids were hurting the little boy.
She got up (Her) cane She picked it up She's swish-swished it She chased them They ran this way and that	She ran after the kids, swishing her cane, and the kids scattered.
There she was doing it "Do it now!" "Why are you Running away?" That's what she said	-She yelled "Come on, try it again! Why are you running away?"

Figure 1.D-ii. An Excerpt from *Matathwidita*, a Havasupai song, as translated by Leanne Hinton.

---

[64] From Hinton's dissertation, "Havasupai Songs," p. 298-301.
[65] Ibid., 296.

The Work of Alfred Kroeber

There are several scholars spoke with singer/storytellers between 50 and 100 years ago. The evidence they collected about how creation stories may have been told consists of fragmented pieces that will be very different from the kind of relatively clear evidence that Halpern provided. We shall see that many scholars wrote down creation stories as they listened to these stories being told. For the most part, these texts were designed to convey the substance and the content of the stories, to name the main characters, and to describe their actions, but not to document how these stories were told. Yet each of these scholars was presumably speaking with a singer or singers who knew *how* these stories were usually told, when and where, and for whom. As I begin to examine more creation story texts, I show that each text contains at least some information concerning how the story was told. It is almost as if the raconteurship of each singer/storyteller was so notable, and so recognized by everyone in attendance, that each researcher found him- or herself drawn to include at least vestigial bits and pieces of information that provide some information about the singer and how he told his story. I will show that when enough creation stories are considered, a picture begins to unfold, one that suggests that the telling of all or most creation stories seems to have consisted of the narration of a sequence of episodes, many of which appear to have been associated with a set of songs. Because creation stories apparently involved the narration of a sequence of episodes, it seems possible that their performance may in some sense have been similar to the way song cycles are performed today.

Of the scholars who studied an ESCR tribe or tribes, the well-known anthropologist Alfred Kroeber stands out for his research into the creation stories of the Mohave, of which he collected a relatively large number in the first decade of the 1900's. Kroeber wrote down the stories as he heard them told, producing creation texts that stand out in part because of their copious details. Invariably at least some of these details shed light on the question of how these stories may have been told. Still another feature of these creations stories texts makes them relevant for the present study. Each of these creation story texts consists of a sequence of episodes. Kroeber also developed a method for showing that most episodes were associated with a set of songs. After each episode, he included a number that indicated the approximate number of songs that was associated with that episode. Because each song contained no more than a handful of words, Kroeber believed the songs were irrelevant and therefore only rarely included any of them. Still, the Mohave creation stories that Kroeber documented constitute a useful body of evidence, relevant for anyone interested in learning more about how these stories may have once been narrated, a subject to be explored in Chapters 2 and 3. Here I will consider the history of Kroeber's study with the Mohave and their creation stories.[66]

Kroeber is known for his studies of the tribes of California. Perhaps less well known, however, is the fact that his interest in stories and literature spanned his entire career and predated his studies of anthropology. Like Herzog, Heidsiek, and Kwiatkowska,[67] Kroeber's initial academic training involved the study of some aspect of the canon of Euro-American literature. Kroeber enrolled in Columbia College in New

---

[66] This is a subject that I expand upon, Chapters 2 and 3, when I consider Kroeber's transcriptions in more depth.

[67] See "Singing and Dancing," this chapter.

York in 1892, and completed a Bachelor of Arts, and a Master's degree, with a thesis

entitled, "The English Heroic Play."[68] In 1896, he began to study anthropology with

Franz Boas. His first seminar in anthropology involved a topic that seems to have

embraced his interest in English literature while also offering him an introduction to the

oral literature of a non-Euro/American culture. This was a class in the translation of

Chinook texts, as taught by Franz Boas. Kroeber received his doctorate in anthropology

in 1901. Funded in part by philanthropist Phoebe Hearst, he then went to California. In

the same year, he received an appointment in the Anthropology Department at the

University of Berkeley.[69] For the next decade, he traveled throughout the state, studying

and surveying the tribes of California.

By 1917, Kroeber had completed his *Handbook of the Indians of California,*

which synthesized the data that he and other scholars had gathered about California

tribes. Kroeber characterized his *Handbook* as containing "a series of tribal

descriptions." [70] Neither this characterization nor the layout of the his *Handbook* (which

is divided into chapters, in most cases, one chapter per tribe) make obvious Kroeber's

---

[68] See Timothy Thoresen's "*A.L. Kroeber's The Theory of Culture: The Early Years*" (PhD diss., University of Iowa, 1971), 2
[69] See Ibid., p.68, as well as his "Kroeber and the Yurok, 1900-1908," that is included in Kroeber's *Yurok Myths,* edited by Grace Buzaljko, (Berkeley: University of California Press, 1976), xix-xxvii.
[70] Kroeber's wife, Theodora, writes that Kroeber had finished his *Handbook* in 1917; but the Smithsonian was unable to publish it, due to the onset of World War I. See p. xvi of Theodora Kroeber's "Foreword" to A.L. Kroeber's and E.W. Gifford's *Karok Myths,* edited by Grace Buzaljko, (Berkeley: University of California Press, 1980), 1-380. See A.L. Kroeber's *Handbook of the Indians of California.* Bureau of the American Ethnology at the Smithsonian Institution, Bulletin 78 (Washington: Government Printing Office, 1925; New York: Dover Publications, Inc., 1976). See the "Preface" to Kroeber's *Handbook,* p. v.

interest in collecting stories, or the amount of time that he devoted to this area of
research.

Even as he prepared the *Handbook* for publication, Kroeber apparently never
ceased to study the oral literatures of several tribes: the Karok, Yurok, and Mohave.
Upon his arrival in California, Kroeber had began to work with the Mohave, who lived in
a desert-like region along the Colorado River, and with the Yurok and Karok, who lived
in the coastal forests in Northern California.[71]   The geographical contrast in the
environments of these two tribal populations may have been one factor that led Kroeber
to select them.   Regardless of his initial motivation, Kroeber continued to study the
literature of these three tribes, off and on, for the rest of his life.[72]   Throughout his career,
Kroeber continued to work with at least one storyteller from Northern California, the
Yurok storyteller Robert Spott.[73]   Like the Karok and the Yurok, Kroeber's work with

---

[71] Timothy Thorensen and Ira Jacknis, each of whom have written about Kroeber's early
career, emphasize Kroeber's work with the Karok but not his work with the Mohave.
They also seem to suggest that his studies of the stories of the Mohave and the Karok and
the Yurok was over, by 1910. See Thoresen's preface, "Kroeber and the Yurok, 1900-
1908," in the posthumous publication of Kroeber, *Yurok Myths* (Berkeley: University of
California Press, 1976), p. xxvii. Thorensen's dissertation reviews Kroeber's theories
until circa 1930, and includes a useful introduction to Kroeber's early years. See
Thorensen, "A.L. Kroeber's The Theory of Culture: The Early Years," (PhD diss.,
University of Iowa, 1971), 15-32; and Ira Jacknis, "Alfred Kroeber and the Photographic
Representations of California Indians," *American Indian Culture and Research Journal*,
20, no. 3 (1996).
[72] For a bibliography of Kroeber's publications, see his *Handbook.* Also see the
biography written by his wife, Theodora Kroeber: *Alfred Kroeber, A Personal
Configuration* (Berkeley: University of California Press, 1970). Also see the online
bibliography at http://sunsite.berkeley.edu/Anthro/kroeber/pub/ (accessed on March 10,
2009).
[73] Kroeber's wife, Theodora, confirmed that Kroeber worked with Robert Spott on a long
term basis, from 1900-1953. See Theodora Kroeber's "Foreword" in A. L. Kroeber,
Yurok Myths, p. 14.

Mohave storytellers began in the first decade of the 1900's.

Kroeber did not begin to publish the stories he had collected until his retirement in the 1940's, however. At times, he seems to have broached the idea of publishing these stories, but apparently ran into resistance of one sort or another. In a 1928 letter to the well-known anthropologist Ruth Benedict, he hinted that he had not published these stories because he had too "many irons in the fire." Perhaps more importantly, he added that his "Editorial Committee" was reluctant to publish them because they were folklore; nevertheless, he asked Benedict if she might be interested in publishing the Mohave and Yurok stories that he had collected. The journal that Kroeber refers to in the following excerpt from a letter to Benedict was probably the *Journal of American Folklore*.[74]

> I do not know whether either collection would be suitable for the Journal. The Mohave would probably run to 150 to 200 printed pages, and the Yurok twice as much. The Mohave stories are only twelve or fifteen in number and a couple of them so long that I never did get them finished. I put one such sample in my Handbook to give some idea of the quality.[75]

Benedict apparently did not write back until June 11, 1934, at which time she asked him if the stories were still available for publication.[76] On July 3, Kroeber wrote to Benedict, saying: "I will get the Mohave myths out of storage next time I am in Berkeley and see how much they need done to them." By August 20th, he had done so and wrote her again, saying:

---

[74] Benedict was the editor from 1925 to 1940. See the "Biographical Note", in the *Guide to the Ruth Fulton Benedict Papers, 1905-1948,* at Vassar College Libraries. See the online finding aid at: http:// specialcollections.vassar.edu/findingaids/benedict_ruth.html (accessed on May 25, 2010).
[75] In this letter, Kroeber also mentions that Benedict had sent Kroeber her survey of "Mohave kinship data." See Kroeber to Benedict, 20 February 1928, Ruth Fulton Benedict Papers, Folder 30.13, Vassar College Library.
[76] Ibid. Benedict to Kroeber, 11 June 1934.

I looked my Mohave tales over. They are more interesting than I remember, and I shall have something to say about them. The type-copy will need checking back against the original note-books for proper names, etc; and there ought to be a map or some device for the geographical framework, which is not only obtrusive but significant. I will get to these things after returning to Berkeley about Sept 1.[77]

In 1942, Kroeber finally began to publish the stories that he had collected. In that

year, *Yurok Narratives* appeared, jointly authored by Kroeber and Yurok storyteller

Robert Spott.[78] Of the twelve to fifteen Mohave stories that he had mentioned to

Benedict, Kroeber published seven in a monograph entitled *Seven Mohave Myths*

(SMM), in 1948, which would be the first of what would become a three-monograph

series of the Mohave stories he collected.[79] The stories that Kroeber included in SMM

were ones that he had recorded from 1903 to 1905, either at or near to two reservations

where most Mohave lived, or at the university's Museum of Anthropology in San

Francisco.[80]

In his *Handbook,* Kroeber used Mohave stories as evidence to support his

description of Mohave culture. In his publications of Mohave stories, the process was

---

[77] Ibid. Kroeber to Benedict, 20 August 1934.

[78] See Robert Spott and A.L. Kroeber, *Yurok Narratives*. University of California Publications in American Archeology 35, no. 9 (1942): 143-256. In the discussion above, I have not included all of the Kroeber's post-retirement of Yurok stories, instead I have focused on his book-length publications. For two of the former, see his "A Yurok War Reminiscence: The Use of Autobiographical Evidence," *Southwestern Journal of Anthropology*, 1, no. 3 (1946): 318-32; and "A Karok Orpheus myth," *Journal of American Folklore*, 59, no. 231 (1946): 13-19. These two publications are, however, relatively brief, more like his survey-period publications.

[79] I abbreviate *Seven Mohave Myths* as *SMM*. See A.L. Kroeber, *Seven Mohave Myths*. *Anthropological Records* 11 no. 1 (Berkeley, California: University of California Press, 1948).

[80] At this point, the museum was still located in San Francisco. Mohave tribal members are enrolled both at the Fort Mohave Reservation in Fort Mohave, Arizona, and at the Colorado Tribes Reservation in Parker, Arizona, near Needles, California. Both reservations are located along the Colorado River. The Colorado Tribes Reservation from four tribes: Mohave, Chemehuevi, Navajo, and Hopi.

reversed. In SMM, Kroeber considered the Mohave through the lens of their creation stories, giving a sense that his understanding of the Mohave may have developed as he studied, recorded, and analyzed their creation stories. The second of Kroeber's publications of Mohave creation stories, *A Mohave Historical Epic* (MHE), appeared in 1951. This publication was devoted to a single epic tale, one that had been told to Kroeber by the Mohave singer Inyo-kutavêre in 1902.[81] To give some idea as to the amount of time that it took him to record a long story, Kroeber reports that *Inyo-kutavêre* continued to narrate his story for six days. Even after six days, *Inyo-kutavêre* had not reached the end of his story; but Kroeber had to stop recording since he needed to return to the university.[82]

Kroeber probably completed his last volume of Mohave stories, *More Mohave Myths* (*MMM*) in 1960, a year before he died,[83] although it was not published until 1972.[84] It contains stories that Kroeber had collected between 1902 and 1910 and also in 1953-54. *MMM* includes an additional 11 Mohave creation stories along with Kroeber's

---

[81] A.L. Kroeber, *A Mohave Historical Epic*. Anthropological Records, 11, no. 2 (Berkeley, California: University of California Press, 1951), 71-176. I will be referring to this publications with the initials MHE.

[82] Ibid., 71.

[83] Kroeber returned to study Mohave creation stories, after he had retired. In her "Preface" to *More Mohave Myths* (MMM), Theodora writes that she along with Kroeber and a graduate student visited the Mohave, in 1953 and in 1954. There, they journeyed up and down the Colorado River, as they studied the places mentioned in the Mohave creation stories. (Regarding geographical places, in Mohave creation stories, see my Chapters 2 and 3.) Writing about this journey in his MMM, Kroeber notes that: "Many songs series were still known and sung among the Mohave in 1953 and 1954, and presumably survive in 1960." See A. L. Kroeber, *More Mohave Myths*. Anthropological Records, 27 (Berkeley, California: University of California Press, 1972), 157. 1960 was probably the year in which Kroeber made this statement.

[84] After Kroeber's death in 1961, his wife, Theodora continued to publish the stories that Kroeber had recorded and had prepared for publication.

analysis of all of the Mohave stories that he published.[85]   Under Theodora Kroeber's

supervision, *Kurok Myths* appeared in 1976.   Finally, in 1980 *Karok Myths* appeared,

containing stories gathered by Kroeber and his colleague E.W. Gifford.[86]

In conclusion, Kroeber eventually published a large number of Mohave creation

stories, some during his life, others posthumously.   In the following two chapters I will

consider the texts collected by Kroeber and others, looking for any evidence bearing on

how these stories were once performed.

---

[85] A.L. Kroeber, MMM, 1-160. For the dates regarding when stories were recorded, see
Chapter 2, Figures 2.B-xvii. and 2.B-xviii.

[86] See Kroeber, *Yurok Myths*, edited by Grace Buzaljko (Berkeley: University of
California Press, 1976), 1-484.; and A.L. Kroeber and E.W. Gifford *Karok Myths*, edited
by Grace Buzaljko (Berkeley: University of California Press, 1980), 1-380.

CHAPTER 2

TRANSCRIBING THE STORIES AND THE SONGS

Since most of what we know about these creation stories comes from the work of scholars in the first half of the twentieth century, their individual methods of recording the stories they heard is of critical importance. Some researchers have explicitly discussed the process of making a transcriptions, both by looking at the transcriptions of others as well as their own. This chapter will consider the two of George Herzog's transcriptions of ESCR songs as well as the transcriptions that the anthropologists Ruth Underhill and Kroeber made of a Mohave creation story.

In remarks that he probably wrote in 1960 upon his completion of MMM, Kroeber characterized his work with the Mohave and their creation stories as having been primarily *descriptive,* meaning both that he had written down the stories as he heard them and also that he had prepared and organized the stories for his readers. Writing about this, Kroeber explained:

> This has been a long undertaking, in time and in pages, and I want to consider in how far it may have been worth the expenditures.
>
> Basically, it has been a "descriptive" job--the conveying to the intellectual world of an organized body of new information. That seems the main service which this volume renders; and I regard the service not deprecatingly but with satisfaction. Intelligible description of course is not random itemization but an organized presentation with sufficient elucidation of background and context to make it meaningful in the culture to which it is presented.[1]

---

[1] A.L. Kroeber, "Prologue/Epilogue" in MMM, p. xi-xii.

As Kroeber indicates in the above quotation, his study of the Mohave and their creation stories was a long term project. Writing in 1988, the historian James Clifford reported that some anthropologists had begun to propose that ethnographic studies need not involve such lengthy periods of observation and analysis. Clifford explained that by 1925--some twenty-five years after Kroeber had begun his study of the Mohave-- anthropologists like Malinowski had already began to develop what seemed to them to be a much more efficient approach towards ethnography. By focusing on the social structure of a group or other key parameters, a researcher could generate an ethnographic description in a relatively short period of time, perhaps in two years or less, even if that anthropologist had had no prior experience with a people. Clifford pointed out that in the latter part of the nineteenth century many researchers did not actually gather the data themselves; instead they drew on ethnographic data that had been culled and synthesized by individuals who knew a particular people intimately, probably because they had lived with them for a decade or more.[2] Because he recorded his own data and thought about the Mohave for so long, Kroeber's study of the Mohave places him somewhere between the nineteenth century anthropologists who studied data gathered by others who knew a people intimately versus anthropologists such as Malinowski who gathered their own data but did so in a relatively short period of time. Kroeber, however, did not discount this style of research, which Clifford refers to as being the "new ethnography." In his review of Margaret Mead's 1930 work *Growing Up in New Guinea,* Kroeber admired

---

[2] See James Clifford, *The Predicament of Culture, Twentieth-Century Ethnography, Literature, and Art* (Cambridge: Harvard University Press, 1988), 23-27.

Mead's ability to get to describe the "principal currents of a culture" by offering "pen-pictures of astonishing sharpness." Still, probably as a reflection of his own experience, in periodically visiting and studying the culture of several tribes over an extended period of time, he wondered how far her knowledge really extended, for she had only spent six months in New Guinea.[3]

In 1984, and at roughly the same that Clifford offered his insights concerning the differences between late nineteenth century ethnographies and the "new ethnographies" of the 1920s, Frederika Randall, of the *New York Times*, noted still other questions that scholars had begun to ask about their profession. Obviously, the creation of an ethnography involved more than the reporting of a factual body of information about a people. As Kroeber had said, it also involved the packaging of that information into "an organized presentation." Randall reported that some researchers were troubled that anthropologists were packaging information since this sounded as if it involved storytelling.[4] Clifford pointed out that the idea that ethnographers had in some sense become storytellers had only been highlighted by the fact that some anthropologists such

---

[3] See Mead, *Growing Up in New Guinea, A Comparative Study of Primitive Education,* (New York, William Morrow, 1930). Also, see Kroeber, review of *Growing up in New Guinea,* by Margaret Mead, *American Anthropologist* 33, no. 2 (1931): 248-250. Also, see James Clifford's brief mention of Kroeber's discussion of Mead in Clifford's *Predicament,* 36.

[4] See Frederika Randall, "Why Scholars Become Storytelllers," The New York Times, January 29, 1984. At the present, this is available online at http://query.nytimes.com/gst/fullpage.html?res=9D0CE6DB163BF93AA15752C0A962948260 (accessed on September 20, 2007).

as Clifford Gertz had produced ethnographies that did in fact read like novels.[5]

Writing in 1996, the anthropologist Robert Aunger pointed out still another reason why anthropologists had begun to question whether or not anthropology was in fact a science. Aunger notes that Freeman (in 1984) and Mead (in 1928) had in fact "come to opposite conclusions about the same society," namely Samoan adolescent sexuality.[6] In response, Aunger argued on one hand that a group of fieldworkers whom he referred to as the textualists had begun to insert sections of their unedited field notes into their ethnographic reports, but without including sufficient analysis or interpretation. Unless a reader had an intimate knowledge of a culture, he or she would have a difficult time making sense of what was essentially raw data. Aunger also argued that some researchers were not removing what he called interpreter bias from their reports. Aunger asserted that this element could be removed by following a methodology he had developed and was designed to account for and eliminate the bias of individual interviewers. P. Steven Sangren disagreed, however. Referring to anthropologists in general, he wrote that "disputes of interpretation have always been with us." Sangren did not think that the adoption of any one approach, including the one suggested by Aunger, was likely to change this.[7]

The questions of whether any raw data should be included in an ethnography, and

---

[5] See Clifford Geertz, "Deep Play: Notes on the Balinese Cockfight," *Daedalus* 101 (1972): 1-37. Reprinted by the Geertz in *The Interpretation of Cultures* (New York: Basic Books, Inc, 1973).

[6] See Robert Aunger, "On Ethnography: Storytelling or Science?," *Current Anthropology* 36, no. 1 (1995): 97.

[7] Ibid. See Sangren's "Comments" to Aunger, on p. 121.

whether storytelling was a necessary ingredient, are ones that ethnographic film makers have grappled with as well. In his 2006 article "Narrative: The Guilty Secret of Ethnographic Documentary?" Paul Henley noted that Margaret Mead had also addressed this issue. When Kroeber characterized Mead's *Growing Up in New Guinea* as presenting the "principal currents of a culture," he implied that her ethnography had conveyed the experience of New Guinean youth in a condensed summary. Such a presentation would presumably leave little space for uninterpreted quotations from Mead's raw field notes. But Henley claimed that Mead believed that raw data should be presented, at least in some contexts. Henley reported that she believed that ethnographic films, for instance, ought to consist of raw, unedited footage. Or as Mead said, "the ethnographic film genre should consist exclusively of films of unexpurgated record, entirely faithful to both the chronology and duration."[8] Henley also explained that many ethnographic film makers had been loath to disagree with Mead's sentiment, for fear that their viewers might conclude that their films were unauthentic. As Henley explains:

> Once you admit that you have manipulated the filmic text, this threatens the very foundation of the claim that you are offering an authoritative representation based on the status of the photographic image as a direct and therefore truthful index of the world.[9]

---

[8] See Paul Henley, "Narrative: The Guilty Secret of Ethnographic Documentary?" in *Reflecting Visual Ethnography: Using the Camera in Anthropological Research* 145 (Leiden: CNWS Publications, 2006), 3. For Mead's article, see her "Visual Anthropology in a Discipline of Words," in *Principles of Visual anthropology*, ed. Paul Hockings. World anthropology (The Hague: Mouton, 1975). For more publications by Henley, see: http://www.socialsciences.manchester.ac.uk/disciplines/socialanthropology/about/staff/henley/ (accessed on March 10, 2009). Also see Ira Jacknis, "Margaret Mead and Gregory Bateson in Bali: Their Use of Photography and Film," *Cultural Anthropology*, 3, no. 2 (May, 1988): 160-177.

[9] Ibid. p. 8.

Through numerous examples of ethnographic films, Henley nevertheless demonstrated

that most if not all film makers do organize their raw footage; furthermore they do so

using what Henley referred to as linear narrative structures. Having filmed a ritual (or

some other ethnographic event) and having possibly also interviewed some of the

participants and/or bystanders, Henley writes that a film maker then generally returns to

his editing room, where he selects segments from his "rushes" and arranges them in a

particular sequence. The final product usually has a well defined beginning, middle, and

end. While film makers use different strategies to create such a structure, Henley argued

that all of elements of a linear narrative are needed. Explaining what he meant by the

beginning of a film, Henley explained that at some point near the beginning of a film, the

film maker must get the audience "on the train." Referring to this process, Henley wrote:

> Once you have got the audience "on the train", they have at least the illusion that
> they know where it is supposed to be going and everything is ready for the main
> body of the film, i.e. the Middle, to begin.[10]

With her research, the anthropologist Cécile Vigouroux has studied the moment-to-

moment decisions that the linguist Kate Riley made as she studied the process of

language socialization in the French-speaking family of Anne, Etienne, and their

newborn child.[11] (From this point on, I refer to this family as being A-E-B.) As A-E-B

ate dinner, Riley videotaped their conversations. On her own, Riley made a preliminary

---

[10] Henley, *Narratives*, 14.
[11] See Cécile B. Vigouroux, "Trans-scription as a Social Activity," *Ethnography* 8, no.1 (2007): 61-97.

transcript of the tape. When she next met with Anne and Etienne, Riley showed them the transcript, which they reviewed and edited together.

As Vigouroux observed Riley at work, both in person and by watching films that she made of Riley working with A-E-B, Vigouroux focused on the moment-to-moment decisions that Riley made as she worked with A-E-B. Vigouroux found that Riley's work involved two spheres of activities. During each, Vigouroux saw Riley as taking in and organizing data in qualitatively different ways. On one hand, Vigouroux noted that Riley spent time observing and listening to Anne, Etienne, and their baby. Attempting to capture the uniqueness of this task, Vigouroux referred to this facet of Riley's work as taking place in *speech event time,* a term that seems designed to capture the experience of a linguist as he or she listens precisely to what a person or persons were saying, while also observing their interactions. In his study of film ethnographers, Henley described a similar process, one involving the relationship between a camera operator and the people that he or she is filming. Regarding the process of operating a camera and taping a ritual activity, Henley stated that sometimes a camera operator falls into a trance-like state, one referred to as *ciné-transe,* during which he becomes closely linked with the people he is filming. Henley wrote that during *ciné-transe,* the camera operator was "in perfect choreographic harmony with the protagonists," that is, the people he or she is filming. Even though the operator is responding closely to the people that he is filming, Henley asserts that the camera operator still continues to make choices. Or, as Henley put it,

> Clearly, the camera-operator, even when in *ciné-transe* and reacting to the intrinsic *mise-en-scène,* continues to make a series of choices as to how to construct the order of his sequence shot and in so doing is imposing his own narrative structure on the event. [12]

It some respects, Vigouroux's *speech event time* seems analogous to *ciné-transe.*

Vigouroux also took note of another process that occurred as Riley worked. Vigouroux saw a difference between what Riley did when she was observing A-E-B versus how she acted as she transcribed their speech and then thought about how to revise her transcript. Vigouroux refers to the latter as being *transcription time.*[13]

Emphasizing the differences between *speech event time* and *transcription time,* Vigouroux explained that when Riley was observing A-E-B (and in *speech event time*) versus what she said and paid attention to when she was working on a transcript (and in *transcription time*). The same was true for Etienne and Anne. As they helped Riley to analyze her transcription, everyone would sit around a table, where they would look at the video tape, on a video monitor. Vigouroux noted that Etienne always took a seat that allowed him to see Riley's transcription as well as the video monitor. As a result, he was able to follow Riley, as she switched between speech *event time* and *transcription time.* In contrast, Anne sat in a position that allowed her to see the monitor but not the transcript. As a result, Vigouroux stated that Anne remained more-or-less stuck in *speech event time,* something that was reflected in the kinds of comments that she tended to make. Stepping back and thinking about the roles that Riley shifted between (from

---

[12] By *mise-en-scène,* Henley seems to be referring to everything that the camera operator sees. Henley, *Narratives,* 9.

[13] The idea is that during *transcription time,* an observer produces a *scription.*

speech time to transcription times), Vigouroux wrote that "while transcribing, Kate [Riley] was doing ethnographic fieldwork and vice versa."[14]

In her discussion of musical transcription, ethnomusicologist Nicole Beaudry focused on still another facet of the process of transcription. Beaudry wrote about the experiences that she had had as she transcribed an audio recording of an Inuit throat game.[15] In Inuit throat singing, two women face each other, their mouths in close proximity. As Woman A breathes in, Woman B breathes out, into Woman A's mouth. In the process, Woman B vocalizes/sings, using the vocal cavity of Woman A's mouth as a resonating chamber. The women then reverse roles.[16] Writing about the sequence of transcriptions that she had made of an audio recording of Inuit throat singing, Beaudry noted that as her understanding of what she was listening to deepened, the type of transcriptions that she produced changed. She maintained that each type was valid, since it reflected the particular phenomena that she was attending to at a given moment. At first, her transcriptions were primarily oriented towards *describing* the sounds that she was hearing. As she became much more familiar with the recording, she adopted qualitatively different forms of notation and symbols. As she explained, her transcriptions became more and more *prescriptive*: they increasingly came to look like a set of instructions that performers could use as they learned to take part in this throat

---

[14]See Cécile B. Vigouroux, "Trans-scription," p. 90.

[15] See Nicole Beaudry, "Toward Transcription and Analysis of Inuit Throat-Games: Macro-Structure," *Ethnomusicology* 22, no.2 (1978): 261-274.

[16] In contemporary throat singing, women stand or sit farther apart.

game.[17]

Beaudry's insights can also be used when thinking about the different transcriptions that any group of scholars might make of the same performance. Since every musician is likely to listen to a piece of music from a different perspective, each will produce a unique or at least slightly different transcription. A reader then might use a collection of transcriptions--each of the same piece--to help him or her to consider that piece but from a variety of perspectives. Perhaps, then, a response to a disagreement between two observers (as in the case of Freeman and Mead) might not simply be about who was right, but about the benefit that readers might be able to derive from hearing multiple, even opposing interpretations of the same people. I believe that Beaudry's ideas can also be applied when thinking about ethnography or, for example, when thinking about the texts that Kroeber and Halpern and other scholars have made of creation stories. On one hand, the question of validity is of interest, since many of the creation story texts that scholars have published bear titles that seem to lay claim to too much authenticity. On the surface, at least, a title such as "The Creation Story of the Such and Such People" might suggest that it presents the actual creation story of the tribe in question. Rather than accepting it as such, it seems much more helpful to remain aware that each text was influenced by the particular interests of a given scholar at a given time. It seems likely that if a group of scholars had the opportunity to write down the same creation story, that each scholar would produce a unique transcription. When

---

[17] Concerning prescriptive versus descriptive forms of notation, see Charles Seeger, "Prescriptive and Descriptive Music-Writing," *The Musical Quarterly* 44, no.2 (1958): 184-195.

taken as a group, even seemingly contradictory transcriptions might allow readers to develop a better sense of the actual story. For these reasons, I will be referring to each creation story text as being a transcription.

Transcription of Songs: George Herzog

The transcriptions of each scholar are likely, then, to focus on certain facets of an event. A useful starting point for considering this phenomenon is George Herzog's writings on ESCR music and his transcriptions of songs, as given in his article "Yuman Musical Style" (YMS). Herzog's contribution to the study of ESCR music was not limited to this one article. He also provided assistance to two other scholars. Kroeber made audio recordings of Mohave singers; and he asked Herzog to listen to and to transcribe at least some of these.[18] In the winter of 1929-30, anthropologist Leslie Spier visited the Maricopa, a Yuman-speaking tribe who live in the vicinity of Phoenix, Arizona.[19] During this visit, Spier also made audio recordings of singers, which he forwarded to Herzog. Seven of Herzog's musical transcriptions appeared in Spier's 1933 publication, *Yuman Tribes of the Gila River.*[20]

---

[18] I do not know when this exchange took place. The ethnomusicologist Richard Keeling writes that examples of Herzog's transcriptions of Mohave songs can be found in Kroeber's papers. See Richard Keeling, *A Guide to Early Field Recordings (1900-1949) at the Lowie Museum of Anthropology. University of California publications* 6 (Berkeley: University of California Press, 1991). See the footnote 8 on p. xvi.

[19] See Leslie Spier, *Yuman Tribes of the Gila River* (Chicago: University of Chicago Press, 1933), 5.

[20] For Herzog's transcriptions, see Spier, *Yuman Tribes*, 274-279. In his *Guide* (see note 18), Keeling lists twelve audio recordings that Spier made of the Maricopa, in 1928. See Keeling's *Guide,* 443-445

During the summer of 1927 Herzog traveled to the ESCR and spoke with singers, most of whom were from tribes where a Yuman language was spoken. Along the Colorado River, in Needles, California, he interviewed and made sound recordings of Mohave singers.[21] In Yuma, Arizona, Herzog seems to have worked with Mohave, Quechan, and possibly also Cocopa singers. Traveling westward, he visited Campo, which is located close to the U.S/Mexican border near Tecate, Mexico.[22] Herzog also visited the Serraño, apparently the only Uto-Aztecan-speaking tribe that he visited. Herzog's study is thus first and foremost a study of the music of singers from some of the Yuman-speaking tribes within the ESCR. In this discussion, I will sometimes use abbreviated terms such as "Yuman songs," or "Yuman singers," when referring to songs that are performed by singers from Yuman-speaking tribes within the ESCR.

In YMS, Herzog offers a number of insights and conclusions about Yuman songs and their performance. As evidence for his assertions, he often refers to one or more of the thirty-nine transcriptions that he included in YMS. Of particular interest here is the possibility that a number of his transcriptions may be inaccurate, at least in certain respects. The issue here is not Herzog's musicianship but that he made mistakes, and possibly because he had not spent enough time observing ESCR singers and dancers. We can begin by considering some of Herzog's general comments about ESCR music,

---

[21] See George Herzog, "United States, Arizona and California, Mohave Indians, 1927." Performers: Sitc'o'm'ai [sic] and John Carter, vocals with gourd rattle or basket drum accompaniment Archives of Traditional Music, Indiana University. Fieldnotes and audio recordings. Accession number, 54-124-F.

[22] Kumeyaay is still spoken by some people at Campo. Kumeyaay and Cocopa and Mohave and Quechan are Yuman languages.

specifically about rhythm. Herzog wrote that "in more than half of the songs the time-unit ('bar') is not constant within the song." As mentioned in Chapter 1, "fancy" songs are songs that contain metric shifts; whereas "single-step" songs utilize a single meter.[23] While Herzog may not have been aware of the difference between "fancy" and "single-step" songs, he must have been referring to "fancy" songs when he referred to metric irregularity. Here is the quotation in question:

> In more than half of the songs the time-unit ("bar") is not constant within the song. The most diverse combinations occur, which reappear without change in subsequent repetitions of the song. Such forms imply a more complex and more flexible feeling for rhythm than is ours, and they do not have to be interpreted as deviations from simple norms to which our rhythmic habits have become limited.[24]

Explaining what he meant by songs wherein the "time-unit ('bar') is not constant," Herzog stated that that in such songs a duple pattern such as ♫♫ is sometimes followed by a triple pattern ♩♪. Or, as he wrote:

> A common practice of this kind is a temporary change from a two-unit to a three-unit rhythm, a continuous movement like ♫♫ changes for a few beats to ♩♪ or vice versa.

This statement is ambiguous, however. Does Herzog mean that the eighth-note tactus remains constant, as shown in Method 1, in Figure 2.A-i? Or, does he mean that the triple pattern (♩♪) has the same duration as the four note duple pattern (♫♫), as shown in Method 2?

---

[23] Regarding "fancy" songs, see "Singing and Dancing" in Chapter 1.
[24] YMS, p. 194.

Figure 2.A-i. Two types of rhythmic variation.

As he continues, Herzog never clears up this ambiguity. The problem seems to be that

Herzog was primarily focusing on the melody and its rhythm. In the quotation below, he

refers his readers to his transcriptions, where he will presumably show how the singers

moved from a duple to a triple rhythm. However, he apparently did not realize that the

melody, and its rhythm, and the pattern of the gourd, and the text, and the dance steps are

tightly integrated. Without this understanding, he was unable to perceive that the

transition from a duple to a triple rhythm uses method 2 rather than method 1 (see Figure

2.A-i).

> Often the same rhythmic configuration is found in subsequent time-units ("bars")
> of different length. This may appear as a shortening or lengthening of the same
> rhythmic figure, by eliding or adding a rhythmic unit (beat). (The last bar of a
> phrase is often set off in this way, as in [transcriptions] Nos. 1, 4, 29, 30). Or, the
> number of beats is kept but their actual time-values are changed; in which case the
> figure appears contracted or expanded. A common practice of this kind is a
> temporary change from a two-unit to a three-unit rhythm, a continuous movement
> like ♫♫ changes for a few beats to ♩♪ or vice versa (See Nos. 5, 14, 26) In
> many songs, the rhythmic unit is a combination of these two elements (as in Nos.
> 12, 21, 25, 27, 30, 32).[25]

---

[25] YMS, p. 194.

Hamini kovara, *a "single-step" song*

Hamini kovara is one of the eleven *Bird* songs that the Mohave singer Sitcomai performed for Herzog.[26] A "single-step" song is a song that uses the same meter (or "step") from start to finish. A scan of Herzog's transcription of *Hameni koreräa* can be seen in Figure 2.A-ii.

The ambiguities that Herzog left unresolved in his discussion of ESCR songs (in YMS) persist in his transcriptions. As suggested in Figure 2.A-ii but as can also be seen in his other transcriptions of ESCR music, Herzog rarely used bar lines. This combined with a time signature of 21/4 would seem to suggest that the song was rhythmically free. On the other hand, 21/4 might also suggest that the song had an underlying rhythmic pulse. With 21/4, did Herzog simply mean to say that the song began with a phrase of twenty-one quarter notes? At the same time, Herzog's metronome reading of ♩=102 certainly would seem to imply a regular tempo, one that could easily be felt and danced to and was therefore possibly more fixed than free. Note, Herzog seems to have made a mistake with his metronome reading. Based on listening to the recording, it should have been ♩.=102.

Overall Herzog's transcription seems to suggest that the pulse of this song was

---

[26] Herzog describes Sitcomai as being forty-five years of age. The songs were recorded at Needles, California. Herzog's fieldnotes are at the Archives of Traditional Music, Indiana University. The field notes are not paginated but are divided into a number of categories. For the brief information that Herzog includes about Sitcomai, see the type-written notes that begin with the heading: "Phonograph records collected by George Herzog, Summer, 1927." The audio recording of *Hamini kovara* is identified as Accession number, 54-124-F, item 31, cylinder 4001, strip A, on the Indiana Archive's copy of Herzog's recording of this song. See footnote 21.

quite variable. I have listened to Herzog's audio recording of this song. The gourd or other percussion instrument is not audible on the tape. While there are moments when the singer Sitcomai distorts the underlying rhythmic pulse, to my ear, the song has a clear triple meter throughout. A basic dance step for this song would likely involve a predictable shifting from foot to the other, on each downbeat (see Figure 2.A-iii). I have therefore re-notated his transcription, adding bar lines, measure numbers, and a time signature of $\frac{3}{4}$ (see Figure 2.A-iv). As shown in this figure, lines 1 and 2 do in fact contain seven measures.

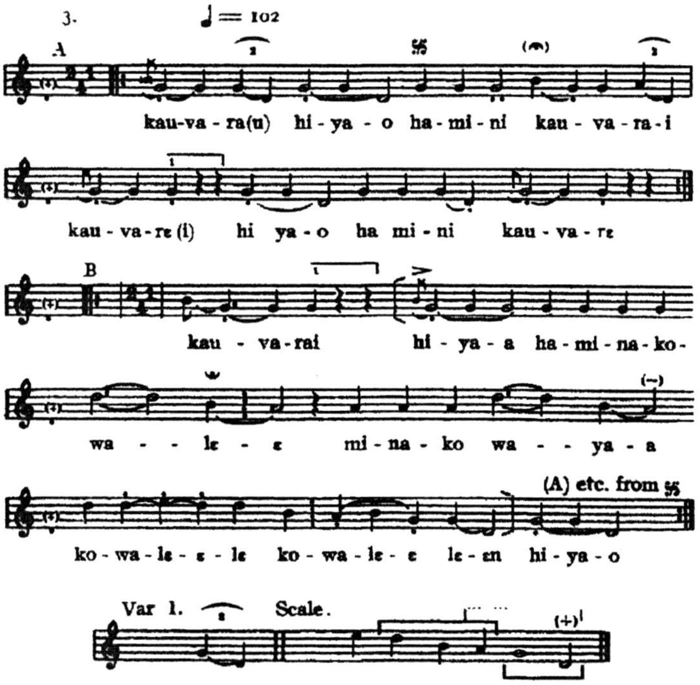

Birds song-series, ninth song. Rattling· ♩ ♩ 𝄽 etc. The record contains: 4A 2B 3A 2B 3A B. The first rendition of A begins at the sign. Ending as in No. 1.

Figure 2.A-ii. A scan of Herzog's transcription of *Hamini kovara.*

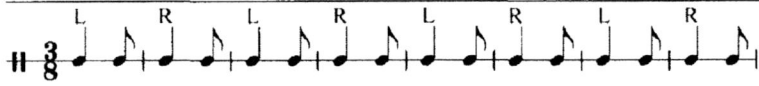

Figure 2.A-iii. Basic dance step for *Hamenι kovara* [27]

Figure 2.A-iv. Herzog's *Hamini kovara*, rewritten with bar lines.

Thus Herzog's transcription can easily be recast to show a song that is in ¾. Not realizing that the dance steps and the melody and the text were linked, Herzog

---

[27] The time signature should be 3/4.

seems to have focused more or less exclusively on the melody and its rhythm, which he then attempted to write out note by note. This led him to make some errors. For instance, he notated measures 2 and 7 as containing two quarter notes in the time of three (see Figure 2.A-iv), which is inaccurate. Herzog's audio recordings are rough, however. It seems possible both that Sitcomai's voice was somewhat raspy and emphatic. At that same time, it sounds as if his voice may have been distorted somewhat during the recording. Still it seems clear that Sitcomai does use a steady tactus but not always. This must have been a factor that contributed to Herzog's confusion when he was trying to decide which rhythms were present in measures 2 and 7. In general, instead of attempting first to write out the melody, it is best to approach the transcription of an ESCR song by first considering its text.

As I consider the text to this song, I also address a related issue, namely the idea that Sitcomai uses different vocal qualities when singing different words. In "Singing and Dancing," in Chapter 1, I considered a *Bird* song, as sung by the contemporary Kumeyaay singer Harry Paul Cuero, Jr. There is a basic difference, however, between Cuero's singing style and Sitcomai's. Whereas Cuero's vocal quality is more or less the same, from start to finish, Sitcomai varies the quality of his voice, depending on the words that he is singing. In measure 5, when Sitcomai articulates the word *ha-me-nii*, he is singing (see Figure 2.A-iv); the frequency of his voice (in Hz) is relatively constant, and the rhythm of his melody is predictable and clear. When he articulates the word *kauvara*, however, the situation is different. As this word is repeated, Sitcomai sometimes *sings* this word, but at other times, he temporarily abandons his regular singing voice. At these moments, his voice becomes more of a shout. The vocal quality

that Sitcomai uses when he sings/shouts the word *kauvara* involves still another

difference. When someone says or shouts the word "Hey!" the lips are open and the

sound seems to be propelled outward. When the same person shouts "Ho!" that person's

lips are closer together. The sound moves outward but it also seems to be projected

backwards, down into the speaker's throat. This latter effect is similar to what occurs as

Sitcomai's sings/shouts the word *kauvara*. Starting with the syllable *kau,* his voices is

suddenly loud, louder than for any other word in the song. Figure 2.A-v gives some

sense as to how much louder Sitcomai's voice is when he sing *kauvara* versus *hamini.* In

this instance, Sitcomai added an extra syllable to *hamini.*

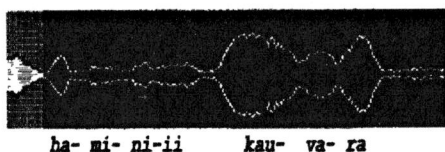

ha- mi- ni-ii   kau- va- ra

Figure 2.A-v. The relative amplitude of *kauvara* versus *hamini.*

Sitcomai's pitches are also harder to define as he sings or shouts the word *kauvara.* He

seems to connect the syllables of this word with one long vocal slide. He begins this

vocal slide with the syllable *kau-*; he slides, progressing to *va,* continues to *ra-,* and

finishes with *i.* The following chart shows that whereas Herzog writes the word in question as *kau-va-ra-i,* I write the same word as *kau-re-rãay-ii.*[28]

Herzog	kau	va	ra	i
Elster	kau	re	rãay	ii

In Figure 2.A-vi, I give an approximation of Sitcomai's vocal glide on *kau-re-rãay-ii,* without going into too much detail.

ha- me-nii   kau- re- rãay-ii

Figure 2.A-vi. The vocal glide on *"kaurerãay."*[29]

Possibly because Sitcomai's voice is loudest when he shout/sings the word *kauvara,* Herzog's transcription shows the song as beginning with this word. On the tape, however, Sitcomai does not begin by singing *kauvara;* instead he starts out by singing the word *hamini* (measure 5 of Herzog's transcription). However, because he did not think to emphasize the words and the dance steps, Herzog was sometimes not able to discern the correct starting or ending points of musical phrases and their accompanying texts. In this case, the fact that he attempted to transcribe these songs after having spent relatively little time listening to and observing the performers firsthand probably prevented him from realizing the importance of the words and the dance steps.

In addition to varying the quality of his voice, Sitcomai sometimes adds or

---

[28] In fact it is difficult to tell whether the second syllable is *re* or *rã.* If it is *rã,* then it has a single trill rather than a double. But I do not hear this second syllable as being *wa* or *va,* the last being what Herzog heard and wrote down.

[29] I also spell *kovara* somewhat differently than does Herzog. See Figure 2.A-viii, p. 100, for my transcription of this song.

subtracts syllables with reach repetition of a word. Here I focus on his variations of the word *kaurerãay.* I have written out the words to this song. (See Figure 2.A-vii)[30] In this figure, the number above each word corresponds to the measure numbers in my transcription (in Figure 2.A-viii). The song has two sections. On the tape, Sitcomai alternates between repetitions of sections 1 and 2. Section 1 begins with the word: *hamenii;*[31] then come two repetitions of the word *kaurerãay.* As can be seen in Figure 2.A-viii, each repetition of *kaurerãay* is slightly different. The first time *Sitcomai* sings/shouts this word, it is: *kau-re-rãay-ii.* The second time it is *kau-re-rãa-a.* Variation on this word also occurs in line 2. Here, the first time *Sitcomai* sings/shouts this word, it has only three syllables: *kau-re-rã.* In lieu of the fourth syllable, he takes a breath.[32] When he sings the repetition of this word *(kaurerãay-a),* furthermore, he is no longer shouting. In addition, the pitches that he is singing are easier to identify. Also noteworthy in Sitcomai's performance are the vocal glissandi that he uses to connect pitches that land on the downbeat with those that occur on weak beats. In Figure 2.A-viii, I have attempted to capture the quality of Sitcomai's glissandi by using curving slur lines. The glissandi do not begin until the slur line starts to curve, not sooner.

---

[30] Finally, as a way of reconciling Herzog's transcription with mine, I rearranged his transcription, beginning with the word *hamini.* See Figure 2.A-ix, p. 101.

[31] I have written out the words to this song, as I hear them. My spelling varies somewhat from what Herzog used.

[32] There is still more variation on *kau-re-rãa-a,* ones that are not shown in Figure 2.A-vii. For example, in line 1, the second of the *kaurerãa's* is sometimes *pau-re-rãa-a* instead of *kau-re-rãa-a.*

Figure 2.A-vii. The text of *Hamenii kaurerãay,* sections 1 and 2

Section 1 of *Hamenii kaureāay*.

	1	2	3	4	5	6	7
1	ha- me-	nii kau-	re- rāay-	ii kau-	re- rāa-	a hey-	yo- o
	8	9	10	11	12	13	14
2	ha- me-	nii kau-	re- rā-	(breath) kau-	re- rāa-	a hey-	yo- o

Section 2 of *Hamenii kaureāay*.

	15	16	17	18
3	o- me- na ko-	wel-	- ley-	ey
	19	20	21	22
4	o- me- na ko-	waay-	- ja-	a
	23	24	25	26	27	28
5	ka- wa- ley- a-	ley	ka- wa-	ley- a- ley- a	haay-	yo- o
	29	30	31	32	33	34	35
6	me- na	nii	kau- rāay-	re- a	rāa-	a hey-	ya- an
	36	37	38	39	40	41	42
7	ha- me-	nii kau-	rā re-	(breath) kau- re-	rāa-	a hey-	yo- o

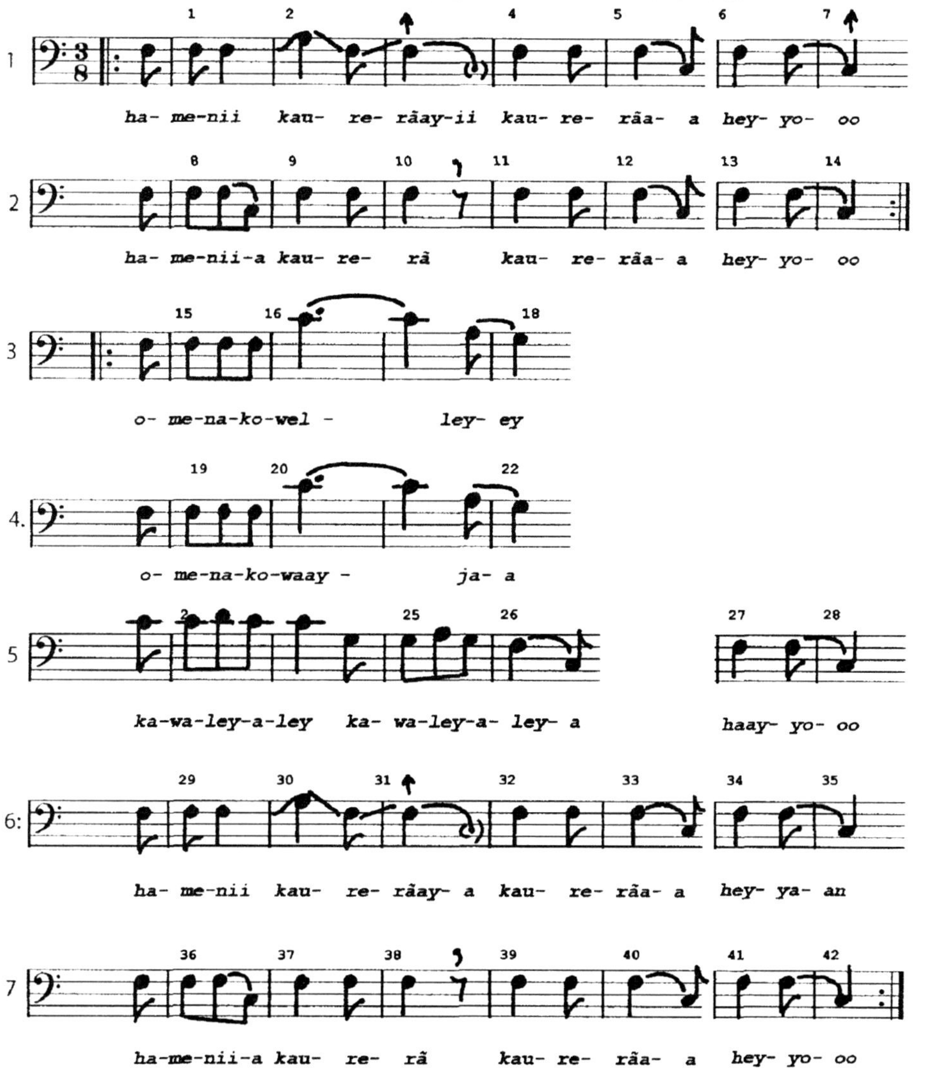

Figure 2.A-viii. *Hameni kaurerãay,* based on the tape.

Figure 2.A-ix. Herzog's *Hamini kovara*, re-arranged.[33]

---

[33] I have rearranged Herzog's measures, showing that his measures correspond to the ones in my transcription (see Figure 2.A-ix).

Huyawa kwena, *a "fancy" song*

Herzog wrote that, "In more than half of the songs the time-unit ("bar") is not constant within the song."[34] With this remark it seems likely that Herzog was referring to "fancy" songs since they contain metric shifts between duple and triple meters. As an example of a song wherein "the time-unit ('bar') is **not** constant," I examine Herzog's transcription of *Huyawa kwena,* also a *Bird* song and also sung by Sitcomai.[35] In listening to Herzog's recording of *Huyawa kwena,* I found that the song was "fancy," that is, it contained metric shifts. Upon listening to a segment of this recording, the Kumeyaay singer Harry Paul Cuero, Jr. reported that he also sings this song.[36] When Cuero sings this song, however, it is not "fancy;" although, the words and the melody are closely related. Cuero explained that the song is based on the spoken words *uunyáw kenáp*, meaning something on the order of, "you know, you can tell." As Cuero explained, it is the participants who know the story and therefore can tell it. In recognition of this, the singers turn their backs to the dancers as they sing this song. Note, Herzog's transcription shows the tempo as being a quarter note equals 184 beats per minute. However, the copy at Indiana plays back much faster and therefore needs to be slowed down. I find that a tempo 184 is still too fast for this song. 150 beats per minute is better. At this tempo, it is also much easier to understand what the singer

---

[34] See footnote 24.

[35] This is the second of Herzog's transcriptions, in his YMS, 100. The Indiana Archive's copy of Herzog's recording of this song is identified as Accession number, 54-124-F, item # 28, cylinder 3998, strip A. Also see footnote 21.

[36] Regarding Harry Paul Cuero, Jr., see my discussion of one of his songs, in "Singing and Dancing," in Chapter 1.

Sitcomai says before singing this song. Ione Dock explained that he is telling his

audience to dance with all their heart and might.

I have included a scan of Herzog's transcription of this song (see Figure 2.A-x).

For the sake of clarity, I have also written out Herzog's transcription (see Figure 2.A-xi).

As can be seen, Herzog's transcription of *Huyawa kwena* is similar in many respects to

his transcription of *Hamenii kaureraay*.[37] These two transcriptions can begin to provide

a sense of some of the questions and issues that Herzog focused on, as he studied these

and other Yuman songs. Both transcriptions demonstrate that these songs have a fairly

narrow melodic range and that both songs contain a number of repeated notes that

effectively establish one note/pitch as a tonal center. For both songs, the central pitch is

"G." In YMS, Herzog wrote that ESCR songs contain sections. In fact, his

transcriptions of both of these songs are divided into at least two sections. Herzog labels

these as sections as *"a"* and *"b."* In the *"b"* sections of both songs, Herzog also

identified a "rise," by enclosing a segment of the melody in brackets. (For the "rise" in

Huyawa kwena, see the bracketed section, in the *"b"* section, in systems 3-4, in Figure

2.A-xi; for the "rise" in *Hamini kovara,* see bracketed section, measures 17-30, in Figure

2.A-iv, p.93.

The idea that Herzog was writing out *Huyawa kwena* without the knowledge

that this song contained metric shifts begins to emerge with his choice for an initial

time signature. Herzog's initial time signature is $\frac{6}{4}$ (see Figure 2.A-xi). As shown in

---

[37] See Figure 2.A-iv and Figure 2.A-xi.

his transcription, the song begins with a phrase that is strung across eight quarter note pulses. The same is true for the next time signature of $\frac{7}{4}$, in line 2. With no bar lines and with time signatures that seem to represent phrases rather than the underlying meter, Herzog again gives the impression that the pulse of this song is quite free, that it might be a mistake to try to represent it with a fixed time signature.

In order to record the metric shifts that are present in a fancy song, the melody along with the words and the dance steps and the percussion pattern all need to be taken into account. As I listened to Herzog's audio recording of *Huyawa kwena*, I realized that this song shifts between duple and triple meters. The percussion instrument on this audio recording is all but inaudible. Thus the audio recording of course contains no direct information about the dance steps. Nevertheless, the melody and the words alone provide sufficient clues, regarding where the metric shifts are and what the associated dance steps might be. My transcription for this song is given in Figure 2.A-xii, p. 107. Again, I have arranged the text so that the transcription shows the segments of the text that are repeated and also where the metric shifts occur.

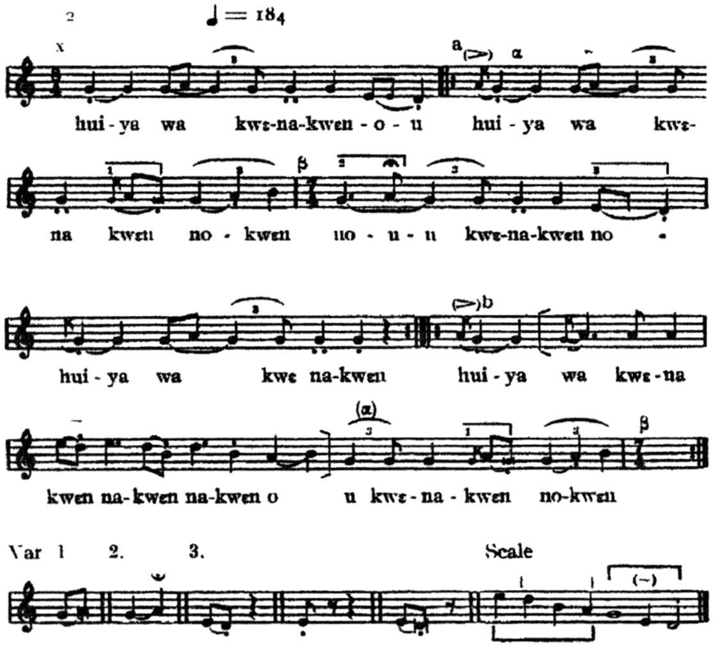

Birds (tciyɛ́rɛ) dance-song series, sixth song. Rattle indistinct. End as before. The record contains x (introduction) 4a b 2a 2b 7a 2b.

Figure 2.A-x. A scan of Herzog's transcription of *Huyawa kwena*.

Figure 2.A-xi. Herzog's *Huyawa kwena*, written out.[38]

---

[38] In system 4, the rhythmic value for the second note for the words *u-kwe-na* should be an eighth note instead of a quarter note (as is the case for *kwe-na,* see the first half of system 3).

Figure 2.A-xii. *Huyawa kwena*, written out, based on the audio recording.

While many Yuman-songs utilize an underlying triple rhythmic pattern, this song begins with a duple pattern, as shown in line 1. I use a time signature of $\frac{2}{8}$. The dance steps would likely have involved a shifting of weight on each new downbeat.

The text to this song provides an important starting point for understanding this song. As Cuero explained, the text of this song is based on the spoken words *uunyáw kenáp,* meaning that the dancers know the story and that therefore can tell it. During speech, the second syllable of each word is accented, as in *uun-**yáw*** and *ke-**náp***. The relationship between the spoken word *uunyáw* (know) and the corresponding sung word, *hu-ya-wa-a* is shown in Figure 2.A-xiii.

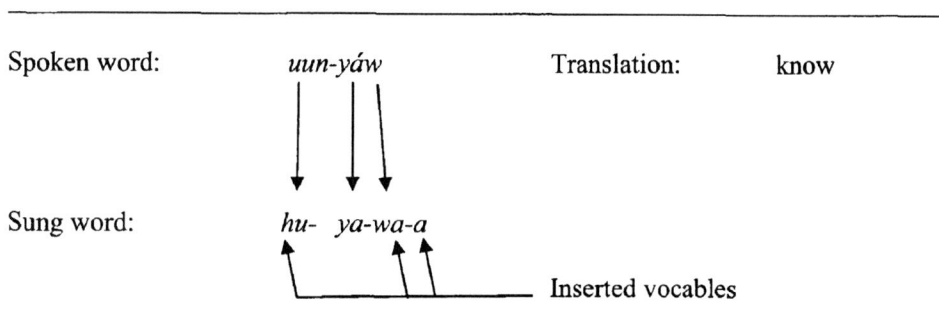

Spoken word:	*uun-yáw*	Translation:	know

Sung word: *hu- ya-wa-a*

Inserted vocables

Figure 2.A-xiii. *Unnyáw* and *huyawa.*

The spoken word *kenáp* (tell) becomes the sung word *kwe-na,* sometimes also appearing as *kwe-no-o-o* (see Figure 2.A-xiv).

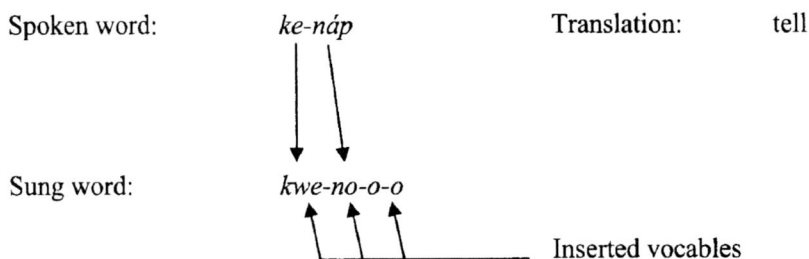

Spoken word: *ke-náp*   Translation: tell

Sung word: *kwe-no-o-o*

               Inserted vocables

Figure 2.A-xiv. *Kenáp* and *kwena (*or *keno-o).*

The patterns of stressed and non-stressed syllable are not always carried over into the song. The accents of the syllables of the spoken word *uun-yáw* are not carried over into the corresponding the sung word *hu-ya-wa-a.* In fact, the opposite is true. In contrast, the pattern of non-stressed and stressed syllables from the spoken word *ke-náp* are replicated in the corresponding sung word *kwe-ná.* Each time Sitcomai sings *kwe-na,* the first syllable, *kwe,* always occurs on an upbeat. The second syllable *na* always occurs on a downbeat. This is shown in Figure 2.A-xv, which contains the initial four measure introductory phrase of this song. In this introductory phrase, each time Sitcomai sings *kwe-na,* the first syllable *kwe* occurs on the upbeat and the second syllable *na* takes the downbeat. Throughout the piece, Sitcomai generates variation by shortening or lengthening the duration of the note on which he sings the syllable *na.* An example can be seen in this introductory phrase. The first time he sings *kwe-na,* the second syllable, *na,* lasts for a single eighth note (see measure 3). When he repeats *kwena,* the

second syllable appears in variation. The *na* becomes *no-o* and the duration is a quarter

note, as seen in measure 4.

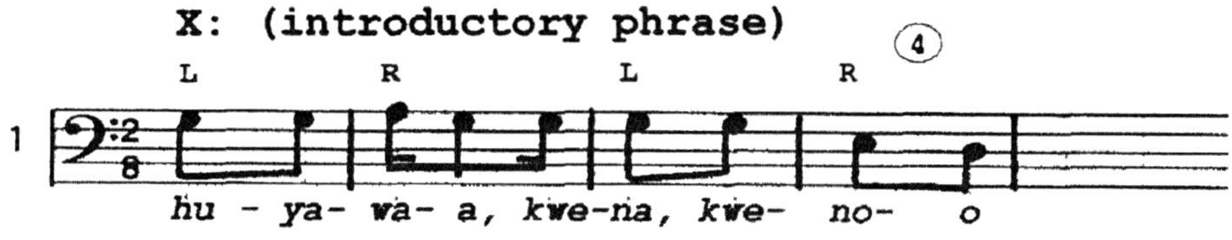

Figure 2.A-xv. *Huyawa kwena,* line 1.

Throughout this song, Sitcomai continues to vary the duration of the second

syllable of *kwe-na.* An analysis of this variation provides an important key to

understanding the shifts from duple to triple meter. After singing the introductory phrase

(line 1), Sitcomai sings the first line of Section A (labeled line 2, in Figure 2.A-xvi).[39]

Line 2 begins much as does line 1. However, whereas line 2 begins in

$\frac{2}{8}$ it shifts to $\frac{3}{8}$. As will be seen, the shift from duple to triple meters is determined by

how Sitcomai sets the word *kwe-na* to the music. At the start of line 2, Sitcomai

holds the *na* (of the first *kwena*) for a single beat. The song is still in $\frac{2}{8}$. With

the next repetition of *kwe-na,* he holds the *na* for two beats. This sets the stage

for the shift from $\frac{2}{8}$ to $\frac{3}{8}$. On the next beat, Sitcomai starts a third repetition of

kwena. The syllable *kwe* takes the upbeat, meaning that measure 8 must contain

---

[39] Following Herzog's labeling convention. See Figure 2.A-xii.

three beats. The song has now shifted from $\frac{2}{8}$ to $\frac{3}{8}$. Sitcomai confirms that this is the

case when, in measure 9, he extends *na* (in the third repetition of *kwena*) so that

it becomes *na-a-a.* Clearly measure 9 is in $\frac{3}{8}$. The dancers are now shifting their

weight every three beats. From now on, every mid-section metric shift will in fact

begin with the word *kwena.*

Section A:

hu - ya- wa- a, kwe-na, kwe- na, kwe- na- a- a

Figure 2.A-xvi. *Huyawa kwena*, line 2.

Line 3 involves a repetition of the words *kwe-na kwe-no.* While these words are similar

to what Sitcomai has sung before, the repetition is not exact. This kind of subtle variation

seems to be standard for ESCR music. The patterns of the stressed and non-stressed

syllables remain the same, however. The syllable *kwe* continues to take the upbeat, *na*

always occurs on the downbeats. On the first *kwe-na,* the second syllable, *na,* lasts for a

single eight note. On the second *kwe-no,* the second syllable, now *no,* is extended. It

lasts for two beats. The difference, however, is that Sitcomai has now switched the meter

back to duple. The song remains in a duple meter for the remainder of Section A.

Figure 2.A-xvii. *Huyawa kwena*, line 3.

Sitcomai's transition from the end of measure 9 to the start of 10 is, however, not clear cut. I show *kwe* as being a grace-note pickup to measure 10. This is, however, only an approximation of what Sitcomai actually does. On the tape, Sitcomai hesitates briefly, just after singing *na-a-a*. When he sings *kwe*, the duration of this syllable is slightly longer than what would be expected of a grace note, but not long enough to be written as a 16th note. This is also one of those moments where Sitcomai's voice is halfway between shouting and singing. Pitches are connected by glissandi, making it difficult--or perhaps inappropriate--define precise pitch or rhythmic values. As he ends Section A, Sitcomai repeats the first word *huyawa*. The next words, *kwe-na kwin,* have been modified slightly, to form an ending formula of sorts; instead of *kwe-na kw-na,* Sitcomai sings *kwe-na kwin.*

Figure 2.A-xviii. *Huyawa kwena*, line 4.

The B Section also starts with a duple meter and with the same words used in section A, namely *hu-ya-wa kwe-na.* In Section A, the first shift from duple to a triple

meter took place over three repetitions of *kwe-na.* In contrast, in Section B, this shift to

triple is accomplished with just two repetitions of *kwe-na.* On the second repetition of

the syllable, *kwe,* (measure 18), Sitcomai's voice suddenly begins to ascend, reaching up

to E. This is the rise. On the next syllable, *na,* Sitcomai's voice ascends still higher, to a

high E. At the same time, the volume of his voice increases markedly and he holds it

for two beats. This signals the shift from $\frac{2}{8}$ to $\frac{3}{8}$, an idea that is confirmed on with the

next repetition of *kwe-na,* on the next upbeat (measure 19) and the following downbeat

(measure 20). In measure 20, Sitcomai again the syllable, *na,* for two beats. In measure

21, the syllables, *no-o-o,* are spread out over three beats. For the duple meter (measures

16 to 18), a singer might his or her weight on each downbeat. When the meter shifts to

triple (measures 19-21), a singer and/or dancers might shift their weight on the downbeat

and then on the upbeat to the next measure.

Figure 2.A-xix. *Huyawa kwe-na,* first line of the Section B.

In the B section, one usually expects more elaboration. Here this takes the form of

further repetitions on the word *kwena.* By varying the melody and by continuing to

change the meter, Sitcomai manages never to repeat himself exactly, even though he continues to sing the same or very similar words. With line 6, Sitcomai briefly returns to a duple meter (measure 22), with the syllable *na* lasting only one beat. Just as quickly, he shifts the meter back to a triple meter (measure 23). Once again, the melody begins to ascend, although not as high this time, only up to an F. Still this rise seems to result in an extension of the value of *na* such that it lasts for two beats. This second repetition of *kwe-na* is followed by still another repetition, now with the slightly different *no-o-o,* one that is also strung out over three beats.

Figure 2.A-xx. *Huyawa kwe-na,* line 6.

The approaching end of section B is signaled, in line 7, with the repetition of a phrase heard in the second to the last line of Section A (see line 3, measures 10-11). The text here again involves repetitions and variations on the words *kwe-na, kwe-no-o.*

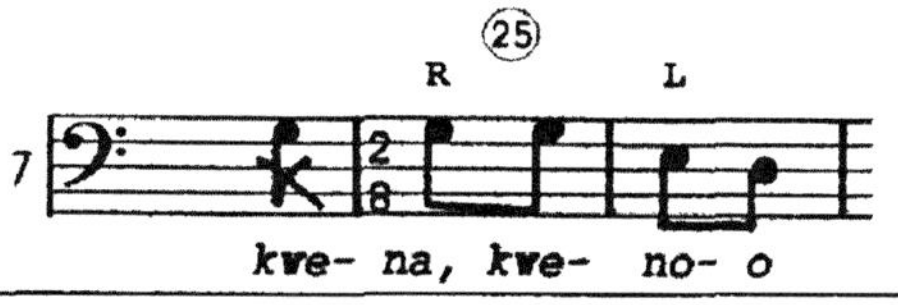

Figure 2.A-xxi. *Huyawa kwe-no-o,* line 7.

Sitcomai brings the B section to a close by repeating the last line of Section A. Again, the last syllable of this section contains the syllable *kwin.*

Figure 2.A-xxii. *Huyawa kwe-na-kwin,* line 8.

In conclusion, an analysis of the words of a song (including the corresponding spoken words, if known) can provide a tool for understanding why certain syllables are stressed while others are not. It would appear, however, that Herzog had not thought to analyze the text in this way. Nor does he appear to have been aware of the dance steps that were associated with this song and its metric shifts; instead, he seems to have focused exclusively on the melody and its rhythm, attempting to write it down, note-by-note. Most of the durational values that he chose are correct. For this reason, I was able to insert the necessary barlines and time signatures (in parentheses), without creating too many inconsistencies in his transcription (see Figure 2.A-xxiii.) I have also included a note-by-note comparison of the first part of this song, as transcribed by Herzog and by me (see Figure 2.A-xxiv). Herzog does make some errors in durational values, all of which occurred in segments of the melody that contain shifting meters. [40] Had he been aware of these shifts, I am sure that he would have addressed them with his transcriptions.

---

[40] In Figure 2.A-xxiii, see measures 8, 15, 19, 20, and 23. Also see the corresponding measures, in Figure 2.A-xxiv.

Figure 2.A-xxiii. Herzog's *Huyawa kwena*, with bar lines, etc.

Figure 2.A-xxiv. The first part of *Huyawa kwena*, Elster versus Herzog.

Transcription of creation stories: Ruth Underhill and Alfred Kroeber

All of the creation-story texts that we have are transcriptions made by one or another scholar at some time in the past. Furthermore, the creation-story text of one scholar is likely to be different, perhaps even markedly so, from that of another scholar. Might this mean that one scholar had studied and spent more time with the Mohave than the other? Or, could the differences between texts be due rather to the fact that each person is likely to examine and to respond to a story from a unique perspective? In this section, I begin by briefly considering the anthropologist Ruth Underhill's study of the Mohave. Like Kroeber, Underhill began to study the Mohave relatively early in her career. Also like Kroeber, she apparently continued to think about the Mohave long after she had retired. And like Kroeber, she wrote down Mohave creation stories. It is not clear, however, that either anthropologist knew the Mohave better than the other. What does seem clear is that Underhill and Kroeber saw the Mohave through markedly different lenses. As a result, their creation story texts and some of their conclusions about the Mohave are quite different. When considered together, however, their creation story texts make it possible to develop a broader understanding of the stories.

Halpern's transcription of *Lightning* showed that the telling of a creation story included the singing of sets of songs, one set after the other (See chapter 1, section 1.C.). Might those performances in the 1930's have resembled in some respects the performance of a song cycle today? Most creation story texts were collected between 1900 and the onset of World War II, at a time when singers knew these stories and how to perform them. The scholars who recorded them were primarily interested in capturing and conveying the "story" part of each creation story. The particulars of *how* a creation story was told were usually set aside. It seems likely that Halpern was aware of this. His transcription of *Lightning* was markedly different from any of the creation story texts that scholars had thus far produced. Because it consisted of a sequence of episodes, many of which were followed by a set of songs, his transcription can be defined as being a song cycle, but one where the singer takes the added step of pausing to speak before singing each set of songs. At the same time, Halpern's text of *Lightning* resembles the creation story texts that other scholars had previously produced.[41] Halpern's text certainly resembles the theme of creation as seen in other creation story texts. In ESCR creation stories, the events described take place at the dawn of the world, when superhuman protagonists support mankind, ensuring that he will continue to develop and evolve. This theme can also be seen in Halpern's transcription of *Lightning.* For example, in *Lightning,* the hero Wonder Boy uses his primordial creative powers to bring more and more phenomena into the domain of man's perception. He does this by talking about what he sees and then by singing a set of songs about it. Episode by episode, man's possibilities expand, as Wonder Boy describes everything that he encounters, from the

---

[41] Sometime between 1935-38, Halpern was enrolled at U.C. Berkeley, where he studied with Kroeber. It seems possible that Kroeber may have shown Halpern his field notes of the Mohave creation stories that Kroeber had collected. While studying with Kroeber, Halpern began his field work with the Quechan. See Margaret Langdon's "Biography of A.M. Halpern (1914-1985)," in Abraham Halpern, *Kar?uk: Native Accounts of the Quechan Mourning Ceremony.* Edited by Amy Miller and Margaret Langdon. University of California Publications in Linguistics 128 (Berkeley, Calif: University of California Press, 1997), p. xv.

tiniest insect to the clouds and the lightning in the skies.

As I consider a selection of creation stories texts, I will show that many if not most are episodic; furthermore, most episodes are associated with a song or a set of songs. Thus the backbone of the song cycle is present. Some ESCR scholars leaned towards presenting a novelized account of a creation story. In these cases, the skeleton of the song cycle tends to be fainter, but it can still generally be discerned. In other creation- story texts such as those of Kroeber, the song cycle structure or form is clearly obvious. There is one main difference between Kroeber's and Halpern's transcriptions. Whereas Halpern always included the texts to the songs, Kroeber rarely did so. As will be seen, even though Kroeber decided that songs should be excluded from his transcriptions, he apparently realized that it would have been inaccurate to make no mention of them at all. He therefore developed an indirect method of showing which episodes were associated with a song or songs.

Kroeber and Underhill, their contrasting orientations

The fifty to one hundred years or more that separated James Clifford from the anthropologists that he studied gave him a distance that made it easier for him to judge the relative strengths and weaknesses of their approaches. The situation must have been different for Ruth Underhill (1883-1984), who in 1952 reviewed Kroeber's (1876-1961) *Seven Mohave Myths* (SMM) and *A Mohave Historical Epic* (MHE) with the knowledge of an insider/scholar.[42]   The fact that Underhill had studied the Mohave was something

that was acknowledged by Kroeber when he invited Underhill to review his SMM and

MHE. Kroeber wrote to her: "You are one of a few people interested in both the

ethnology and the literary aspects, and one of the fewer still who know the [Mohave]

tribe" (in Figure 2.B-i).[43]

Underhill responded by reviewing SMM and MHE. In her review, Underhill

stated that she had edited the chapters that Kroeber had written about the Mohave, for his

Handbook.[44]   Thus her work on the *Handbook* had to have occurred sometime before

1925, when it was published. This may also have been her first introduction to the

Mohave and to the tribes of California. In the 1930s, Underhill studied anthropology

with Franz Boas and Ruth Benedict, among others, at Columbia University.[45] As part of

her studies, Underhill did fieldwork with the Papago, who reside in several locations,

primarily in the Southeast portion of Arizona and also in Sonora, in Mexico. Underhill

worked closely with Chona, an elderly Papago woman,[46] recording her life story and

---

[42] See Ruth Underhill's review of Seven Mohave Myths and A Mohave Historical Epic is
in Midwest Folklore II, 2 (1952): 127-8.

[43] The Underhill papers at the Bailey Library and Archives, at the Denver Museum of
Nature and Science, Manuscript Collection, BOX 22, Correspondence, 1951, December
23, from Kroeber to Underhill.

[44] Ibid. In her review of SMM and referring to the Mohave, Underhill states that:
"Kroeber sketched their characteristics in two intriguing chapters of the *Handbook of the
Indians of California* (BBAE, No. 78, 1925, Edited by the reviewer) and his statements
are amplified in the present volume."

[45] See the online guide to Underhill's papers at the University of Denver, http://library.du.
edu/about/collections/specialcollections/Underhill/ index.cfm#Scope (accessed on
September 20, 2007).

[46] The Papago are also known as the Tohono O'odham. They reside in Southern Arizona,
near to Tucson, and in parts of Sonora, in Northern Mexico.

eventually publishing it in 1936 as *Papago Woman*.[47] From 1932 to 1946, Underhill

worked for the Bureau of Indian Affairs Department of Indian Education.[48] It was in the

1930's that Underhill's interests came even closer to coinciding with Kroeber's, with her

decision to study the Mohave. As part of this work, she listened to Mohave singers tell

their stories. At this time, she heard at least two of the stories that Kroeber would

eventually publish in *Seven Mohave Myths* (SMM).[49] Two newspaper articles, both

published in 1981, when Underhill was ninety-eight, suggest that she like Kroeber had

continued to think about and study the Mohave throughout her life. One of these articles,

published in *The Pantagraph,* reports that Underhill had agreed to start a new

collaborative project with the Mohave. As part of this effort, tribal members had agreed

to compose a series of pamphlets about Mohave culture. Underhill would oversee the

project, along with Edward Swick, a Mohave tribal historian whom she had previously

met during her 1930's visit to the Mohave. As part of this project, Underhill would also

review her field notes. Referring to Underhill's initial fieldwork with the Mohave, the

article in the *Pantagraph* states: "During that time, she compiled reams of notes on the

Mohaves and Swick says those will prove invaluable as most tribal elders of the 1930s

---

[47] See Underhill, *The Autobiography of a Papago Woman*. American Anthropological Association, Memoirs no. 46 (Menasha, Wisconsin: The American Anthropological Association,1936).

[48] Underhill became the Assistant Supervisor of Indian Education, from 1934-1942; and the Supervisor, from 1942-1948

[49] See Underhill's review of *Seven Mohave Myths*.

have died."[50]

When Underhill first traveled to visit the Mohave in the 1930's, it seems likely

that she may have expected to see a people whose culture coincided with the description

that Kroeber had given in his *Handbook*. In his *Handbook,* Kroeber had focused on

providing summary information about Mohave creation stories but not detailed accounts.

With SMM and MHE, the situation changed. For the first time, Kroeber presented his

detailed transcriptions of some Mohave creation stories (there are seven stories in SMM,

and one long epic in MHE). Prior to reading SMM and MHE, Underhill may not have

realized how different her experience of the Mohave was from Kroeber's. As she

reviewed Kroeber's detailed transcriptions of these stories, Underhill found that she

disagreed with the way Kroeber had presented the stories. Her most ardent criticism of

Kroeber's transcriptions centered around the idea that Kroeber had stripped them of their

emotion and drama. Recalling her own experiences as she listened to Mohave singers tell

stories, Underhill explained, "some of the tales, as heard by the reviewer, put a great deal

more stress on drama and dialogue than Kroeber's version."[51]

---

[50] See "Mohave Indians to write history as never before," *The Pantagraph,* September 17, p. C9. Also, see "Dr. Underhill to help tribe write history," *The Rocky Mountain News,* August 20, 1981, p. 13. Underhill's papers are held by the University of Denver. The Denver Museum of Nature and Science also has some of her materials, includes the two newspaper articles referred to above. Apparently Underhill gave most if not all of her Mohave notes back to the Mohave, before she died; but it is unclear whether she gave these to the Colorado River Indian Tribe or the Fort Mohave Tribe.

[51] See Underhill's review.

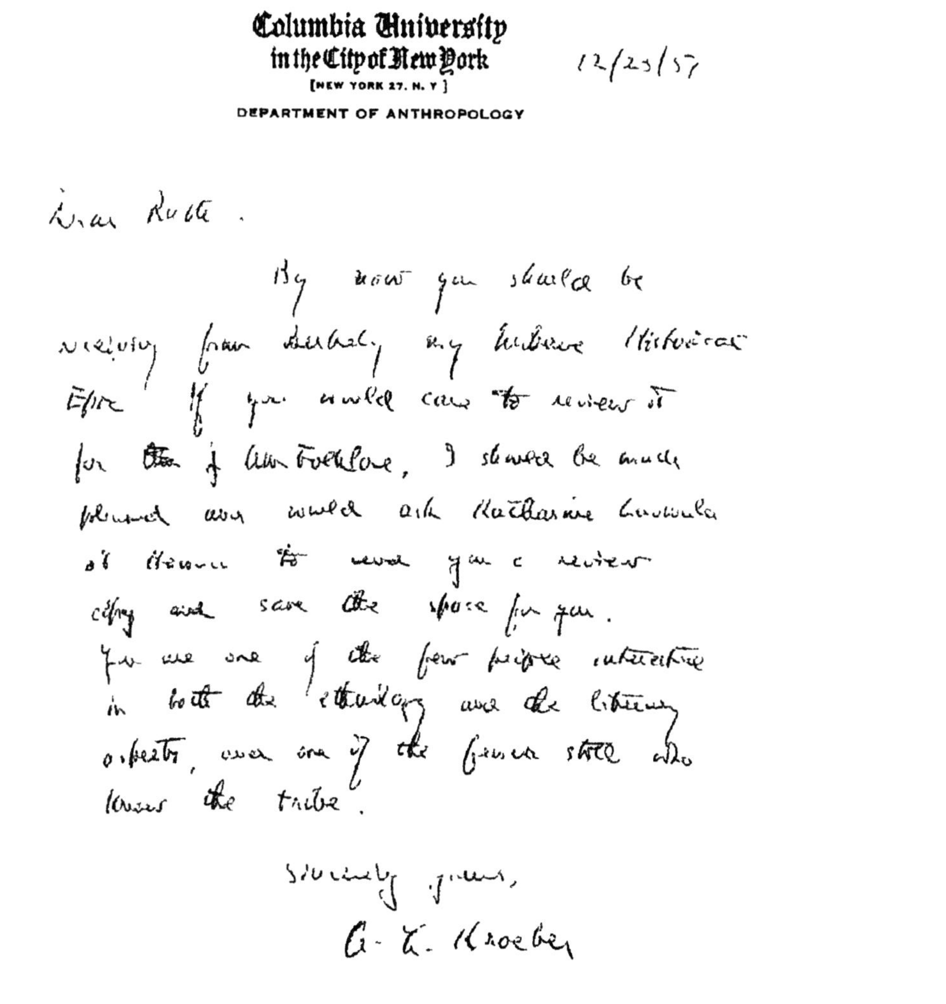

Columbia University
in the City of New York
[NEW YORK 27, N. Y.]
DEPARTMENT OF ANTHROPOLOGY

12/23/51

Dear Ruth.

By now you should be receiving from Berkeley my Mohave Historical Epic. If you would care to review it for the Jour. of Am. Folklore, I should be much pleased and would ask Katharine Luomala at Hawaii to send you a review copy and save the space for you. You are one of the few people interested in both the ethnology and the literary aspects, and one of the fewer still who knows the tribe.

Sincerely yours,
A. L. Kroeber

Figure 2.B-i. Letter, from Kroeber to Underhill.
12/23/51

[Dear Ruth,

By now you should be receiving my Mohave Historical Epic. If you care to review it for the Journal of American Folklore, I should be rather pleased to write and would ask Katherine Luomala in Hawaii to send you a review copy and save the space for you. You are one of a few people interested in both the ethnology and the literary aspects, and one of the fewer still who know the tribe.

Sincerely yours,
A.L. Kroeber]

Possibly because she knew that Kroeber still had more Mohave creation stories to publish,[52] Underhill included in her review an alternative way of presenting these stories. Her critique and her suggestions take the form of a brief summary of the story of *Cane,* the first of the creation stories in SMM. Underhill's summary of *Cane* suggests a story whose plot is crystal clear. There is no question as to who the main characters are: they are two brothers, one older, one younger. The conflict that emerges between them is clear: the older suffers in silence but with growing resentment, as the younger brother selfishly takes all of the available women for himself. Similarly the resolution is straightforward: The younger brother faces his destruction, literally at the hands of his older brother. Thus it appears that Underhill favored a novelistic style when it came to presenting Mohave creation stories. What follows is the section of Underhill's review of SMM that contains this summary:

> A modern Longfellow, itching to re-shape a primitive tale in the idiom of his own time and culture, could hardly find a more striking subject than appears in the first of Dr. Kroeber's Seven Mohave Myths. Here two brothers, left alone at the dawn of the world, go out to seek wives. (A Mohave is allowed as many as he can support.) In true Indian style, no description of their characters is given; yet we gather from the action that the elder, endowed with medicine power, is unloved by women while the younger, selfish and petulant, is embraced by every girl he meets. The elder suffers his inferiority without any of the paragraphs of analysis we should find in a modern work. In one situation after another, he yields to the younger, even after worsting him in a fair fight. Then, in his own good time, he afflicts his rival with a fatal disease and, during his death throes, removes his bones to make shinny balls and hide-scrapers.

> Underhill did allow that Kroeber had provided a "clear plot summary" for each

---

[52] In fact, more of Kroeber's transcriptions of Mohave creation stories would appear in *More Mohave Myths,* published posthumously in 1972.

story; but, she argued that Kroeber's transcriptions were difficult to read, this because she

believed that Kroeber had included numerous ethnographic minutiae. For example,

Underhill pointed out that Kroeber had included some songs in his transcriptions. She

argued that these should have not been included. Based on her own experience, the

words to each song mainly consisted of vocables:

> Perhaps the songs with which the narrative is punctuated in the usual
> Southwestern manner, might give emotional release. If so, this must have come
> chiefly from sound, for the reviewer, who took a number of them in text, can
> report that they consist mostly of meaningless syllables, with a key word here and
> there.

Underhill's criticism of the songs that Kroeber included in SMM and MHE is

exaggerated, however. What Underhill failed to point out, or may not have realized, was

that Kroeber in fact agreed with her. This was a sentiment that he had expressed as far

back as 1925, in the *Handbook.* Demonstrating that he had not changed his mind, in

SMM Kroeber rarely included songs. For example, he included only nine of the

approximately ninety songs that went with *Deer* and only two of the 182 songs from

Cane.[53] As a way of demonstrating why the songs should be included, Kroeber had

provided, in his *Handbook,* examples of a number of songs taken from a variety of

Mohave creation stories. As an example, consider three of the songs that he provided

from *Raven,* as shown in Figure 2.B-ii. Like the other songs that Kroeber provided as

examples, these three *Raven* songs contained relatively few words. Kroeber therefore

argued that they were extraneous, a sentiment that he expressed, when he said, "It is clear

that very little of the plot gets into the songs." Referring to the three *Raven* songs

---

[53] See *Deer* and *Cane* in SMM.

Kroeber wrote:

> It is clear that very little of the plot gets into the song: insufficient to render it intelligible to those who have not learned or heard the story; although the words themselves may be readily recognizable.[54]

#1	ahnalya	gourd rattle
	ialya	I show
	viv'aum	standing
#2	ahnalya	gourd rattle
	idhauk	I hold
	amaim ichiak	upward raise it
	viv'aum	standing
#3	idhauk	I hold it
	akanavek	I tell of it
	viv'aum	standing
	achidhumk	I look hither
	achikavak	I look thither
	viv'aum	standing

Figure 2.B-ii. *Raven* songs from Kroeber's *Handbook*.
Source: Kroeber's *Handbook,* p. 758.

Kroeber's conclusion that "It is clear that very little of the plot gets into the song" only makes sense when one considers a song or a small number of songs in isolation, without providing any sense of their meaning with regard to the story as a whole or to some part of the it. In fact this is precisely how Kroeber treated these three *Raven* songs and the others that he provided as examples. Contributing to this picture is the fact that Kroeber provides word-for-word translations for these songs and others. Without an attempt to move beyond this rudimentary approach, his translations could only confirm his contention, namely that the songs should be excluded. I have listened to singers speak

---

[54] See Kroeber, *Handbook,*758.

about their songs and can report that the meaning of their songs cannot be conveyed solely through the use of a simple, word-for-word translation. As a way of responding to Kroeber's treatment of these songs, I have therefore included my own free translation, in Figure 2.B-iii.

From Kroeber		My free translation
1. ahnalya	Gourd rattle.	My gourd rattle. I stand and show it.
oalya	I show.	
viv'aum[55]	Standing.	
2. ahnalya	Gourd rattle.	My gourd rattle. As I stand, I hold it and thrust it upwards.
idhauk	I hold	
amaim ichiak	upward raise it	
viv'aum	standing	
3. idhauk	I hold it	I hold it. As I stand, I tell of what I see. I look hither. I look thither, as I stand and tell my story.
akanavek	I tell of it	
viv'aum	standing	
achidhumk	I look hither	
achikavak	I look thither	
viv'aum	standing	

Figure 2.B-iii. Three *Raven* songs and two approaches to their translation.

More than anything else, Kroeber's treatment of these songs may reflect the fact that he was primarily interested in writing down the stories. He may have seen any other task, including thinking about the songs, as a potential diversion, one that might have prevented him from accomplishing his chosen task. At the same time, Kroeber's and Underhill's mutual conclusion that the songs contained little of value suggests that neither of them realized that some significant part of the story was likely conveyed through the songs. Had Underhill or Kroeber realized that a set of songs could be used to

---

[55] Songs 2-4 are from Kroeber's *Handbook.* See Figure 2.B-ii

explore a topic from a variety of vantage points, it seems possible that they, like Halpern, would have included the songs alongside or with the accompanying spoken narrative. It seems likely that these three *Raven* songs belong to a set. Even without any consideration of the story of *Raven*, it seems obvious that each of these songs describes a performer, as he stands up and tells his story; furthermore, in these songs the gourd is more than a percussion instrument per se. As the singer holds his gourd, his gourd seems to somehow enhance his ability to tell his story. This is a subject that the performer considers in a slightly different way with each song. I will consider three songs in more detail below, when I consider Kroeber's transcription of *Raven*.

In addition to his unnecessary addition of songs, Underhill argued that Kroeber had muddied the plot, making it impossible for most readers to understand, because he included so many minor "incidents." In his transcriptions, Kroeber in fact not only included numerous incidents but also the names of the places (oftentimes in Mohave) where each incident occurred. Underhill found these Mohave place names to be burdensome detail. Or, as she explained:

> One can imagine this story re-told against the Wagnerian background of the dawn-world and with our modern awareness of the effects of jealousy, inferiority, and childhood influences. At least, one can imagine it after reading Kroeber's clear plot summary, dramatic paragraph headings, and acute literary comments. Without them, the reader, unless particularly interested in Indians, might bog down among the many incidents in which the plot is embedded or tire of the unpronounceable place names which suffice a Mohave instead of poetic description.[56]

Underhill disagreed with still another of aspect of Kroeber's account of the

---

[56] See Underhill's review.

Mohave. In his *Handbook,* Kroeber reported that a number of the Mohave singers whom

he had interviewed told him that they had dreamt of creation while still *in utero.* Later,

as adults, they would speak and sing about the events that they had experienced. These

were events that had taken place in what Underhill refers to as the "dawn-world," in the

above quotation. As Kroeber explained, during these dreams, the singers were projected

back to the time of creation. Or as Kroeber wrote:

> Over most of native North America the acquisition of power by dreams or visions
> of spirits is the basis of shamanism; and where religion is simple, it is largely
> constituted of shamanism. The Yuman tribes, however, have evolved the special
> belief that these visions are of the spirits and great gods of the beginning of the
> world. This group of tribes in their philosophy transcend time and project their
> souls back to the origin of things. This act they call dreaming. The most basic
> and most significant of these dreams are not those of adolescence, but those which
> one had before birth--while still in the mother's belly, they say. It is these
> prenatal dreams which the newly born baby and the child may forget, but which
> come back to the growing boy and the man when he hears others singing or
> telling similar experiences.[57]

Based on her conversations with Mohave singers, Underhill concluded that

Kroeber's observations were incorrect. Writing about this, Underhill wrote, "This

remarkable attitude might be subject to discussion and later investigators, including the

reviewer, have not found it to be so clear cut."

Raven is one of the creation stories that Kroeber included in SMM. His

transcription of *Raven* provides an example of the kind of clear-cut remarks that he had

provided concerning dreams and creation stories. On March 19, 1903, Pamitš, a Mohave

singer, told this story to Kroeber. Emphasizing the idea that his story did in fact consist

of events that he had experienced, Pamitš sometimes added comments to this effect

---

[57] From Kroeber's "Introduction," in *Seven Mohave Myths,* 1.

(such as "and then I saw"), as he told the story. Regarding how Pamitš had learned the

creation story *Raven*, Kroeber wrote:

> Pamitš said to me: "I was a baby boy [meaning a foetus] when I dreamed this
> singing; it was given to me by the Ravens. Now I am a man, but have not
> forgotten it. I dreamed it before I ever was born. If I had been born when I
> dreamed it, I would have forgotten it. No, I did not learn it from other Mohaves;
> and I did not hear any of them sing it. In fact, no one else sings like this, for it
> was I that dreamed it myself."[58]

Kroeber's transcription of *Raven* provides a useful example in considering some

of the key objections that Underhill raised: that Kroeber should not have included songs,

that he had included too many incidents and Mohave place names, and that his report that

singers had learned their songs in dreams must have been exaggerated. All of the

Mohave creation stories that Kroeber transcribed begin during the time of creation.

Raven begins just after the creator Matavilya has died.[59] Two brothers, both

identified as Ravens (*Aqāqa*), are among those present. Whereas Wonder Boy is the

protagonist in *Lightning*, in *Raven*, the protagonists are two Ravens. Like Wonder Boy,

these Ravens want to ensure that mankind continues to evolve. The Ravens do this by

teaching mankind about war. In the story, recorded by Kroeber, the Ravens speak

directly to Pamitš.

All of Kroeber's transcriptions consist of a sequence of episodes, which he

numbered sequentially.[60] In addition, many of the episodes in Kroeber's transcriptions

are followed by a number that indicates the number of songs associated that episode.

---

[58] SMM, 37.

[59] Matavilya, the creator, appears throughout Kroeber's transcriptions of Mohave creation
stories.

[60] Kroeber's term was stations.

Shorter than many of the other stories that Kroeber collected, *Raven* contains only thirty-

two episodes.

---

3. Then he said:[6] "Listen to what we tell. We have dreamed
well. We can divide the dark and the stars.[7] You do not know
it, but you will have war. We did not learn that from
Matavilya: we dreamed it. We are telling what is so: You will
see. We are brave and tell of things which we have dreamed."
(4 songs.)[8]
    4. Now as they sang, they had no gourd (rattles). They
said: "We have no gourds. That will not do. When people make
war and kill an enemy and dance, it will be well that they
such things." Now they were about to make a gourd to give to
me.[9] They said: "We have none yet but we can make it." Then
the older one stood up, turned to the west, to the north, to
the east, and to the south.[10] Then he had a gourd in his right
hand. He said: "It will be well, when a man sings, to use
that. Everyone will like to hear it." (4 songs.) [11]

---

[6] "Said to me," in the narrators words.

[7] Referring to wars of the Mohave against the Halchidhoma
and Cocopa.

[8] The words of the first of these songs about dreaming are:
sumāk imank akanavek.

[9] Viz., to the narrator.

[10] Clockwise circuit beginning with the west.

[11] The words of these four songs are: 1, ahnālya hidhauk
imat-kievek kanavek, gourd hold when-have tell; 2, ahnalya
oalya viv-aum, gourd I-show standing; 3, ahnalya hidhauk
amaim-itšiak viv'aum, gourd I-hold upward-raise-it standing;
4, idhauk akanavek viv'aum atšdhumk atšikavakek viv'aum, I-
hold-it I-tell-of-it standing look-here look-there standing.
Atšidumk and atšikavakek may refer to upstream and downstream
(north and south).

Figure 2.B-iv. Showing episodes 3 to 4 from Kroeber's transcription of *Raven*.[61]

Figure 2.B-iv shows episodes 3 and 4, from Kroeber's transcription of *Raven*.

Pamitš began episode 3 with the words "Then he said." Kroeber explains that these

---

[61] See Kroeber, SMM, 39.

words could be restated as "Then he said to me," meaning that the Ravens were speaking directly to Pamitš. As the Ravens begin to speak, they first describe their qualifications. They say to Pamitš, "We have dreamed well." In and of itself, this demonstrates that the Ravens have special powers. Next, they begin to teach. Speaking about war, they say: "You do not know it, but you will have war." Episode 3 ends with the notation "(4 songs)," indicating that this episode was associated with four songs. In a footnote, Kroeber explains that the first song is about dreaming. He also provides the following words for this song: *"sumāk imank akanavek."* Using a dictionary written by the linguist Pamela Munro and others, I was able to find entries that seem to correspond to most of the words in this song. It seems likely that the song means something like, "The stories I tell came from my dreams."[62] (See Figure 2.B-v.)

English:	dream	come or start from	tell
Mohave:	sumach	imank	kanavek[63]

Figure 2.B-v. A possible translation for the first song of episode 3.

Kroeber does not provide the words to any of the other songs for episode 3; but it seems possible that these songs may have touched on some of the other subjects that are mentioned in this episode, such as the idea that the Ravens can "divide the dark and the stars," or that man will one day wage war.

In episode 4, the Ravens speak about singing and playing the gourd. In Kroeber's

---

[62] See Pamela Munro, Nellie Brown, and Judith G. Crawford, *A Mojave Dictionary.*
UCLA Occasional Papers in Linguistics no. 10 (Los Angeles, California: Department of Linguistics, University of California, 1992.)
[63] *Kanavek,* "tell," is not listed in *A Mojave Dictionary.* Therefore I used what seemed to be a related word, *kuunav* that also means "tell."

transcriptions of Mohave creation stories, it is not uncommon to see references to singing

or dancing in the spoken sections. It seems possible that such references may have

helped to tie each spoken section together with the associated songs. Episode 4 in fact

contains a number of such references to singing and playing the gourd. This should be

expected, for it is in this episode that the Ravens point out that man has not learned to

play the gourd. They rectify this problem in this episode. Or, as the Ravens say:

> "We have no gourds. That will not do. When people make war and kill an enemy and dance, it will be well that they have such things." [64]

To create gourds, the Ravens draw on their supernatural skills and powers. The older

Raven stands up. After reaching out to the four directions, he magically produces a

gourd. As this episode comes to an end (and while still speaking to Pamitš), the Ravens

say, "It will be well, when a man sings, to use that. Everyone will like to hear it."

Kroeber included four songs for episode 4. Three of these songs are ones that

Kroeber had included in his *Handbook* (as an example of why songs need not be included

in his transcriptions).[65] As mentioned earlier, Kroeber's treatment of these three songs

was cursory. The same is true in SMM. He included the songs (now four instead of

three), but in a fashion that made them difficult to read or understand (see Figure 2.B-vi).

By presenting these songs in this fashion, Kroeber seems to reinforce his conclusion that

these and other songs had little to offer.

---

[64] See episode 4, Figure 2.B-iv.
[65] See Figure 2.B-ii.

11 The words of these four songs are: 1, ahnālya hidhauk imat-
kievek kanavek, gourd hold when-have tell; 2, ahnalya oalya viv-aum,
gourd I-show standing; 3, ahnalya hidhauk amaim-itšiak viv'aum, gourd
I-hold upward-raise-it standing; 4, idhauk akanavek viv'aum atšdhumk
atšikavakek viv'aum, I-hold-it I-tell-of-it standing look-here look-
there standing. Atšidumk and atšikavakek may refer to upstream and
downstream (north and south).

Figure 2.B-vi. Showing how Kroeber presented the songs, for episode 4.[66]

When these songs are arranged and presented in a manner that is easier to

comprehend (see Figure 2.B-vii), it becomes clear that they probably constitute a set, or

possibly a part of one.

1.	*ahnalya hidhauk imat-kievek kanavek*	Gourd hold. When-have, tell.[67]
2.	*ahnalya oalya viv-aum*	Gourd, I show, standing.
3.	*ahnalya hidhauk amaim-itšiak viv'aum*	Gourd, I hold upward. Raise it, standing.
4.	*hidhauk akanavek viv-aum atšdumk atšikavakek viv'aum*	I hold it. I tell of it, standing. Look here. Look there, standing.

Figure 2.B-vii. Four Songs from *Raven*, in SMM.
Source: footnote SMM, p.38, footnote 11.

In Figure 2.B-viii, I include my translation of these four songs.[68] In this type of

aaa translation, it becomes much easier to see that each song touches on the topic of

holding and playing the gourd, but from a slightly different perspective. The spoken

section of episode 4 ends as follows: "It will be well, when a man sings, to use that.

Everyone will like to hear it." It thus appears that these four songs have a significant

message to convey. The first song of this set begins, with the singer telling his story as

[66] See Kroeber's SMM, p. 39.
[67] I have added punctuation to the English translation, in an attempt to clarify Kroeber's translation.
[68] I included three of these songs, in Figure 2.B-iii.

he holds his gourd. The gallant tone begins to appear in the next songs. Song 2 focuses on the act of showing the gourd, while standing. In song 3, the singer raises his gourd up into the air, still standing. With the fourth song, Pamitš puts it all together. Here is Kroeber's translation for this song 4 (from his *Handbook):* "I hold it. I tell of it, standing. I look hither. I look thither, standing."[69]

In these songs the singer is restricted to a relatively small number of words; nevertheless, as he moves from one song to the next, he seems to add progressive layers of meaning. As the songs are performed, a picture gradually emerges of a singer who is raising and showing his gourd for everyone to see, as he stands and sings and tells his story.

---

[69] See Figure 2.B-ii.

	From Kroeber		My free translation[70]
	Mohave	English	
1.	ahnalya hidhauk imat-kievek kanavek[71]	Gourd hold. When-have, tell.	I hold my gourd. As I play my gourd, I tell my story.
2.	ahnalya ialya viv'aum[72]	Gourd rattle. I show. Standing.	My gourd rattle. I show it, as I stand.
3.	ahnalya idhauk amaim ichiak viv'aum	Gourd rattle. I hold upward raise it standing	My gourd rattle. I hold it. I thrust it upwards, as I stand.
4.	idhauk akanavek viv'aum achidhumk achikavak viv'aum	I hold it I tell of it standing I look hither I look thither standing	I hold it. I stand and I tell my story. I look hither. I look thither, while standing. And I tell my story!

Figure 2.B-viii. Two contrasting ways of presenting the songs from episode 4.

---

[70] This is my free translation.
[71] Song 1, the Mohave and the English, are from SMM. See Figure 2.B-vi.
[72] Songs 2-4 are from Kroeber's *Handbook.* See Figure 2.B-ii

Kroeber's and Underhill's transcriptions of Vinumulye

Although it appears that Underhill never published any Mohave creation stories, she did spend time working on an undated manuscript that she entitled "The Battle at Spirit Mountain." This title bears a special significance; since Spirit Mountain, which is located next to the Colorado River, some thirty miles north of Needles, California,[73] is viewed by Yuman-speaking peoples throughout the ESCR as being the place of creation. The Denver Museum of Nature and Science has two drafts (both undated) of Underhill's "The Battle at Spirit Mountain." In the following discussion, I will be referring to these as Drafts 1 and 2. Draft 1 contains numerous corrections, including words and section that have been crossed out as well as handwritten remarks.[74] All of the corrections from shown in Draft 1 have been entered into Draft 2. Draft 2 is somewhat shorter, Underhill having removing some portions of the story.[75]

Consider, for example, Figure 2.B-ix, which shows the start of Draft 1. This excerpt shows the first title "The Battle at Spirit Mountain," followed by "translated from the Mohave by Ruth Underhill." In first sentence of the text that follows, Underhill explains that "The Battle at Spirit Mountain" is based on the creation story *Vinyimulya hupacha:*

---

[73] See *Spirit Mountain,* p. 3.

[74] This remains the case, even though Draft 1 has no pagination. Draft 1 consists of eight separate pages. For the purposes of this discussion, I have numbered the pages of Draft 1 in the order in which they appear. The pages from Draft 2 were paginated, 1-5. When I received these documents, from the Bailey Library and Archives, at the Denver Museum of Nature and Science, Draft 1 was labeled "AR-M237_080134." Draft 2 was "AR-M237_092830."

[75] See footnote 87.

Excerpts from the song-narrative <u>vinyimulya hupacha</u> which recounts the adventures of the ancestor of the Thorn clan.[76]   For purposes of comparison, also see Figure 2.B-x, a facsimile of the same excerpt from Draft 2; Figure 2.B-xi gives a clearer transcription.

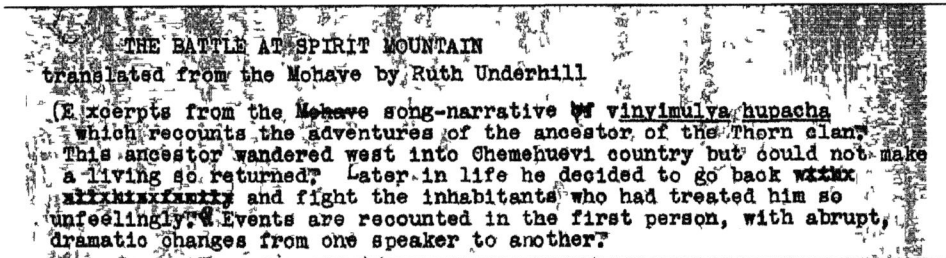

Figure 2.B-ix. An excerpt from Draft 1 of Underhill's *Vinyimulya hupacha*.
Note: Underhill does not include explanatory prose other than the initial note, shown in this and following two figures.

---

[76] See Figure 2.B-xi.

TH BATTLE AT SPIRIT MOUNTAIN

Translated from the Mohave by Ruth Underhill.

(Excerpts from the song-narrative vinyimulya hupacha which
recounts the adventures of the ancestor of the Thorn clan.
This ancestor wandered west into Chemehuevi country but
could not make a living so returned. Later in life he
decided to go back and fight the inhabitants who had treated
him so unfeelingly.

Events are recounted in the first person, with abrupt, dramatic
changes from one speaker to another.)

Figure 2.B-x. An excerpt from Draft 2 of Underhill's *Vinyimulya hupacha*.

THE BATTLE AT SPIRIT MOUNTAIN

Translated from the Mohave by Ruth Underhill.

(Excerpts from the song-narrative <u>vinyimulya</u> <u>hupacha</u> which recounts the
adventures of the ancestor of the Thorn clan. This ancestor wandered west into
Chemehuevi country but could not make a living so returned. Later in life he
decided to go back and fight the inhabitants who had treated him so unfairly.

Events are recounted in the first person, with abrupt, dramatic changes from one
speaker to another.)

Figure 2.B-xi. The same as Figure 2.B-x, copied in Times Roman.

Kroeber transcribed a story that he referred to as *Vinumulye-patše*. The Mohave

singer Hiweik-kwini'īlye told this story to Kroeber, on April 23, 1904.[77] Kroeber

identified this story as being *Vinumulye-patše,* but he also explained that *Vinumulye-patše*

---

[77] See Kroeber's SMM, p. 24.

was shorthand for *Vinumulye-hapātše*[78]. Because *"tš"* stands for a "ch" sound, *hapātše* and *hupacha* (from Underhill's title) amount to two different ways of spelling the same work. Therefore *Vinyimulya hupacha* (Underhill's title) and *Vinumulye-hapātše* (Kroeber's title) probably refer to the same story. In a crossed-out section of Draft 1 of this story, Underhill wrote, "Excerpt from narrative ata malyae (reed)." *Cane* is another Mohave creation story, one that Kroeber included in SMM.[79] In *Cane,* two brothers clash. Eventually the older kills the younger. Or as Underhill explained:

> In one situation after another, he [the older brother] yields to the younger, even after worsting him in a fair fight. Then, in his own good time, he afflicts his rival with a fatal disease and, during his death throes, removes his bones to make shinny balls and hide-scrapers.[80]

Underhill's *Vinyimulya hupacha* is a different story. Underhill's *Vinyimulya hupacha* is, however, quite similar to Kroeber's *Vinumulye-hapātše.* Because the stories contained in the transcriptions of Underhill and Kroeber are similar in many respects, their transcriptions provide an opportunity to consider the differing ways in which these two scholars responded to the Mohave and their creation stories. In the following discussion, I refer to this story as *Vinumulye.*

As the story begins, two groups of Mohave live side-by-side. In their respective transcriptions, Underhill and Kroeber refer to these groups by different names. In Underhill's transcription, one of these groups is identified as the Thorn clan, and the

---

[78] Meaning that *Patše* corresponds to *hapātše.*

[79] See Kroeber's SMM, 4. Kroeber writes the title as *Ahta-'amalya'e.* The corresponding entry in *A Mojave Dictionary* is "Cane Song, *Ahta Malyae.*" See p. 220.

[80] See the previous discussion regarding Underhill's review of Kroeber's SMM. Also see footnote 49.

leader of this group as "Thorn leader." For an unspecified reason the Thorn clan is forced or chooses to leave, and they travel until they settle somewhere in Chemehuevi territory. Unfortunately the land that Thorn leader and his people have moved to is arid and unproductive. The resulting disquiet of the Thorn clan is expressed through the voice of Thorn leader, who dreams of the foods that his clan was once able to eat. Underhill portrays Thorn leader's remembering in vivid terms, as she did in her summary of *Cane*. Remembering the food that he and his clan members once ate, Thorn leader states:

> *Beans, corn, pumpkins, you ate and you were filled*
> *You lived there, you are glad*
> *You mashed the food, you made it into cakes*
> *You roll them up and set them on a stick,*
> *Their odor filled my nose* [81]

Thorn leader also speaks about how plentiful game was in his homeland. In this excerpt, he states that his group used to live at Spirit Mountain.[82]

> *Don't you see it afar, the Spirit Mtn, my land!*
> *There I lived and hunted.*
> *The rat, the cotton tail, the chuckwalla, I hunted as I lived there*
> *I killed them, I ate them. I had my fill when I stayed there*
> *Now I will tell of it for I dreamed it and it came before my eyes*

Thorn leader and his clan are apparently known for their prowess as warriors. They realize that they are certainly strong enough to return home and to once again take control of their lands. Thus Thorn leader and his people decide to return home. In her review of SMM and MHE, Underhill objected to Kroeber's excessive use of Mohave names; yet in her manuscript she incorporates them. In the following excerpt, each of the

---

[81] This is from page 2 of Draft 2.

[82] This excerpt is taken from part of the text that Underhill had crossed out. See Draft 1, page 3

names mentioned seems to be the name of one of those who stayed behind. Thorn leader

and his clan are ready to kill anyone who may try to prevent them from returning home.

Expressing this sentiment, Thorn leader says,

> *Huakykumari, Apotkwinamakm, Umasitcama, Nyimasavlyalyuvava.*
> *They live there now and we shall kill them.*
> *They are afraid. But we shall go there.*[83]

What follows is the first page of Draft 2 of Underhill's transcription of *Vinumulye*. It

includes the events just discussed (see Figure 2.B-xii).

THE BATTLE AT SPIRIT MOUNTAIN

Translated from the Mohave by Ruth Underhill

(Excerpts from the song-narrative <u>vinyimulya</u> <u>hupacha</u> which recounts the adventures of the ancestor of the Thorn clan This ancestor wandered west into Chemehuevi country but could not make a living so returned Later in life he decided to go back and fight the inhabitants who had treated him so unfairly

Events are recounted in the first person, with abrupt, dramatic changes from one speaker to another.)

Thorn leader speaks [84]

My land, my curving land! I bring it back, I dream of it
Huakykumari, Apotkwinamakm, Umasitcama, Nyimasavlyalyuvava
They live there now and we shall kill them
They are afraid But we shall go there
They will flee, look you
For there is none who is my equal

Figure 2.B-xii. The Start of Underhill's Transcription of *Vinumulye*, from Draft 2, page 1.

Having left their homeland, the people of the Thorn clan eventually settle in a

barren land. They therefore dream of the abundance of their homeland, of returning

---

[83] This is from the start of Draft 2, also part of the excerpt in see Figure 2.B-xii.

[84] Note, the above is a semi-diplomatic transcription. I have retained Underhill's layout, spacing, etc. but in contemporary typescript.

home once again, and engaging in war in order to seize it once again. Underhill's

transcription of *Vinumulye* contains moments in which the Thorn people return home

and begin to fight, as described here:

> *Now we cross the water, we arrive at the other side.*
> *I will pursue them, I will come up with them, I will kill them.*
> *Their leaders will I kill, their leaders only.*
> *At the Place where Hail has been, at the Place where the Travelers Drink.*
> *I come upon the enemy, the enemy fears us.*
> *Now, go the upper way!*
> *Now Ahuailyevitc, surround the enemy!*

As they engage in battle, the Thorn people find themselves faced with a bitter dilemma:

to fight means to slaughter people who they once lived with and loved. In Underhill's

depictions of moments of battle there is a rapid shifting between the desire to vanquish

the enemy and moments in which the Thorn people recognize their brethren and realize

that they do not want to kill them, as shown here:

> *Now Humastcama (an enemy) stop! Shoot at me! We will kill each other.*
> *Now Nyamasav nyayuyava, where are you going?*
> *Where are you going forsooth!*
> *Stop! We will kill each other.*
> *Never, perchance shall we see each other again.*
> *Look you, it is the end!*
> *For with the arrow and the bow you are not my equal.*

For the Thorn people, the drive to kill their enemies appears to be a deeply ingrained.

When Thorn leader and his people suddenly lose their desire to fight, Thorn leader's

daughter becomes enraged. At this point, the voice of the narrator shifts from Thorn

Leader to his daughter.[85]

> *(The two parties now fight and the speaker is victorious. But he does not*

---

[85] This is from Underhill's transcription of *Vinumulye,* Draft 2, page 2

kill the enemy, and some escape. For this his daughter who is in the
party chides him.)
Daughter speaks:
You pursued the enemy, you followed after them.
I followed you and I came hither.
With all my strength I ran.
I thought that you and he would kill each other
And I would have died by her side.
But instead you only looked at them.
You were in love with their faces, with their bodies.
You are not hunting to kill.[86]

Having expressed her frustration with her father, the daughter leaves, at least for a while.

Thus far, the overall effect of Underhill's manuscript is that of a well integrated story, one that appears to have a clear beginning, middle, and end; an easily recognizable conflict; and a well-defined set of protagonists and antagonists. After the departure of the daughter, the form of the story begins to change. Underhill abandons her clear beginning, middle, and end structure. In the remainder of her transcription, Underhill jumps back and forth between the different parts of the story. The story becomes episodic, thus mimicking the structure of a song cycle. While there are no notes in her manuscript stating she had decided to move beyond the role of a transcriber, it appears that Underhill decided to work with the song cycle form, as a sculptor works with clay. As the different parts of the story are reintroduced, Underhill adds new details. The recurring parts include: Thorn Leader, as he dreams of returning home; Thorn Leader, as he thinks about those who stayed behind and how they will be afraid if he returns; descriptions of the two clans, as they begin to fight; moments during which the daughter expresses her thoughts and feelings, and lastly moments of repose, during which

---

[86] Ibid.

Underhill introduces themes taken from songs about the sounds of birds or other natural phenomena.

The storyline is not always consistent, however. On one hand, as "The Battle at Spirit Mountain" continues, we learn (in Draft 1) that Thorn Leader's daughter may not have grown angry because her father and his clan lost their desire to slaughter their fellow men. As this part of the story is represented, we also learn, however, that the daughter may have reacted with disappointment and anger because her father scolded her. In the excerpt that follows, it seems that after leaving her father, the daughter may have lived for two years with some other group of people (presumably the Chemehuevi), before deciding to return to her father. Here Underhill's style is pointedly dramatic. The daughter begins by saying that her father "chided her."[87]

> *He chided me. He did indeed.*
> *I go. I go. I go. I leave my people.*
> *I think I shall reach some other place.*
> *Perhaps they will send me for wood, they will send me for water.*
> *I go outside and stand there thinking.*
> *Could I do it? Is there any way?*
> *What if I should go to the enemy who have fled?*
> *They might take me prisoner.*
> *They might send me for wood. They might send me for water.*
> *I go back inside the house. I pile up the small dish of embers and hide it.*
>
> *I carry it behind the house. And I go back inside.*
> *I go out again. I ponder. I will listen, which way to go.*
> *I go out and stand there. I think. I stand outside and think.*
> *I will go.*
>
> *(The daughter wanders for two years, finally decides to return)*

---

[87] Draft 1 describes the daughter's actions in much more detain than does Draft 2. "He Chided Me, "Excerpt #3 of Underhill's Transcription of *Vinumulye*, From Draft 1, page 4.

My father! Where may he be?
I shall go to him.
He may be dead, he may be alive.
I go. I think of him. I go again.[88]

As the story becomes more episodic, Underhill begins to use songs--or at least the kind of content often found in some songs-- as a kind of transition point between different parts of the story. Moments of action such as dreaming about returning, or actual moments of fighting, are followed by periods of rest. It is in these moments of repose that Underhill introduces themes that are typically found in songs. Some of the words used seem as if they might be song texts.

As Draft 1 continues, the reason for the daughter leaving is once again that her father and his fellow warriors were reluctant to fight:

Daughter speaks:
Because you did not kill these enemies, I ran away.[89]

Underhill then introduces a moment of rest, during which she mentions, "the middle of the night." The narrator also says, "It is almost light." By referring to the night or the time that precedes dawn, Underhill manages to allude to topics that are the subject of some songs but without actually mentioning any songs. Here is the section that follows:

Now they camp, they sleep.
The girl sleeps, she wakes, she looks, she sits up.
The middle of the night. It is almost light.
The middle of the night.

This moment of repose leaders directly to a moment of action. The daughter wakes. Awake, at night, she once again begins to worry about her father.

---

[88] This excerpt is taken from page 4 of draft 1.
[89] Draft 1, p. 6.

Daughter speaks:
"My father, wake!
You sleep: you may have an unlucky dream.
You may prove unequal to the enemy."
The old man (or father) is thinking of the enemy.
He does not sleep. "How am I going to kill them?"
He does not sleep.
"Wake! Do!
By sleeping no one feeds himself.
By the enemy you might be overcome."

Night gives way to dawn, however. The text that follows, "The birds wake, they cried,"

is similar to what might be found in a song text.

"The birds wake, they cried," she says.
"It is as though they spoke. They know," she says.
"They hear the morning. It is the yellow warbler.
It is as though it spoke, you hear?
It feels the dawn," she says. "Do you hear?"

This moment of quietude once again gives way to another of the recurring themes, this

time that of war. It is no longer Thorn leader who speaks. Now the narrator sounds more

like a superhuman protagonist, one interested in teaching man a lesson.

Above, all over, I see the stars.
Here and there, all over, you see?
Long, long ago He made them, and He finished them, you see!
They will speak to you. By that you shall know,
You shall plan how to kill, you plan how to capture.
What He has done, I will tell.
I finished, I leave my telling.
Those who come after me shall tell it also.

This is followed by another moment of repose. This time, Underhill is using lines that

sound as if they might actually have come from songs. Now the songs are about birds

who wake up and then begin to sing: the owl, the nighthawk, and the mockingbird.

The owl sleeps, it wakes, it cries.
It knows the morning as it sits there.

The Nighthawk comes out toward us
Crying as it comes.
It knows the morning, it comes crying.
The Mockingbird wakes, it speaks
It tells of the morning, it talks, it speaks.

The quail sleep. The light is coming, they wait.
The eat something. They eat, I know them.

The red stinging ants, the stinging ants, they sleep.
The light they see, they know it, they wait.

Thus far I have touched on most but not all of the parts in her Underhill's transcription of

Vinumulye. In what follows, Thorn Leader once again speaks about war and returning

home. The remainder of the story (not all included here) focuses on this theme:

Thorn leader speaks:
The sun comes out.
The enemy who I pursued, they will I chase.
They cannot all have good dreams nor all have bad.
I will kill them. I will pursue them.
The enemy, the man-woman, I will pursue.

The fight:
There, face that way! Shoot at them:
if you turn back, they will shoot your back and they will laugh.
Face forward, shoot! Face forward, shoot!
Do not run, do not turn back!
If you turn back, they will shoot your back

Kroeber's transcription of Vinumulye

In her manuscript "The Battle of Spirit Mountain," Underhill uses the kind of

novelistic style that she advocated in her review of Kroeber's SMM and MHE. The

protagonists are easily identified. The conflicts are well defined. At the same time,

Underhill incorporates elements of the song cycle form. into her "The Battle of Spirit

Mountain." While she does not adhere to this form strictly, the story becomes episodic at a certain point. The different part of the story each have a different theme. Thus in the moments of repose and between incidents, Underhill introduces themes and even texts that are typical of songs. Additionally, she also includes what appear to be the texts of some songs. In contrast, Kroeber's transcription of *Vinumulye* adheres closely to the song cycle form. Like all of his transcriptions of Mohave creation stories, Kroeber's transcription of *Vinumulye* consists of a sequence of numbered episodes. Kroeber's V*inumulye* has twenty-nine episodes, most of which are associated with a set of songs.[90] His transcription shows that at least 160 songs were associated with V*inumulye*. Some episodes clearly contain more songs than others. For example while episode 19 has thirty songs and episode 21 has forty, most episodes in this story contain generally no more than five songs.

The story begins with a factual account of the journey of Umas-kwitŝit-patŝe and his faction [episode 1] (see Figure 2.B-xiii). Episodes 1-3 detail the journey of Umas-kwitŝit-patŝe, from his homeland, *Aha-kwa'i* (located between Fort Mohave and Needles) to the Providence Mountains, *Avi-kwe-havase*. As can be seen in episodes 1-3, each episode is associated with at least a few songs. Kroeber appears to have made little or no attempt to dramatize the story, but seems instead to have written it out as it was told to him.

---

[90] For the purposes of brevity, I will sometimes write Kroeber's V*inumulye* rather than Kroeber's transcription V*inumulye*.

1. Umas-kwitŝit-patŝe lived at Aha-kwa'i[1] with his people. At that time the river was near that place. He was the only one of them to talk to the rest. Then he and his people crossed the river to the western side to Amaṭ-kusayi.[2] (4 songs.)[3]

2. Then they went up on the mesa, and from there into the mountains at IƟave-kukyave. (2 songs).[3]

3. Then they went to the large mountains, Avi-kwe-havase,[4] the Providence mountains. (2 songs.)

4. They had found that land and kept it for their own. They lived there a year. Now Umas-kwitŝit-patŝe was a Mohave, and his relatives were Mohave in this country. He said: I want to go back to my relatives." Then he returned by the way he had come, going back to Aha-kwa'i with his people. When he returned, all the Mohave said: "I think he has come to make war." They talked of war. They were afraid of him, for he was very large. Then he went back to the Providence mountains with his people. Now he was a man who dreamed well.[5] He knew what the people were saying about him: he dreamed it. They were saying: "I wish Umas-kwitŝit-patŝe would come again. We would cook wheat[6] for him, and put meat into it, and make good food for him." No one sent for him to come but he knew what they wished. Then he was ready to come to make war. So he started with his people, but he did not go straight. He went part way to Hatalompe[7] far down to Aha-kwatpave.[8] (An indefinite number of songs.)

[1]Aha-kwa'i is at the "Old Gus" ranch, below Milltown, on an overflow pond or slough (an old river arm), at the foot of the mesa on the east edge of Mohave valley, upstream from Needles and downstream from Fort Mohave. At the time of the story, the river lay close to Aha-kwa'i.

[2]Downstream from Hatŝioq-vatveve.

[3]The narrator stated that he usually omitted the songs credited to pars. 1 and 2 and began with those referring to the Providence mountains. Ieave is arrowweed.

[4]"Blue Mountains," as they appear from the Mohave country.

[5]Sumatŝ-ahotk.

[6]Frequently considered native by the Mohave.

[7]Six miles south of Beal, the point at which the Santa Fe railroad leaves California on its way east.

[8]On the Colorado on the east side, below Ehrenberg. He had to cross the river to reach it, of course.

Figure 2.B-xiii. Episodes 1-4, from Kroeber's transcription of *Vinumulye.*[91]

In Kroeber's transcription, the group who leave is not identified as being the Thorn clan,

[91] Kroeber's SMM, 24.

in Underhill's transcription, but rather a faction of the *Owitŝ* clan who decide to leave and travel away from away their homeland.[92]   Their leader's name is Umas-kwitŝit-patŝe.[93] The faction of the *owitŝ* clan that remains behind, is led by Savil-yuyave, Umas-kwitŝit-patŝe's brother. The members of Savil-yuyave's faction are frightened when they hear that Umas-kwitŝit-patŝe, who is such a big, strong warrior, is planning to return. In Kroeber's transcription, when Umas-kwitŝit-patŝe and his group *do* return, they do not fight with Savil-yuyave and his group; instead they embark on still another extended journey. Kroeber provided what for him was a relatively long summary for this story. Here is an excerpt from the first part of his summary:

> The tale is simple. The Mohave hero Umas-kwitŝit-patŝe, with his people, leaves his home in the northern part of Mohave valley, for the Providence mountains, off to the northwest in Chemehuevi territory, and lives there a year. There is no farming possible in this desert range, but the story is silent on subsistence. The chief wants to return to make war, and, after a brief visit home, leads his people to the river at the south end of Mohave valley, and then makes a long detour downstream.[94]

In her transcription, Underhill focused on portraying the feelings and the thoughts of the main characters. We learn Thorn Leader's about dreams of tasty food and plentiful game provide a motive for his return. Thorn Leader also explains that in order to return he will have to fight, meaning that he will have to vanquish those who stayed behind.

---

[92] The words *"owitŝ"* is sometimes translated as being the "cloud" or "wind clan but seems to have no relationship to the word "thorn."

[93] An ŝ sounds something like an English "ch."

[94] As his summary continues, Kroeber provides more details about the travel sequence. Thus the Thorn clan makes "a long detour downstream to Ehrenberg, in Halchidhoma land; from there they turn back until they reach the foot of Mohave valley." See Kroeber, SMM, 24. To the best of my knowledge the Halchidhoma, a Yuman-speaking tribe, no longer exist as a separate tribe.

We also see that when it comes to fighting, he and his clan ultimately turn away in disgust. In contrast, in Kroeber's transcription the narration focuses much more on the facts of the narrative and much less on the emotions. Consider, for example, this excerpt, taken from episode 4 (see Figure 2.B-xiii). Umas-kwitŝit-patŝe wants to go back but his thoughts about whether or not he might face resistance are not mentioned. He simply returns.

> Now Umas-kwitŝit-patŝe was a Mohave, and his relatives were Mohave in this country. He said: I want to go back to my relatives." Then he returned by the way he had come, going back to Aha-hwa'i with his people.[95]

When Umas-kwitŝit-patŝe returns, those who stayed behind are indeed afraid. The narrator does discuss their fears. As episode 4 continues, the narrator explains:

> When he returned, all the Mohave said: "I think he has come to make war." They talked of war. They were afraid of him, for he was very large.

Again, there is no fighting. Umas-kwitŝit-patŝe and his people simply turn around and go back to where they have been living. Or as the narrator said, "Then he went back to the Providence mountains with his people." Again, there is no fighting.

After recovering from their initial fears, those who stayed behind begin to wish that Umas-kwitŝit-patŝe would return. We hear about this from Umas-kwitŝit-patŝe, not those who stayed behind. But Umas-kwitŝit-patŝe is a dreamer. It is through his dreams that he discovers that that those who stayed behind actually want him to return. Why? His cooking is excellent. Episode 4 continues with,

---

[95] This is from episode 4. The geographical place *Aha-hwa'i* is first mentioned in episode 1. (See Kroeber, SMM, 24.) It is the Mohave place where Umas-kwitŝit-patŝe and his people lived before they left on their first journey. See footnote 1 of episode 1 in Figure 2.B-xiii.

> Now he was a man who dreamed well. He knew what the people were saying about him: he dreamed it. They were saying: "I wish Umas-kwitŝit-patŝe would come again. We would cook wheat for him, and put meat into it, and make good food for him." No one sent for him to come but he knew what they wished.

Umas-kwitŝit-patŝe, however, is ready to make war. He does not go home, to make war; instead he goes someplace else.

> Then he was ready to come to make war. So he started with his people, but he did not go straight. He went part way to Hatalompe far down to Aha-kwatpave.

The protagonists do not fight in Kroeber's transcription, not as they did in Underhill's. On the other hand, as Kroeber's transcription continues, a conflict does emerge between Umas-kwitŝit-patŝe and his daughter, Ilya-owitš-maikohwere. The cause of this disagreement is very different than in Underhill's transcription. In Kroeber's transcription, we learn that the daughter's name is Ilya-owitš-maikohwere. The conflict between father and daughter centers around the fact that Ilya-owitš-maikohwere had recently reached puberty. For this reason, her father Umas-kwitŝit-patŝe tells her that she may no longer sleep near to him and his wife. Explaining this further, Kroeber writes: "He wanted her to have a lover and marry, and feared that no man would steal to her while she lay close to her parents."[96] The daughter responds to this with anger and leaves. The dispute between father and daughter occurs in episodes 18-20 (see Figure 2.B-xiv).

---

[96] Excerpt #1 from Kroeber's transcription of *Vinumulye-Patše*, in Figure 2.B-xiii.

18. Umas-kwitŝit-patŝe had a daughter, Ilya-owitš-maikohwere. He said: "Now that you are big enough, do not sleep near me. Sleep at a distance. Sleep in the corner of the house."[22] The girl was angry at his saying that and ran off. (4 songs.)

19. She went east until she came to Hawi, where she slept. Then she went to Avi-hoalye, the Walapai mountain.[23] There were many girls among the (Walapai) people living there, and she went with them and stayed with them a year. She liked it there. (30 songs.)

20. After a year she went back. When she returned, she was ashamed and sat outside the house. She did not go indoors to her parents. She was painted red. The people she had been with, the Walapai, had given her the paint. The Mohave do not know how to paint like that. So they did not know who she was. She sat with her head bowed. Then Umas-kwitŝit-patŝe cane out. "That is my daughter," he said. (10 songs.)

[22]He wanted her to have a lover and marry, and feared that no man would steal to her while she lay close to her parents. There is nothing disgraceful in this suggestion, to the Mohave, who scarcely make a distinction between lover and husband. The old people frequently exhort the young to enjoy themselves while they can.

[23]Hoalye means yellow pine. The name Walapai, hawaly-ipai in Mohave, seem to be derived from this word.

Figure 2.B-xiv. Episodes 18-20, from Kroeber's transcription of *Vinumulye*.[97]

Kroeber, then, wrote out each Mohave creation story as a sequence of episodes, most of which were associated with a set of songs. Possibly because the task of writing out the stories took all his time, or possibly because he was first and foremost interested in the stories, Kroeber did not attempt to analyze the place of the songs in any substantive fashion. In footnotes, however, he does provide the texts of some songs. With her "The Battle of Spirit Mountain," Underhill also gives some consideration to the songs. She weaves together themes taken from some songs along with the story of Thorn Leader and his traveling clan. Neither Kroeber nor Underhill seemed to have been aware of how

[97] Kroeber. SMM, 25.

singers were able, with a set of songs, to describe a subject from a variety of points of view. Nor does either scholar mention the idea that the information conveyed in a set of songs complemented that which was conveyed in the associated spoken section; instead, Underhill and Kroeber both focus on the "story" part of the story. They do so in different ways, however, reflecting their individual responses to the Mohave. With her review of Kroeber's SMM and MHE, Underhill argued that a creation story text should convey the underlying thoughts, emotions, and actions of the main protagonists, an idea that she puts into practice in her "The Battle at Spirit Mountain." Kroeber, on the other hand, steadfastly presents the stories as a sequence of episodes, as they were dictated to him by each singer.

Neither scholar attempted to present everything that they knew about a story or even everything that they had heard. Whereas Kroeber's Mohave creation-story texts appear to be "descriptive," in the sense that he appears to be writing down what each singer told him, this is not entirely true. He did not, for instance, attempt to explore what part of a story might only be understood by considering the interplay between the parts of the story that were told and those that was conveyed through the songs. Thus the issue is not simply that he decided to exclude most songs from his transcriptions, but that he seems not to have realized that a study of how stories were told might significantly add to his understanding of each story. Underhill, on the other hand, seems to have been ready to set aside the stories as she heard them, in order to weed out details that she saw as burdensome. With this in mind, she seems to have been ready to exclude most songs, incidents, and geographical place names, all of which would have been likely included in a narration, by a Mohave. In lieu of these details, Underhill developed speeches through which she explored the motivation of the protagonists and their actions.

Kroeber's his audio recordings and his thoughts about performance

While, with his creation-story texts, Kroeber did not attempt to explore the interplay between the parts of a story that were conveyed by speaking and the parts that were communicated through the songs, it was not because he lacked information about the songs. As will be seen, in the following discussion, the opposite was true. Kroeber in fact made hundreds of wax cylinder recordings of Mohave creation story songs. Having said this, it still seems likely that Kroeber probably set aside these audio recordings in favor of focusing on writing down each creation story. In *A Mohave Historical Epic* (MHE), published in 1951, Kroeber paused, at one point, to discuss how he wrote out the epic tale that was the subject of this monograph. In the process, he gave some idea of the amount of time required to write down a story. The storyteller was the Mohave Inyokutavêre, and he knew the story of the origin of the Mohave clans. In 1902, Inyokutavêre told his story to Kroeber. As Kroeber explains,

> At Ah'a-kwinyevai[98], in a sand-covered Mohave house, we found the old man we
> had come to see, Inyokutavêre, "Vanished-pursue," who was reputed to know
> about the origin of clans. He admitted that he did, and would tell me the story. It
> would take a day, he said, when I asked about the length. As that day was partly
> gone, I arranged to come back in the morning.[99]

The Mohave singer Jack Jones served as the interpreter. In the following quotation,

---

[98] *Ah'a-kwinyevai* is located, "across the river from Needles and two or three miles inland." MHE, 71.
[99] For a larger excerpt of the same quotation, see Figure 2.B-xv

Kroeber explains that it took Jones as much time to translate the story as it did for

Inyokutavêre to tell it. Referring to Inyokutavêre and explaining this process, Kroeber

wrote:

> Each of three to four hours total narration by him and as many of translation by
> Jack and writing by me.[100]

Kroeber in fact met with Inyokutavêre for six days, before deciding to return to Berkeley.

His transcription of Inyokutavêre's epic story contains 197 episodes but no songs.

At Ah'a-kwinyevai[101], in a sand-covered Mohave house, we found the old man we had
come to see, Inyokutavêre, "Vanished-pursue," who was reputed to know about the
origin of clans. He admitted that he did, and would tell me the story. It would take a
day, he said, when I asked about the length. As that day was partly gone, I arranged to
come back in the morning.

 Of course he did not realize that it would take Jack about as long to English to me
his telling in Mohave as that took him, and I overlooked the fact, or had long since
learned not to be too concerned about inaccuracies of time estimates by natives.
However, he went on for six days. Each of three to four hours total narration by him
and as many of translation by Jack and writing by me. Each evening he believed, I
think honestly, that one more day would bring him to the end. He freely admitted,
when I asked him, that he had never told the story through from beginning to end. He
had a number of times told parts of it at night to Mohave audiences, until the last of
them dropped off to sleep. When out sixth day ended, he still, or again, said that a day
would see us through. By then I was overdue at Berkeley; and as the prospective day
might once more have stretched into several, I reluctantly broke off, promising him,
and myself, that I would return to Needles when I could, no later than next winter, to
conclude recording the tale.

 By next winter Inyokutavêre had died.

Figure 2.B-xv. Excerpt from Kroeber's MHE.[102]

  It seems clear that Kroeber must have devoted a significant amount of his time to

the writing out of Mohave creation stories. He does not discuss the process that he used

---

[100] See note 99.

[101] A Mohave place name, "across the river from Needles and two or three miles inland."
MHE, 71.

[102] MHE, 71.

when writing down stories that had songs. He does however mention that he always worked with a translator, since most of the singers only spoke Mohave. It seems likely that the process that Kroeber used to record stories that had songs was similar to the one he used to write down Inyokutavêre's story. When the singer had come to end of each episode, Kroeber then asked the singer to say how many songs were associated with that episode; but he makes no comment regarding when he made audio recordings of songs. Did he record songs after a singer had reached the end of an episode? There is no way to know, based on what Kroeber writes in his publications.[103]

In fact, before the appearance of his *More Mohave Myths* (MMM), which was published posthumously in 1972, Kroeber made no mention of the fact that he had made audio recordings of Mohave singers. To demonstrate that he did in fact make a number of audio recordings, I provide a brief reckoning of these recordings. In MMM, Kroeber included a list all of the audio recordings that he had made of Mohave singers/storytellers.[104] In addition, Kroeber made a separate list of the Mohave creation stories that he collected.[105] These lists show that Kroeber had in fact made hundreds of audio recordings of songs. He also made a much smaller number of audio recordings of singers telling portions of their stories. Kroeber's first visit to the Mohave was in 1900, but he does not say what he did on this trip. In 1902, when he again visited the Mohave, he wrote down three stories, but did not make audio recordings (see Figure 2.B-xvi).

---

[103] *Handbook*, SMM, MHE, or MMM.
[104] See MMM, 157.
[105] Ibid., 156.

Singer	Story
N^{y}avarúp	Origins
N^{y}avarúp	First Berdache
Inyókutavére	Mohave Historical Epic

Figure 2.B-xvi. Mohave creation stories, recorded in 1902.

In the following year, Kroeber returned to write down still more stories. This time, he

brought along audio recording equipment. As he explained:

> Between 1903 and 1910 I recorded at Needles or in San Francisco, or had
> recorded for me, on Edison or Columbia paraffin phonographs cylinders, 25 parts
> of 7 Mohave myths,[106] and some 470 Mohave songs from 20 song cycles, which
> were stored in the University's Museum of Anthropology.[107]

Kroeber went on to explain that about half of his audio recordings were transferred to

magnetic tape in 1957; the rest were too damaged to transfer. Still more information

about the audio recordings that Kroeber made comes from the work of the

ethnomusicologist Richard Keeling, who studied Kroeber's audio recordings as well as

other audio recordings held at the Lowie Museum of Anthropology. In 1991, Keeling's

catalogue appeared as *A Guide to Early Field Recordings (1900-1949) at the Lowie*

Museum of Anthropology (Guide).[108] The *Guide* is based on the information written on

the carton of each wax cylinder together with the data that Kroeber supplied when he

entered each recording into the university's catalogue of recordings. On the basis of this

data, Keeling was able to connect an audio recording with its corresponding Mohave

creation story. Keeling is also often able to indicate the set that a group of songs belongs

---

[106] "25 parts of 7 Mohave myths" refers to the recordings that Kroeber made of singers as
they spoke and told parts of their stories. See Kroeber, MMM, 157.

[107] Ibid.

[108] See Richard Keeling, *A Guide to Early Field Recordings (1900-1949) at the Lowie*
Museum of Anthropology. University of California Publications 6 (Berkeley: University
of California Press, 1991).

to. On the other hand, the information in the cartons and in the university catalogue apparently did not allow Keeling to match a particular set of songs with a given episode in Kroeber's transcription of the same story; but even without this kind of specific information, the *Guide* provides an excellent resource for learning more about Kroeber's transcriptions of Mohave creation stories.

Figure 2.B-xvii (p. 173 to 175), which contains information taken from Kroeber's MMM as well as from Keeling's *Guide,* provides a chronological list of the Mohave creation stories that Kroeber transcribed, showing the name of each story, the singer who told it, the monograph that each story appeared in, and the date (if available) of the audio recording. The audio recordings shown in Figure 2.B-xvii are ones that Kroeber apparently made while writing down the associated story.[109] Figure 2.B-xviii (p. 176), on the other hand, shows recordings that Kroeber or the Mohave Leslie Wilbur made of songs only. Apparently the recordings listed in this table were made with the intent of collecting a selection of the songs from each of the associated song cycles but not while writing down the story.

Taken together, Figure 2.B-xvii and Figure 2.B-xviii demonstrate that most of Kroeber's fieldwork took place during the first decade on the 1900's. Figure 2.B-xvii also provides an overview of the stories that Kroeber worked on. Kroeber's published transcriptions include fifteen Mohave creation stories: seven in *Seven Mohave Myths;* an

---

[109] Or possibly after he had written down the story. Kroeber does not say which was the case.

eighth, in *A Mohave Historical Epic;* and another seven in *More Mohave Myths.*[110] Six

stories involved narration without singing. They are: *Coyote, The First Berdache, A*

Mohave Historical Epic, Mastamho (Origins), and *Origin of War.*[111] Twelve stories

contained both narration and songs. These include: *Akak, Cane, Chuhueche, Deer,*

Nyohaiva, Raven, Salt, Satukhóta, Tortoise, Tumanpa, Vinumulye-Patše, and Yellak.

Two were what Kroeber referred to as "singings," or "dancings:" *Hacha* (Pleiades) and

Chutaha. They involved singing and dancing but no spoken narration. In these cases,

Kroeber apparently did not write down these stories. Kroeber states that each was

associated with a lengthy narrative, but he did not publish these narratives. A

performance of *Hacha* or *Chutaha* apparently involved singing and dancing to a small

number of songs, over and over, throughout the night.[112]   Thus Kroeber published a

large number of Mohave creation stories, many which included songs. He recorded a

relatively large number of the songs for certain song cycles. As shown in Figure

2.B-xvii, Kroeber recorded sixty-one of the 182 songs associated with *Raven,* and 42 of

the 110 songs from *Nyohaiva.* He also recorded the singer telling part of the beginning

and the end of *Nyohaiva.* He recorded 140 songs from what appears to be a total of 180

songs from *Cane,* as well as one example of the singer telling part of this story. Kroeber

also hired William Kretschmer, a professional musician, to transcribe many of the songs,

---

[110] Kroeber lists 10 different stories in MMM but two of these are repetitions: *Cane* and *Origins.* In another, story #16, Kroeber presents fragments of various stories.
[111] *Coyote* does contain a few songs but is clearly not a full-fledged creation story/song.
[112]Kroeber discusses how these were performed. See Kroeber, *Handbook,* 756, 764-765. See MMM, 158, where Kroeber shows the Mohave singer, Jo Nelson who had recorded songs from *hacha* and chutaha. In his *Guide,* Keeling lists the two *hacha* songs under accession numbers 24-590 through -591; and chutaha, as 24-592 through –593.

which he himself then analyzed. Probably as he prepared MMM for publication, Kroeber wrote the following, regarding these musical transcriptions:

> These notational transcripts are in my possession, and I have analyzed part of them for structure, variation, scale, and the life. Many song series were still known and sung among the Mohave in 1953 and 1954, and presumably survive in 1960.[113]

Thus it seems clear that Kroeber had at his disposal material that would have allowed him to reconstruct and describe how a singer or singers performed their stories. Thus, he was not forced to focus on the "story" part of each of the creation stories because he lacked other kinds of data, including data about the songs.

Kroeber did provide some information about how some of the stories were told. He noted, for instance, that each song cycle had a distinct dance step and rhythmic pattern. These two variables, combined with the use of a particular method for generating the rhythmic pattern, apparently made each song cycle distinct. Or as, he explained:

> Each story had its appropriate dance step, as it had its characteristically recognizable songs, and its prescribed rattle, struck basket, palm slap, resonating pot, or other accompanying beat.[114]

Kroeber also offered some comments concerning the dance that was used during a recitation of some of the creation stories. In a performance of *Nyohaiva*, Kroeber noted that the women danced "in a ring around the singer." Kroeber also reported that the singer used a stick as the percussion instrument; further, the singer sometimes marked off the beat by letting this stick drop to the ground. Other times, his gestures--moving the

---

[113] See MMM,157.
[114] SMM, 2. Also, see his *Handbook,* 755

stick forwards or backwards--helped to establish the rhythmic pattern. Or as Kroeber, writes:

> Nyohaiva is sung standing. At any rate while women dance in a ring around the singer, he leans on a stick, which he sometimes thrusts forward and waves to the rhythm of his song, sometimes drops through his hand to strike the ground. There is no rattle or musical instrument.[115]

Kroeber also described how *Raven* was danced to, Kroeber writes:

> I did not see an actual Raven dance, but it was illustrated for me as follows. The women bend their knees somewhat so that their skirt hem is lowered perhaps four or five inches. Then they sag and rise in the knee an inch or two, without moving their feet or even rising on their toes. The body is inclined slightly forward, the head is erect, the eyes wide open and looking level (not lowered as by the Plains Indian women); the arms hang straight down, almost stiffly, the wrists perhaps being bent back a trifle. When the women move forward and back, they shuffle their feet forward (or back) an inch or two at each step, without raising them from the ground.[116]

Kroeber seems to have stumbled, however, when confronted with the task of describing precisely how a singer told his stories. Mohave singers were clearly willing to dictate their stories to Kroeber; but he apparently did not ask Mohave singers to show him how they told their stories; instead he seems to have asked singers whether they ever told their stories, from start to finish. When confronted with such a question, it seems possible that singers may have reacted with at least some surprise. Kroeber provides one example, when the interpreter and the singer would not respond to his query, regarding whether the singer ever told his story from start to finish.

With the help of Jack Jones, a Mohave singer and interpreter, Kroeber wrote down two song cycles, *Nyohaiva* and *Yellak (Goose)*. Both were told by the Mohave

---

[115] SMM, 27.
[116] SMM, 37.

singer Aspa-sakam, in November, 1905. Kroeber apparently did not ask Aspa-sakam to demonstrate how he told these stories; instead Kroeber writes that he asked Jones and Aspa-sakam whether Aspa-sakam had ever told his stories from start to finish. Kroeber reports that neither Aspa-sakam nor Jones would provide a direct answer to this question. Kroeber concluded that neither had understood what he had asked. As Kroeber explained:

> neither he [Aspa-sakam, the singer] nor the interpreter [Jack Jones] seemingly could be made to understand clearly my questions whether he had every sung *Goose* a whole night through, or whether he had ever sung it or *Nyohaiva* continuously from beginning to end.[117]

Having failed to get an answer, Kroeber then made a surprising leap in logic. He concluded that Aspa-sakam never told his stories, from start to finish. The following is a continuation of the above quotation. Referring to Aspa-sakam, Kroeber writes:

> It is doubtful whether he had ever sung either *Goose* or *Nyohaiva* through consecutively at any one time or occasion.[118]

In the above quotation, Kroeber makes no mention of singing along with spoken narration; instead he seems to have attempted to ask whether or not the performers sang all or most of their songs, for either *Goose* or *Nyohaiva,* at any one occasion. Yet Kroeber does not seem to have gotten a clear answer. In another of his comments, Kroeber touched on the subject of singing in combination with spoken narration. With the following quotation he seems to be saying that in a public setting (such as at a dance or funeral) a singer may have sung his songs but without speaking about them. On the

---

[117] The names of song cycles are not in italics in the original. SMM, 27.
[118] SMM, 27.

other hand, he seems to suggest that in the privacy of his home a singer would sometimes narrate an episode and then sing the associated set of songs. Such performances were always incomplete, however. Or, as Kroeber writes:

> Theoretically, when it is not a matter of a dance or a funeral, a man both narrates and sings, telling an episode and then singing the songs that refer to it, until his audience drops off to sleep.[119]

In still another quotation, Kroeber reiterates the idea that a singer, in the privacy of his house, might sing and tell a part of his story but never the whole thing. This time Kroeber adds that most people knew the songs but not the stories. That may mean that the singers sang their songs at community events but without including any spoken narration. Thus the community knew the songs but not the stories. With the following quotation, it appears that Kroeber is not attempting to describe performance per se; rather he seems to be arguing that there is no reason to speak about it. Here is the quotation in question:

> Sometimes a night is spent by a singer entertaining a houseful of people with alternate recital and singing: but such occasions seem not to have been common. Many singers declare that they have never told their whole tale through, and sung their songs from beginning to end at one sitting. It is in accord with this statement, that some men appear to know the whole of a song cycle but only parts of its myth; and that to the public at large all the songs are more or less familiar, but stories much less known. [120]

As shown in this section and also in the preceding one Kroeber argued that the songs were unimportant. When he wrote that singers never told their stories from start to finish, he was in effect making a larger statement. He was arguing that there was no need

---

[119] SMM, 2.
[120] Kroeber, *Handbook,* 755.

to spend time documenting how the stories were told and that it was sufficient to preserve each story in the form of a text. On the other hand, as he met and spoke with Mohave singers in the first decade of the 1900's, he was speaking with individuals who not only knew their creation stories but how to tell them. He seems to have preserved at least some performance-related information. All of his transcriptions of Mohave creation stories are divided into episodes. In the creation stories that had songs, he indicates the number of songs that were associated with each episode. This by itself seems to suggest that a singer may have sung and told his way through such a story. In addition, even stories that did not include songs (such as the story of the origin of the clans, in MHE) are divided into a sequence of episodes. It seems possible that this might mean that the telling of stories in an episodic fashion was a widely used style or technique among the Mohave. With respect to creation stories that had songs as well as narrative, Kroeber seems to have split the episodes into two parts: the part that was spoken and the part that was sung. When viewed from this perspective, Kroeber's transcriptions appear to consist of the spoken parts of each episode, but strung together to form a long narrative.

Ione Dock: "They'd Sing and They'd Tell."

Ione Dock, an accomplished Mohave storyteller, dancer, and valued tribal elder, was one of the tribal members with whom I had the privilege of working and speaking with. Before her death in 2007, at the age of 78, Dock spent a significant amount of her time going to inter-tribal events. She entered dancing contests, frequently winning them. She also devoted much of her time to encouraging young people to study and learn about their cultural practices. Dock was especially interested in preserving cultural knowledge, so that in the future younger people would have access to it. Like many other Mohave, Dock came from a family of singers and storytellers. Dock's training in traditional Mohave culture began at an early age. As a child, she spent the summer months living close to the Colorado River, at which time her uncle Pete Sherman joined her and her family. Sherman sang and narrated *Satukhota,* a Mohave creation story, one that Kroeber published in *More Mohave Myths* (1972). Writing about his meeting with Sherman, Kroeber wrote:

> On Sunday, February 8, 1953, I sat down at Parker[121] with a seventy-three-year-old Mohave to inquire into place-names and related matters. He was named Avé-pūya "dead rattlesnake," in Mohave, Pete Sherman in English...He wore his long hair tied up in a blue bandana, which he would not remove for photographing. He was approachable, friendly, on the phlegmatic side, with a twinkle in his eye. He lived perhaps a mile to two from reservation headquarters, in a house of his own adjacent to that of his married niece.[122]

Dock remembered the twinkle in Sherman's eyes. During the summer months, Dock she also recalled that each night her uncle Sherman would tell her stories. She also grew up listening to other members of her family sing and dance. Dock's mother, Nellie Brown was a talented singer and dancer. She assisted the linguist Pamela Munro as Munro gathered words for *A Mojave Dictionary.*[123] Nellie Brown along with Dwayne Drennan,

---

[121] Parker, Arizona
[122] MMM, 99.
[123] See *A Mojave Dictionary.*

another of Dock's uncles, sang *Deer* together.[124]   Sarah Russell, Ione Dock's daughter, is

also interested in her culture. Sarah Russell has led a group of Mohave female teenage

dancers who performed throughout the ESCR.

I asked Dock about some of Kroeber's observations about Mohave singers and the

performance of Mohave creation stories. Dock had never heard that singers dreamt of

creation, as Kroeber reported. She did, on the other hand, state that some individuals

were known to be gifted, that is, they had *sumáč 'ahót*, "great dreams." However, she

had never heard that singers specifically dreamt of creation or that they had these kinds of

dreams in utero. Dock did report that each clan had its own creation story and that these

creation stories were part of the knowledge that was passed on from one clan member to

another. Dock explained that she along with her uncle Pete Sherman belonged to the

Musa clan (the mesquite screw bean clan). *Satakót* was the song that members of Musa

clan sang.[125]

Dock disagreed with much of what Kroeber had suggested about how Mohave

creation stories were told. She did not agree, for instance, with his statement that singers

rarely if ever performed their entire song cycles. The opposite was true. She did say,

however, that singers would shorten or lengthen their performances, in effect including

more or fewer episodes, depending on when and where they were performing, and for

---

[124] Margaret Langdon, a well known linguist who worked at UCSD, taught many
students, some of whom studied the Mohave. Langdon's papers, along with the notes
and field tapes of many of her students, have now been transferred to UC Berkeley and
should at some point be available for study. At least one of her students had the
opportunity to speak with and record Nellie Brown and Drennan singing *Deer*.
[125] Here I have attempted to write *Satakót,* as said by Dock, with the accent on the last
syllable.

whom. At funerals, Dock explained, a rendition of a story might go on for two or three days, until the ceremony ended. This is a statement that Lorraine Sherer, who grew up with the Mohave, agreed with. In her 1965 book *The Clan System of the Fort Mojave Indians,* Sherer wrote that the Mohave had something on the order of 30 different clans.[126] At a funeral, singers from a large number of clans might be heard, each singing a different song cycle. Shearer also emphasized the idea that these performances lasted for an extended period of time. At the funeral for a chief, for instance, Sherer wrote that the concurrent performances of different singers--each one telling his own creation story--would continue for four days and nights.[127]

Regarding how song cycles were performed, Dock stated that the singers always told their story/song cycles in the same fashion. Thinking specifically of her uncle Sherman, Dock explained that, "He'd sing, then he'd tell." He would sing a set of songs. Then, he would stop and explain their meaning. When singers performed at funerals, Dock explained that it was often difficult to understand what they were singing or saying. Apparently as they spoke over a period or two or more days and nights singers utilized a type of formulaic speech. Dock described her uncle Sherman's spoken narration as being short and choppy, meaning that what he was saying and singing was hard for most people to understand, including herself. Dock heard a number of other Mohave singers

---

[126] Kroeber identifies nineteen different clans. See his A Mohave Historical Epic, 115.
[127] Sherer taught in the Education Department at U.C.L.A. See Lorraine Sherer's, *The clan system of the Fort Mojave Indians* (Los Angeles: Historical Society of Southern California, 1965). For an online version of this book see http://www.elmerfudd.us/dp /mojave/clan/clan.htm (accessed on May 14, 2009.) For a finding aid to Sherer's papers in the Special Collections Research Library at UCLA, see http://content.cdlib.org/view ?docId=kt2j49p9cr&doc.view=entire_text&brand=oac (accessed on May 14, 2009).

sing and tell their stories at funerals. She noted whereas each of the singers from Sherman's generation had their own style of singing and telling that all were difficult to understand. Dock remembered, for instance, hearing the Mohave singer Emmett Van Fleet sing and tell *Uta'ut* at funerals.[128] Recalling his performances, Dock stated that when he spoke that he sounded as if he "had a mouthful of something."

At a funeral, the people from a particular clan would gather together and listen to and participate in the rendition of their clan's creation story. The members of a clan rose to sing and dance to each set of songs. When the set was finished, they would sit down and listen as their singer recounted the events that they had just sung about. Singers along with everyone else attending took periodic breaks. During these breaks everyone would share communal meals, one for dinner, probably at midnight, and another for breakfast, around dawn. Aside from these breaks, singers would continue to sing and tell their stories until the cremation had taken place.

As this chapter has shown, as they studied ESCR music and stories, scholars have of course focused on certain topics or questions, but sometimes without attempting to

---

[128] As far as I can see, Kroeber did not record *Uta-ut*. Guy Taylor, a Los Angeles-based radio recording engineer, did record Emmett Van Fleet's singing *Uta-ut*, in 1972. 525 songs were included. These tapes along with others that Taylor made were re-discovered upon his death. At that time, the San Francisco-based writer Phil Klasky became interested in Van Fleet's tapes. He arranged for the language laboratory at the University of California at Berkeley to transfer the tapes to cassette. Klasky then met with the Mojave elder Llewellyn Barrackman who listened to the tapes and translated them. For information regarding Klasky, see: http://www.nativeland.org/mcs.html. Accessed on May 16, 2009). The original Van Fleet tapes are at the UCB language lab. Van Fleet's tapes may be heard at the lab but not copied without permission from the Barrackman's. For more information, please listen to the documentary produced by The Kitchen Sisters. See this URL: http://www.npr.org/programs/lnfsound/stories/000225.stories.html (Accessed on May 16, 2009).

provide information about the larger picture or context within which a performance took place. Possibly because he saw ESCR music as being primarily vocal music, Herzog wrote down song melodies and their rhythms. This focus turned out to have been too narrow. Clearly, a fuller picture of the music emerges when one takes into account the interplay between the melody, its rhythm, the associated dance steps, the words, and the rhythm of the gourd. For his part, Kroeber chose to focus on writing down the text of each story. This focus did not allow him to explore how the songs complemented the story. As is demonstrated in the excerpts that Halpern published of *Lightning,* Halpern took the single additional step of including the songs along with the associated narrative. In doing so, Halpern clearly suggested that a performance of *Lightning* involved speaking as well as singing. On the other hand, Halpern's transcription of *Lightning* does not provide any information about what people did as they listened. Dock, on the other hand, reported that everyone had a chance to participate. The members of a clan were able to support their singer by performing alongside of him as he continued to sing and dance and speak, for as long as was necessary. When it comes to learning more about music past and present, much can be achieved by studying the creation-story texts from a century ago. While Underhill criticized Kroeber for including what she believed to be unnecessary details, it is such details that often provide clues regarding how a particular story may have been told. For instance, the idea that a singer, as he spoke, directly referred to the songs that he was about to sing (or had just sung), is one that can be inferred by studying Kroeber's transcriptions (and Halpern's transcription).

Figure 2.B-xvii Mohave Creation Stories in Kroeber's SMM, MHE, and MMM

Year	Month	Day	In[1]	Singer[2]	Title	Pl[3]	Sta[4]	Spok[5]	Songs[6]	Wax Cyl[7]	In Seq[8]	In Guide[9]
1900	One week[10]			?	?							
1902	Mar	10-11	MMM	Nʸavarŭp	Origins	N	50					
		12	MMM	Nʸavarŭp	First Berdache	N						
		??	MHE	Inyókutavére	"Epic"	N	197 +					
1903	??	19	SMM	Pamitš	Akaka (Raven)	N	32		186	61	yes	587, 603-65
		21	SMM	Yellow-Thigh	Deer	N	26		90			
		22	SMM	Mähtšit-nyuměve	Coyote	N						
	Jun	21	MMM	Musk Melon	Origin of War	N	18					
	Nov	16, 24	SMM	Joe Nelson	Mastamho	SF	102	por				585
1904	Mar	23	SMM	Heweik-kwini'ílye	Vinumulye-Patše	FM						586
	Apr	24, 27	SMM	Tšiyêrek-avŭsuk	Cane	N	104		182			

Figure 2.B-xvii. Mohave Creation Stories in Kroeber's SMM, MHE, and MMM
(All notes appears as endnotes, after Figure 2.B-viii.)

Year	Month	Day	In[1]	Singer[2]	Title	Pl[3]	Sta[4]	Spok[5]	Songs[6]	Wax Cyl[7]	In Seq[8]	In Guide[9]
1905	Nov		SMM	Aspa-sakam	Nyohaiva	SF	36	Beg:757 End:799	110	42 songs	yes	757-99 (1364-1369)
	Nov		MMM	Aspa-sakam	Yellak: Goose	SF	82	Por:666	427	23	yes[11]	666-756
			Hand		Goose: outlined[12]							
1908	Feb	21, 24, 25, 27	MMM	Tšiyêrek-avûsuk	Cane	N	76	Por:1290	180?	140	1+ per sta.	1152-1290
			MMM	Falcon Grazes	Tumanpa Short	SF	55		123			
	?	1&3	*Hand*	Kunalye	Epic, parts of[13]	N						
	Mar	3	MMM	Hakwe	Yellak II	N	89		4-500	17 songs	?	1337-52
1910	Dec		MMM	Achyora Hanyava	Chuhueche	SF	85	Por:2016	169	12		2016-28
	Dec		MMM	Achyora Hanyava	Salt	SF	25		117	4		2012-15
	Dec		MMM	Achyora Hanyava	Tumanpa Short	SF	55		123	12		1985-2009
1953	Feb	8	MMM	Avé-pûya	Satukhóta	P	78		152			
1954	Jan	31	MMM	Perry Dean	Tortoise II	P	76		309			

Figure 2.B-xvii. Mohave Creation Stories in Kroeber's SMM, MHE, and MMM, Continued

Year	By	Singer	Title	Spoken[14]	Cyl[15]	In *Guide*[16]
1903	Kr	Baby Head	Alysha		3	596-99
	Kr	Baby Head	Chutāha		2	592-93
	Kr	Baby Head	Four rattle beats of singing		1	
	Kr	Baby Head	Hacha		1	590-91
	Kr	Baby Head	Satukhota	Port[17]	1	595
	Kr	Baby Head	Tumanpa			588, 602
	Kr	Baby Head	Vinumulye-Patše		3	589, 600-1
			Nyohaiva[18]		1	594
1905	Kr	Hakwe	Yellak Goose		1	
1908	Kr	Achyora Hanyava	Chuhueche	End[19]	8	1291-1302
	Kr	Aspa-sakam	Yellak		16	
	Kr	Bill Mellen	Tumanpa Vanyume		10	1303-12
	KR	Doctor's Sack	Tortoise		12	1313-24
	Kr	Guy Howard	Chiyere (Birds)		12	
	Kr	Guy Howard	Flute[20]		1	1370-72
	KR	Vinimulye	Kutene[21]		12	1325-36
	LW	Achyora Hanyava	Chuhueche		12	1610-21
	LW	Achyora Hanyava	Tumanpa Short	portion	12	1622-33
	LW	Atsyeq	Frog		12	1562-73
	LW	Bluebird	Speaking?[22]	portion	1	1634
	LW	Doctor Sack's half brother	Salt		12	1550-61
	LW	Kunalye	Alysha		12	1598-1609
	LW	Kunalye	Deer		12	1574-85
	LW	Kupahwai	Ohwere		12	1586-97
	LW	Unnamed woman	Playing Jew's Harp		1	1635
1910	Kr	Achyora Hanyava	Curing songs		2	2010-11

Figure 2 B viii Additional audio recordings, made by Kroeber or the Mohave Wilbur Smith[2]

Note: the following are the endnotes for Figure 2.B-xvii and Figure 2.B-xviii.

[1] Abbreviations: Seven Mohave Myths (SMM), Kroeber's Handbook (Hand), A Mohave Historical Epic (MHE), and More Mohave Myths (MMM).

[2] Most singers had more than one name. In this figure, I have included their Mohave names, where available. For more about this, see SMM, MHE, or MMM.

[3] "Pl," indicates the place where the story was recorded. Regarding where recorded: N stands for Needles, California; P for Parker, Arizona; and SF for San Francisco. The sessions took place in the Museum of Anthropology, in SF.

[4] "Sta," the number of stations in a story. In this discussion, I have been using the term "episode" instead of "station," which Kroeber uses.

[5] "Spok," whether Kroeber made an audio recording of a portion (por) of the spoken part of the narrative. Kroeber provides a list of his recordings in MMM, p. 158. In this list, he provides the year recorded, the name of the singer, the title of the story, the number of cylinders used. He also indicates whether or not the songs were recorded in sequence. Additionally, he indicates whether or not he recorded a portion of the spoken narrative. Kroeber provided still another list, in MMM, p. 156. Here he lists the stories that he had written down and transcribed. When an recording (based on its year, the singer, and the title of the story) coincided with its transcription (based on the same criteria,) I included the information about the recording in. Otherwise, I included the list of audio recordings in the accompanying figure "More audio recordings, made by Kroeber or the Mohave Wilbur Smith."

[6] "Sngs," the number of song in this story;

[7] "Wax Cyl," the number of wax cylinders that Kroeber recorded.

[8] "In Seq," yes, if the recordings were recorded in sequence (rather than taken as samples, from representative parts of the story).

[9] In *Guide*, indicates whether or not the recordings were transferred to modern media. If they are listed in Keeling's *Guide,* then this means that they are still available

[10] Kroeber writes that his first visit to the Mohave occurred later part of 1900. However, he does not say what he did during this visit. See MMM, p. 4. His fields notes might provide more information about this first trip. See, for instance, Kroeber's Mohave: Notebook (7), 1900-02, folder 6, microfilm reel-frame 103:9. Guide to the A. L. Kroeber Papers, 1869-1972. Bancroft Library, UCB. Note, the Bancroft Library mistakenly lists Kroeber as having died in 1972. He died in 1961. The online guide is at: http://content. cdlib.org/view;jsessionid=WBrYRsmFfph5t2_M?docId=tf3d5n99tn&chunk.id=c002256 &brand=oac.

[11] In his *Guide,* for instance for Yellak, Goose, p. 26-35, Keeling provides some information about, presumably taken from the wax cylinder box. This information, in turn, shows that many of the songs are brothers and that they were sung for Kroeber, in sequence. This information usually includes a descriptive word or two about the topic of each set of brother songs. In this fashion, Keeling's *Guide* provides more information about the songs than Kroeber does; on the other hand, it is not always easy to correlate the titles (for songs) that Keeling provides with particular sections/stations in Kroeber's transcriptions.

[12] In the Handbook, p. 766-68.

[13] In MMM, p. 72, Kroeber writes that Kunalye, an old Mohave man, told him parts of the story of the origin of the clans on March 1 and 3, 1908. Kroeber published Kunalye narrative in the *Handbook,* p. 772-75. Also see the version that Kroeber recorded in 1902 and published as *A Mohave Historical Epic.*

[14] "Spoken," indicates whether or not some portion of the spoken narration was recorded in addition to a selection of songs.

[15] "Cyl," indicates the number of wax cylinders that were used, when recording songs from this song cycle/story.

[16] "In *Guide,* " the information came from Keeling's *Guide.*

[17] "Port." Indicates that a portion of the spoken narrative was recorded on an audio recording.

[18] Ibid.

[19] "End," meaning that the part of the spoken narrative that was recorded was taken from the end of the story.

[20] Keeling provides some information about these three selections that are played on a flute. The first two are both entitled: "Yuma's Crying"; the third is "Courting tune, played at night."

[21] Ibid.

[22] Ibid.

CHAPTER 3

SELECTED CREATION STORY TEXTS FROM

THE EXTENDED SOUTHERN CALIFORNIA REGION

It is apparent from Kroeber's and Underhill's differing ways of transmitting the story of *Vinumulye* that collectors recorded stories with different emphases. Most importantly for this study, some collectors had more interest than others in the songs that formed part of at least some performances. While Kroeber reported that some Mohave creation stories were not associated with any songs, each of the texts that I consider in the following chapter suggests that a performance of the story involved singing or spoken narration in conjunction with singing. As will be seen, some of these texts contain quite a bit of information about how the story may have been performed, while others contain much less information. These latter would have made a poor starting point; but when these texts are considered together, a pattern emerges concerning how these stories may have been told. These texts come from different parts of the area, with an examination of Kroeber's transcription of Deer, a Mohave creation story. From here I move south, down the Colorado River to Yuma, Arizona. In 1922 Frances Densmore, who visited and wrote about the music of many different Native American groups, traveled to Yuma, Arizona, where she spoke with a number of singers, including among the Quechan singer Charles Wilson. I consider Densmore's transcription of Wilson's *Lightning* song. Next I move westward, to consider the transcription that the anthropologist Duncan Strong made of the Cahuilla creation story in 1925. Lastly, I consider the work of Constance

178

Dubois, a writer and scholar who spoke with singers from Kumeyaay- and Luiseño speaking tribes and transcribed their creation stories in the first decade of the 1900's.

Kroeber's Transcription of *Deer*

In March of 1903, the Mohave singer Yellow-Thigh told the story of *Deer* to Kroeber. Like his other transcriptions of Mohave creation stories, Kroeber's transcription of *Deer* contains information suggesting that a performance may have involved both spoken narration and singing. His transcription consists of a sequence of twenty-six episodes, many of which are associated with a song or songs. Kroeber estimated the total number of songs to be ninety. While Kroeber did not make audio recordings of the songs,[1] he did include the words for nine *Deer* songs (see Figure 3.A-i). Kroeber did not attempt to argue that these or other *Deer* songs contained information that was integral to an understanding of *Deer* but rather the opposite.[2] I, nevertheless, show, however, that a fuller understanding of *Deer* emerges when these nine songs are considered alongside of the story.

---

[1] Keeling's *Guide* shows, however, that the Mohave singer Leslie Wilbur did record twelve *Deer* songs, as sung by the Mohave singer Kunalye, in 1908. However, the recordings are simply listed as songs 1-12, with no information provided that would link a song to a given part or episode in the story. See Keeling, *Guide,* 172. See also my tables of Kroeber's transcriptions of Mohave creation stories and audio recordings, at the end of Chapter 2.
[2] See "Brother Songs" in Chapter 1.

Descriptions of each song[3]	Song texts [4]
1. The very first song of the cycle, where the Deer are made at Dark-Mountain far in the west (par. 5).	Deer sings: West it-is-night, tell. *Inyahavek tinyamk kanavek.*
2. First song of Hoalye-ketehururve (par. 25), next to the last step in the journey, and the last at which the Deer sing.	Mountain-Lion tell-(of). *Hatekulye kanavek.*
3. Same place, second song.	Arrow from-above tell. *Ipa amaimiyak kanavek.*
4. Same, third song.	I-shall-not-die arrow-from-above fall-on-me it-does-not-pain. *Ipui-mote' ipa'-maimiate ninyupakem hirra'a-môṭ(e).*
5. Same, fourth song, last by the Deer.	Belly-in-shoot arrow-from-above. *Ito-nye-kyam ipa'-maimiak.*
6. Apparently Jaguar sings at Land-blood-have:	Track-them old-man (=brother). *Himekeseik kwora'āk-oêve.*
7. The same:	Do-not-desist chasing continue. *Intomaku-moṭe itavere(m) viewêmeθ(a).*
8. The same:	Kill-them continue brother. *Hatapui viuêmhe kwora'āk-oêve.*
9. The final song of the cycle. Still by Jaguar:	Brother divide-it flesh horns hide sinew. *Kwora'āk-oêvitš atšwoδavek himaṭva hikwĩve tšaθwilve kosmave.*

Figure 3.A-i. Nine *Deer* songs.[5]

[3] As provided by Kroeber.
[4] See note 3.
[5] Kroeber, *Seven Mohave Myths,* 42.

Like the other Mohave creation stories that Kroeber transcribed, *Deer* begins with

a reference to the creator Matavilya and also to Mastamho, the creator's son or successor.

In *Mastamho,* another Mohave creation story, Kroeber explained Mastamho's role as a

teacher of mankind:[6]

> Essentially Mastamho thinks of what will be good for one or more of these tribes,
> causes it to come into existence, and then explains it to the people or has them
> practice it.

No subject was too unimportant for Mastamho. Again, writing about the story of

Mastamho, Kroeber explains,

> One long section ... is devoted to the institution of night and sleep, to the building
> of houses and shade groups, and the setting aside of playing fields.[7]

In *Deer,* Mastamho's does not teach mankind directly; instead, he creates two

lions, both of whom have supernatural powers.[8] These lions are brothers, one older, and

the other younger. After they receive their special powers, they still retain aspects of

their lion-life natures, continuing to behave like the supreme carnivores that they are. At

the same time, the lions are now teachers, their actions meaningful to mankind. Speaking

about the *Deer* story, the Mohave elder Ione Dock explained to me that the story of *Deer*

is one that teaches man to accept his own fragility.

With their new powers, the lions first burrow through the earth, looking for an

appropriate patch of soil that they will use to fashion two deer. Tunneling through the

ground, they first emerge at "Hatekulye-naka, above Avi-kwatulye," both places that

---

[6] See the story of *Mastamho,* transcribed by Kroeber in 1903 in SMM, 50.
[7] Kroeber, SMM, 50.
[8] They are called *numeta* and *hatekulye.*

Kroeber plots on a map that details the travel sequence in *Deer*. The lions, however, are not satisfied:

> Here they raised themselves out of the ground as far as their breasts, turning their heads to look around. Seeing only mountains all about, they said: "This is no place for us," and went underneath began.[9]

In episode 2, the lions continue their travels, passing through still other places: "Avi-kwin-yehore, Avi-ku-tinyam, Kwilykikipa, and Kwamalyukikwa." Finally, they come upon the kind of soil that they are looking for. Mimicking the actions of the creator, the lions fashion two deer out of clay: a male and a female. In episode 3, the lions pause to learn some skills that they will in the future share with mankind. They discover how to make flint arrowheads and how to fabricate bows and arrows. They also learn to refine a poison, made of "rattlesnake, scorpion, black-widow spider, and tarantula." This mixture is placed on the tip of an arrowhead. An animal that has been shot with such an arrow will no longer be able to run quickly, allowing it to be captured. The lions prophesize that certain people will dream about them (the lions). During these dreams, the lions will tell these people how to make arrowheads, bows and arrows, the appropriate poisons, etc.

In the fourth episode, the focus returns to the deer. The lions generate wind and rain that they use to clean off the newly born deer. In episode 5, the deer begin to wonder about and to observe the world around them. They pause to wonder, for instance, what happens to the sun each night. Where does it go? The female deer seems to think that there is some risk that it might not come back. She says: "the wind and the clouds are

---

[9] They "went underneath," that is, they went into the ground and began to burrow again.

taking it away. And there is no place for it to go." The male, on the other hand, does not seem afraid. He seems to know that the sun will rise again, after setting each night. As both deer face to the east, the male deer proclaims,

> Here darkness is coming. When it comes it will bring the stars and the moon in sky. Then we will know which way to go east."

Figure 3.A-ii shows the first five episodes. As can be seen in this excerpt, four songs were associated with episode 5. Of the nine *Deer* songs that Kroeber included, the first is associated with the above quotation, taken from episode 5. Kroeber's translation of this song shows the deer gazing into the night and singing about what it might mean.

> West it-is-night, tell.
> *Inyahavek tinyamk kanavek.*

While this song does not introduce new information, it conveys a directness of expression, not found in the corresponding spoken narrative.

Figure 3.A-ii. Excerpt from the *Deer* Story, episodes 1-5.

1. When Matavılya dıed and Mastamho took hıs place[2] he gave supernatural powers to Jaguar and Mountaın Lıon,[3] two brothers. No one saw them whıle they dug a hole ınto the ground and dısappeared. They traveled underground toward the wınd.[4] At Hatekulye-naka,[5] above Avı-kwatulye,[6] they emerged. Here they raısed themselves out of the ground as far as theır breasts, turnıng theır heads to look around. Seeıng only mountaıns all about, they saıd: "Thıs ıs no place for us," and went underneath agaın.

2. They contınued westward, below the surface, untıl they came to Avı-kwın-yehore, Avı-ku-tınyam, Kwılykıkıpa, and Kwamalyukıkwa.[7] There Jaguar proceeded to make Deer. He put hıs hand ınto the ground: but the earth was not good. Then he thrust hıs hand farther down untıl he found good clay. Then, just as lıttle gırls have clay dolls, he made a Deer, wıth legs and neck and horns and all parts. He made a Doe also. So the two Deer came ınto exıstence.

3. Now ıt was dark where Jaguar and Mountaın Lıon were.[8] Then they saıd: "There are flınt arrow-poınts."[9] Some persons wıll dream of those. Then they wıll make them; they wıll make bows also." Then they measured a bow. They measured ıt a fathom ın length. It was too long. So they measured ıt somewhat shorter, and saıd: "That ıs good: ıt wıll be rıght for the Walapaı and Yavapaı." They prepared sınews and feathers for the arrows. When they had fınıshed everythıng else, they saıd: "Rattlesnake, scorpıon, black-wıdow spıder,[10] and tarantula[11] are the poısons to use. We wıll tell the Walapaı and the Yavapaı about them. They wıll take these four poısons, mıx them wıth a plant and wıth red paınt. They wıll paınt theır arrow-poınts wıth that and theır bows and arrows too. Then ıf they pursue game, ıt wıll not be able to run fast."[12]

---

[2]At Ha'avulypo.

[3]Numeta and Hatekulye.

[4]North, mathak.

[5]"Mountaın Lıon's naka."

[6]"Lızard-Mountaın," stıll at El Dorado Canyon on or near the Colorado, as ıs Ha'avulypo also.

[7]West of San Bernardıno, Calıfornıa; that ıs, ın Serrano or Gabrıelıno terrıtory. The second name means "dark Mountaın."

[8]Spoken of as a house, but conceıved merely as a round space of darkness.

[9]Avı-rrove sohêna.

[10]Haltota, a poısonous spıder, probably the black wıdow.

[11]Kwatšmunyo-'ıpe ın Mohave, "but they called ıt hanekasave."

[12]The Mohave say that the Walapaı who have dreamed of Jaguar and Mountaın lıon follow thıs practıce. If anyone but the owner takes hold of the bow, hıs hand swells. They also tıe to theır moccasıns a small pıece of deerskın[,] contaınıng thıs poıson. Among the Mohave, on the other hand, certaın men, who wısh to be lucky ın gamblıng, tıe to theır haır a small concealed bag of rattlesnake teeth and paınt. Thıs ıs, however, lıkely to render them crıpples.

Excerpt from the *Deer*, episodes 1-5.

4. Now Jaguar and Mountain lion took the two Deer that they had made and said: "They are finished. We will make wind blow on their bodies and cause it to rain over them. The rain will wash out all bad smell and make their flesh good." They made it blow and rain on the Deer and said: "Now that we have made wind and rain, all their bad smell has disappeared. Their meat is good. And now they will be able to go anywhere and never become cold."

5. The two Deer stood looking westward. Then they faced south, east, and north.[13] They wanted to know the land, and where the sun and the night came from. Now they knew that, for the male was wise. He said: There is the sun. It is going down." But the female said: "No, the wind and the clouds are taking it away. And there is no place for it to go to; perhaps there are only mountains, perhaps only sea there. Perhaps it will go behind the mountains, or descend into the fog at the sea." Then they both looked toward the east, and the male said: "Here darkness is coming. When it comes it will bring the stars and the moon in the sky. Then we will know which way to go east." (4 songs.)

[13]Anti-clockwise circuit, starting in the west.

Excerpt from the Deer Story, episodes 1-5, Continued

Having created the deer, the lions begin to follow them and to stalk them. Kroeber's transcription does not focus on the suffering of the deer *per se*. Dock explained, however, that as this story was told the listeners identified with the deer. By episode 24, the deer begin to realize that they are being watched.[10] In fact not only are the lions watching them, they are also corralling and leading them. The terrain is covered by trees torn out by their roots and large broken rocks, all left behind by the lions; yet the deer stay on the same path. The lions, however, have begun to erase their tracks, using wind, thus making it harder for the deer to sense their presence; and as the deer continue to travel, the lions move ahead

[10] See Figure 3.A-iii, for episodes 24-26.

24. They went on eastward. Jaguar and Mountain Lion had indeed gone before them; the Deer followed. They did not see Jaguar and Mountain Lion, but they saw what they had done, pulling out trees by the roots and breaking large rocks, so that the Deer could follow them. The male said: "See, they have pulled up trees, and broken stones and rolled them about." Then after a time they saw no more tracks: Jaguar and Mountain Lion had made the wind blow so that the footprints were effaced. The Deer went on nevertheless. When Jaguar and Mountain Lion came to Hoalye-ketekururuve,[50] Jaguar, the older brother, sat down on the west side, Mountain lion, the younger, on the east. The two Deer did not know they were sitting here, and taking up his bow and arrow, made a slight noise, the Deer heard it, and he did not shoot. But Mountain Lion shot and hit the male. Deer said: "They have failed: they did not shoot me in the right place: they shot up into the sky, and the arrow only dropped on me. I was struck, but I have no pain." Then both Deer ran off eastward. (9 songs.)

25. Jaguar and Mountain Lion still sat there. Jaguar said: "Go follow; kill them." So Mountain Lion went, and his older brother followed. They did not see the tracks of the Deer, but they followed them. They went up on the mesa. Jaguar said to his younger brother: "Keep on: follow; do not stop. I want to teach the people here, the Walapai and Yavapai, to hunt. Some among them will dream and then they will be deer hunters. Do not stop. We could kill them here, but I do not want that. We will wait until we come to Amat-ahwat-kutšinakwe and Amaṭ-axwaṭ-kw-iδau;[51] then we will kill them. We will kill them there: there will be blood on the rocks: I want to name those places for that."

26. Then when they came to Amat-ahwaṭ-kutšinakwe and Amaṭ-axwat-kw-iδau, the make deer had fallen down dead. Now Mountain Lion stood to the east of him, Jaguar on the west. Jaguar said: 'You know why I have pursued him: I want only the skin and horns and sinew. You can have the meat: I do not want it." But Mountain Lion said: "No, we will divide it. I want the right horn. I too want some of the things you want." Then Jaguar said: "I wanted to divide it, but you did not want to. Well, you can have it all." And he went off to the side and stood there.[52] So he had none of it. He went away to the north, to Amaṭ-ke-hoalye, the Walapai Mountains. But Mountain Lion stood by the Deer and tore his body open with his claws. He put his hand inside and took out the heart. Then he went north, holding that. He did not take meat or skin or sinew or horns. He left them and he went to Ahta-kwatmenve.[53]   (8 songs by Jaguar and Mountain Lion)

The female Deer went on the Avi-melyehweke.[54]

---

[50] East of the Walapai Mountains. This would be in or near the Big Sandy Wash, still in Walapai Country, but not far from Yavapai territory.

[51] Amata, land, place; ahwaṭa, blood, red; iδau, have, hold.

[52] An older-younger brother quarrel typical of the myths, usually with the younger having his way.

[53] East of Kingman, below Hackberry, in the heart of Walapai territory.

[54] One of the four mountains mentioned above, which Deer said were named to him by Jaguar and Mountain Lion (note 39).

Figure 3.A-iii. Excerpt from the *Deer* Song: episodes 24-26.

It is in episode 23 that the deer first begin to suspect that they are being followed by lions. In episode 5, the two deer did not agree as to what caused the skies to become dark at night. Similarly, in episode 23, the deer see the tracks of the lions, but they disagree on how old they are. The female deer suspects that the tracks are very old. She says, "You see the tracks, but they are not new. They have been here a long time; they were here when the earth was made." Disagreeing, the male deer says: "No they have been here two or three days. You will see." Continuing to reaffirm her point, the female deer suggests that the tracks may date to the time when the earth was first moist. She says, "No, they were here a long time. Ever since the ground was still moist and they first walked on it." But the male deer counters with, "No, you will find out. They have seen us; they are watching us now."

As Episode 23 ends, the voice shifts away from the deer. Now an unspecified narrator (possibly the singer) speaks. He describes the actions of the deer. His comments lead directly into the eleven associated songs. The narrator says,

> It was on the Walapai (Hualpai) Mountains that they saw the tracks and stood and talked like this (11 songs).[11]

As the story continues, the lions move ahead, until they are able to setup an ambush. The following is excerpted from episode 24. "The Deer went on nevertheless. When Jaguar and Mountain Lion came to Hoalye-ketekururuve,[12] Jaguar, the older brother, sat down on the west side, Mountain lion, the younger, on the east."

---

[11] SMM, 45.
[12] Hoalye-ketekururuve, a Mohave place. See note 50 in Figure 3.A-iii.

The deer eventually walk to a point that lies directly between where the two lions lie waiting. The younger lion, Jaguar, picks up his bow and arrow in preparation for shooting, but makes a slight noise. The deer hear this noise but do not run away, "The two Deer did not know they were sitting here, and taking up his bow and arrow, made a slight noise, the Deer heard it, and he did not shoot." The older lion does shoot, however. He releases his arrow, wounding the male deer who at first says that he feels nothing. Here is how this action is described in Kroeber's transcription. As can be seen, Kroeber has no trouble conveying intensity or action at these moments, "But Mountain Lion shot and hit the male. Deer said: 'They have failed: they did not shoot me in the right place: they shot up into the sky, and the arrow only dropped on me. I was struck, but I have no pain.'"

As episode 24 ends, the narrator says, "Then both deer ran off eastward," and Kroeber indicates that nine songs were associated with this episode. Of the nine songs that Kroeber included, four of these are associated with episode 24 (see Figure 3.A-iv).

1st	Mountain-Lion tell-(of).
	Hatekulye kanavek.
2nd	Arrow from-above tell.
	Ipa amaimiyak kanavek.
3rd	I-shall-not-die arrow-from-above fall-on-me it-does-not-pain.
	Ipui-mote' ipa'-maimiate ninyupakem hirra'a-môt(e).
4th	*Belly-in-shoot arrow-from-above.*
	Ito-nye-kyam ipa'-maimiak.

Figure 3.A-iv. Four songs from episode 24.

Because these four songs all deal with the same or similar subject matter, it seems possible that they also belong to the same set. The first of these is sung at Hoalye-ketehururve, where the deer argue about the age of the tracks of the lions.[13] With the first song, the deer refer to the lions but in general terms.

> Mountain-Lion tell-(of).
> *Hatekulye kanavek.*

In the next two songs, the male deer reports that he was hit by an arrow but not fatally, in fact he feels no pain at all. The corresponding part of the story is as follows,

> Deer said: "They have failed: they did not shoot me in the right place: they shot up into the sky, and the arrow only dropped on me. I was struck, but I have no pain."

While the next two songs cover the same material as is presented in the narrative, they do so in a manner that might better be conveyed through poetry or song. I do not try to retranslate these songs, for when the meanings of these songs are considered within the

---

[13] Kroeber writes that this song was associated with episode 25. This cannot be correct since the place Hoalye-ketehururve is mentioned in episode 24 but not in 25. See Figure 3.A-i.

context of the story, even Kroeber's word-for-word translations suffice. With the first

song, the male deer describes the arrow as having come from someplace up in the sky:

> Arrow from-above tell.
> *Ipa amaimiyak kanavek.*

In another song, the deer admits that he was hit but still argues that the wound is not

fatal:

> I-shall-not-die arrow-from-above fall-on-me it-does-not-pain.
> *Ipui-mote' ipa'-maimiate ninyupakem hirra'a-môt(e).*

It is with the third of the arrow songs that the deer realized that he has been mistaken.

This is information that is not included in episode 24.

> Belly-in-shoot arrow-from-above.
> *Ito-nye-kyam ipa'-maimiak.*

Episode 24 ended with the tepid remark, "Then both deer then ran off eastward,"

a remark that does not suggest that the male deer may be about to die. This soon

becomes obvious, however, in Episode 25. At the start of this episode, Jaguar, the

younger lion, says to the older, "Go: follow, kill them!" It is as this point that Jaguar

explains why the lions are hunting the deer. Jaguar says:

> "Keep on: follow; do not stop. I want to teach the people here, the Walapai and
> Yavapai, to hunt. Some among them will dream and then they will be deer
> hunters. Do not stop. We could kill them here, but I do not want that. We will
> wait until we come to Amaṭ-ahwaṭ-kutšinakwe and Amaṭ-axwaṭ-kw-iðau; then
> we will kill them. We will kill them there: there will be blood on the rocks: I
> want to name those places for that."

In episode 26, the expected at last begins to occur. The older lion does disembowel the

male deer, but these are no ordinary lions. Their main goal is to teach mankind. As the

story draws to an end, neither lion actually eats the deer; instead they each go their separate ways.

No songs follow episode 25, but eight songs follow episode 26, four of which Kroeber included. Since these songs deal with the same subject matter, it seems possible that they belonged to a set of songs (see Figure 3.A-v). As he exhorts the older lion to track down the deer, Jaguar sings each of these. Here is Kroeber's translation for the first song.

> Track-them old-man (=brother).
> *Himekeseik kwora'āk-oêve.*

With the next, the younger lion again exhorts the older. This time, he is urging him not to give up the chase.

> Do-not-desist chasing continue.
> Intomaku-moṭe itavere(m) viewêmeθ(a).

The next song focuses on the act of bringing down the deer.

> Kill-them continue brother.
> *Hatapui viu*êmhe kwora'āk-oêve.

The last song focuses on the act of dividing up the meat.

> Brother divide-it flesh horns hide sinew.
> *Kwora'āk-oêvitš atšwoðavek himaṭva hikwīve tšaθwilve kosmave.*

Although Kroeber only included nine out of the approximately ninety songs that were associated with *Deer,* an analysis of these nine songs leads to a fuller understanding of the story. In Chapter 1, I considered a set of *Lightning* songs, each of which describes the stars in the sky, in a slightly different manner.[14]   With that set of songs, the singer

---

[14] See "Brother Songs," in Chapter 1.

seems to share some of the pleasure and the insights that can result from thinking of the different ways that one might describe the motion of the stars. *Deer,* however, focuses on the harsh realities of the hunter and the hunted. Here, the singer also appears to capitalize on the fact that a set of songs can be used to describe a topic in an incremental manner, but the effect is quite different. In *Deer,* we learn that a set of songs can be used to describe events as they unfold. We see this as the male deer sings a set of songs that communicate his growing realization that his wounds will in fact be fatal (see Figure 3.A-iv). Similarly, with the last four songs, Jaguar encourages Mountain lion to catch and bring down the male deer. As each song is sung, we can imagine the Mountain lion moving closer and closer to his prey (see Figure 3.A-v).

1st	Track-them old-man (=brother).
	Himekeseik kwora'āk-oêve.
2nd	Do-not-desist chasing continue.
	Intomaku-moţe itavere(m) viewêmeθ(a).
3rd	Kill-them continue brother.
	*Hatapui viu*êmhe kwora'āk-oêve.
4th	Brother divide-it flesh horns hide sinew.
	Kwora'āk-oêvitš atšwoδavek himaţva hikwīve tšaθwilve kosmave.

Figure 3.A-v. Four songs from episode 26.

Frances Densmore's Transcription of *Lightning*

In 1922, Frances Densmore traveled to Yuma, Arizona, located along the Colorado River, where she worked with Quechan, Cocopa, Mohave, and Yaqui musicians. A musician herself, Densmore spoke with singers and made audio recordings of some of their songs. She also made musical transcriptions of the many of the songs

that she had recorded, many of which she included in her article *Yuman and Yaqui Music*

(*YYM*), in 1932.[15]   She also made notes about the percussion instruments that singers

used. Whereas the predominant percussion instrument today is the gourd rattle, when

Densmore visited the ESCR, a larger variety of instruments were still being used. These

included a hand-woven basket that, when turned upside down, was used as a drum.[16]

Densmore reported that singers sometimes used a basket as a percussion instrument,

creating rhythmic patterns by rubbing their hands over it. In addition, singers used sticks

to rub or strike this basket. One of Densmore's photographs shows two types of drum

sticks, one made of a bundle of long, thin arrowweed stalks.[17]   A shorter, stubbier stick

was made from willow sticks.[18] Each type of stick must have produced a different sound.

Concerning the use of these sticks and mentioning other percussion instruments,

Densmore added,

---

[15] See Frances Densmore, *Yuman and Yaqui Music* (Washington: U.S. Government
Printing Office, 1932). In 1951, as a companion to *Yuman in Yaqui Music,* Densmore
released *Songs of the Yuma, Cocopa and Yaqui: From the Archive of Folk Song,* a long
playing vinyl recording that presented a selection of some of the songs that she had
recorded, in 1922. In this recording, she included two *Lightning* songs, both sung by
Charles Wilson. In the liner notes to this recording, Densmore identifies one of these
songs as being "Song Concerning the Ocean" (Cat. no. 1211, ser. no. 55.) This is the last
of the *Lighting* songs that Densmore included in *YYM,* making it possible to compare her
recording of this song with her musical transcription. See her *Songs of the Yuma, Yaqui,
Cocopa: From the Archive of Folk Song. Folk music of the United States.* (Washington,
D.C.: Library of Congress, Division of Music, Recording Laboratory, 1951).
[16] 16 ½ inches in diameter and 5 ½ inches deep. Ibid, p. 24. For the photograph of the
baskets and the "drum" sticks, see plate 22, just after page 24.
[17] 25 ¼ inches in length. Each bundle might consist 10-15 thin sticks.
[18] About 15 inches long. In the photograph, these sticks look like they might be between
1" and 2" inches in diameter.

The basket drum may be beaten with the palm of the hand, with one or more willow sticks, or with one or two bundles or dry arrowweed. The rattles comprise a small gourd rattle, a large gourd rattle, a dew-claw rattle, and a rattle made from a spice box.[19]

Densmore also provided a photograph of two gourds, one used by Cocopah singers (larger in diameter)[20] and one used by Quechan singers (much smaller).[21]   Singers also stamped their feet. Recognizing the foot as a percussion instrument, Densmore added, "What may be termed a 'foot accompaniment,' is used also in the 'Human being dance.'"[22]   Densmore also provided a list of some of the song cycles, showing the type of percussion instrument that was used for each one (see Figure 3.B-i).

Legend	Accompaniment
Concerning a bird--------	Basket struck by bundle of arrowweeds.
Concerning a coyote-----	Basket struck by bundle of arrowweeds.
Concerning a deer-------	Basket struck by palm of hand and willow sticks.
Concerning a lightning--	Basket struck by willow sticks.
Concerning the frog-----	Basket struck by palm of hand and willow sticks.
Corn dance---------------	Large rattle.
A social dance-----------	Large rattle.

Figure 3.B-i. Examples of percussion instruments.[23]

Offering a general comment about the use of these drum baskets and sticks, Densmore said,

> It was said that a good story-teller would tell these stories whenever requested to do so. Thus at a gathering anyone might take up a collection, provide the basket

---

[19] Ibid., p. 21.

[20] Ibid., plate 24. See "Singing and Dancing," in Chapter 1.

[21] See note 20.

[22] *Human being* is song cycle. Ibid., p. 21.

[23] As provided by Densmore, Ibid. p. 21. There seems to be an inconsistency in this chart. Whereas bird, lightning, deer, frog, and corn dance all refer to song cycles, by the same name, Densmore does mention a coyote song cycle, in her index to *YYM;* but this seems like a mistake. In YMM, however, Coyote is the topic of songs in various other song cycles, including *Bird* and *Deer.*

and sticks, tobacco and some food, and get him to tell one of the stories. On such occasion the story-teller leads the singing and pounds on the basket, and those who know the songs "help him" by singing with him. [24]

In her musical transcriptions, Densmore did not attempt to capture the unique sounds that singers made with these percussion instruments or the techniques that they employed (rubbed versus struck). As she made her transcriptions, Densmore seems to have relied upon her audio recordings. Densmore found, however, that her audio recordings did not pick up the sound of the struck basket. In place of the basket, she asked singers to use a wooden box. In many of her musical transcriptions, Densmore did indicate the rhythm of the percussion instrument in straightforward divisions of the beat.

The situation is the same with respect to the words. Densmore recognized that the words were in some sense an integral element, but she did not include them in her musical transcriptions. Concerning the words, Densmore reported that, "In Yuman songs, the tempo of the voice and the drum or rattle is always uniform and the two are synchronous."[25] She also observed that each song contained one or more periods. Writing about this, she stated,[26]

> The characteristic form of Yuman songs, as indicated, is a "period formation" with one, two, or occasionally three long periods and a short period containing the more pleasing part of the melody.[27]

Densmore seems to have realized that an analysis of the words in conjunction with the melody could lead to a better understanding of the repeated sections (or periods) in each

---

[24] Ibid., p. 14.
[25] Ibid., 21.
[26] Ibid., 28.
[27] By the "pleasing part of the melody," Densmore seems to have been referring to the section of the melody that contained the rise.

song. Her comments, however, suggest that she may have been willing to include words

that could be translated but probably not vocables. With the following remarks, she

explained that she had in fact decided not to include the words,

> Unusual difficulties surround the transcription and analysis of Yuman songs. The
> form of a melody is determined to some extent by the words of the songs, and the
> present material contains many songs connected with legends and embodying part
> of the narrative. The words of these songs, as already stated, are in a language
> which is obsolete, the singer repeating words by rote. The integrity of these
> words was proven by the rendition of No. 109 by Cocopa and a Yuma, the words
> as well as the melody being the same on the two phonograph cylinders. It is not
> practical to undertake the placing of such words or syllable beneath the notes of a
> transcription.[28]

Based on these conclusions, and others, Densmore decided to include the melody and its

rhythm, in her musical transcriptions. She often also included the rhythm of the

percussion instrument. In her transcriptions, the periods that she indicates seem abstract,

without the words.

An example will prove useful when considering the kinds of information that

Densmore included for each story. The Quechan singer Charles Wilson who sang

Lightning was one of the singers with whom Densmore spoke. Here, I consider

Densmore's transcription of *Lighting*.[29] In his transcription of *Lightning*, Halpern

identifies the protagonist as being Wonderboy. In her transcription, Densmore refers to

the protagonist as being White Cloud. It is difficult to compare the stories contained in

their respective transcriptions, since Densmore and Halpern both published excerpts

---

[28] Ibid., 17.

[29] Charles Wilson was apparently a relative of the Quechan singer William Wilson, who
also sang *Lightning*. Halpern transcribed W. Wilson's rendition of *Lightning*, in the
1930's. See "Brother Songs," in Chapter 1.

rather than the entire story. Having said this, it seems clear that the overall thrust of the actions of White Cloud/Wonder Boy, seems to be the same in both transcriptions. A super-human being, Wonder Boy's makes his home in the sky and he can control thunder, lightning, and the winds.

While Densmore did not include the words for any of the songs with her musical transcriptions, she did include a descriptive title, along with a brief summary of the associated narrative, for each song. The titles and the brief narrative that Densmore provided for three songs can serve as an example (see Figure 3.B-ii). As can be seen, with each song White Cloud declares that his power resides in the skies: in lightning, in thunder, and in wind.

Densmore's terse description, "The words of the songs are summarized in the title and are frequently in the first person," does not acknowledge how effective these titles and summary descriptions are in summarizing the story. In fact, when these titles and the summary remarks that Densmore provided for each song are taken together, the result rivals the kind of information that other scholars provided with their creation story texts.

1.	White Cloud Declares His Power	White Cloud says that he will be known by the lightning, thunder, and rain in the sky, and that these will be continued, though he may go away. During these next three songs, he calls the clouds, the lightning, and the high winds. They come at his command and fill the heavens.
2.	White Cloud Demonstrates His Power (a)	None
3.	White Cloud Demonstrates His Power (b)	In the next song, White Cloud has returned to his home. He stands there singing this song.

Figure 3.B-ii. Three *Lighting* songs in which White Cloud talks about his power.

It is for this reason that I refer to the total information that Densmore provided for

Lighting as being a transcription. Shown in Figure 3.B-iii are the thirteen songs that

Densmore included in her transcription of *Lightning*. When the narratives that Densmore

provided for each of these songs are pieced together, the result is a summary of the story,

one that focuses on the journey of White Cloud and all that he perceives. As the story

begins, White Cloud is in the desert near Indio, California, traveling towards a mountain,

identified only as "Dark Mountain." After arriving there, White Cloud journeys up into

the sky, where he finds a place that he will call his home. Next, he proceeds to

demonstrate his ability to create thunder, lightning, wind, and rain. After journeying to

the ocean, where he observes waves crashing against the coast, his travels are complete.

White Cloud finishes his journey with the final statement: "This is the beginning of the

clouds, the high winds, and the thunder. I alone can command them to appear."

Like the other scholars whose writing I have considered, Densmore did not attempt to describe the way a singer told his story; nevertheless, her comments include clues that shed some light on this question. In the following quotation, Densmore does not actually say that a performance involved singing as well as spoken narration. On the other hand, she does write, "The story is told in the common language of the present time." This seems to at least imply that the singer provided some spoken narration. She also states that "the songs, which are sung at intervals, are in the old language which is not understood by anyone." Here is the quotation in question:

> The story is told in the common language of the present time and the songs, which are sung at intervals, are in the old language which is not understood by anyone, the words of the songs being learned with the melody and sung by wrote. A general knowledge of their meaning is received by tradition. The words are said to embody a part of the narrative but they are not descriptive. The legend is usually concerning a journey and the song appears to contain the choice bits and delightful little episodes, while the details of the journey are carried by the narrative. The songs appear to represent the poetry and the narrative the prose in a varied performance which give great pleasure to these Indians.[30]

While she did not describe a performance, she did offer some indications as to when song cycles were performed. The songs were sung at night. Densmore explained that each part of the night "had its songs." Some songs were sung early in the evening, others after midnight, still others were sung before the sun rose. In the following quotation, Densmore explained that she asked each singer to make a selection of his songs,

> No attempt was made to record all the songs of any cycle and the singer was asked to choose a number from the portions sung at different parts of the night. It was the custom to divide the night into parts (before and after midnight) and each half of the night had its songs. There was an order of the songs within these parts,

---

[30] Ibid., 13.

certain songs being sung early in the evening, at about midnight, and "along toward morning.[31]

Densmore recognized that songs were sung in sets. She seems to have aimed at recording one song from each set. In her discussion of *Lighting,* she explained that each of the songs in a set had the same melody,

> The songs are in groups of three, each group having the same tune but with different words. Only one of a group was generally recorded, though in one instance an entire group of three with the same were found on the phonographic cylinders.[32]

So the songs in a set used the same melody, each song had different words. Writing about a *Lightning* song that she entitled "On Top of His Own Mountain," Densmore added still another insight concerning the nature of the songs in a set. Each song, she explained, addressed the same subject. With the first song, White Cloud describes a mountain that he sees. Next, White Cloud reports that he is traveling towards the mountain. In the next song (or songs), he has named the mountain. Or, as Densmore explains,

> The melody of the three next recorded songs is the same. In one of these songs, White Cloud says that he has seen a certain mountain (near the present site of Indio) and is traveling toward it. In the next three songs he named the mount, calling it Avi'tinya'm, which means Dark Mountain. The melody was repeated accurately, and the transcription is from the second of the group.[33]

Densmore reiterated the idea that the songs in a set referred to the same subject, when she spoke about still another set. With each of the songs in this set, White Cloud describes his power. Or, as Densmore explained,

---

[31] Ibid., 15.

[32] Ibid., 112.

[33] Densmore may be referring to Indio, California. Ibid., 114.

White Cloud says that he will be known by the lightning, thunder, and rain in the sky, and that these will be continued, though he may go away. During the next three songs he calls the clouds, the lightning, and the high winds. They come at his command and fill the heavens.[34]

In conclusion, the breadth of information provided by Densmore in *Yuman and Yaqui Music* is considerable. Like the other scholars whose transcriptions I have considered, Densmore did not set out to describe actual performances; yet she was speaking with singers who presumably performed their songs and narrated their stories. Her discussion is peppered with bits and pieces of information that probably provide at least some information about how the stories were told. Densmore never says that a performance involved both singing and spoken narration; nor does she say that a performance involved singing alone. She does, on the other hand, explain that the songs were sung in sets. She also writes that the songs in a set had the same melody, dealt with the same or similar subject matter, but had different words. Because she emphasizes that there was a difference between what was conveyed during narrative versus the songs, it seems possible that a rendition of *Lightning* may have involved both spoken narration and singing.

---

[34] Ibid., 119.

	Titles of songs	The associated narrative
1.	"I Have Arrived in the Sky"	None
2.	"The Sky is in Darkness"	As the story begins, White Cloud is somewhere near Indio, California, traveling towards a mountain that he identifies as Dark Mountain, Avi'tinya'm.[35]
3.	"On Top of His Own Mountain"	"In explanation of the following song it was said that while the Wonder-boy has [sic] traveled through the night Coyote has continually seen the daylight. Coyote has [sic] continually seen the daylight. Coyote danced and sang this song."
4.	Song of Coyote	"When White Cloud left Dark Mountain he went up into the air, making a path in the sky. At last he found a place in the air which pleased him so well that he called it his home."
5.	"At the End of the Path in the Sky"	White Cloud mistakes "swirling clouds" for smoke; next, he speaks with a bird, asking it about its wanderings. Then, he "expresses himself as satisfied with all that he has seen and says that he will now demonstrate his own magic power which be shown in the sky."
6.	White Cloud Declares His Power	"White Cloud says that he will be known by the lightning, thunder, and rain in the sky, and that these will be continued, though he may go away. During these next three songs, he calls the clouds, the lightning, and the high winds. They come at his command and fill the heavens."

Figure 3.B-iii. The story of *Lightning,* based on the song titles and the corresponding summaries that Densmore's provided.

---

[35] Note: in some cases I have summarized the narrative for each song. In other instances, I have used excerpts from Densmore's remarks. These are enclosed with quotation marks.

7.	White Cloud Demonstrates His Power (a)	None
8.	White Cloud Demonstrates His Power (b)	In the next song, White Cloud has returned to his home. He stands there singing this song.
9.	"White Cloud is Singing in the Sky"	White Cloud has decided to travel again. He intends to go toward the south, and in this song he tells of the proposed journey.
10.	"I Will Go Toward the South"	As he passed a certain place in the sky, he saw a woodpecker and said, "Now I know that creatures such as you live and roam in a place like this."
11.	Song of the Woodpecker	In the sky next following song he has gone still farther and come down to the oceans, where he sees great waves throwing waves of mist into the air. He is now on the earth and he sings this song.
12.	Song Concerning the Ocean	In the final song he says, "This is the beginning of the clouds, the high winds, and the thunder. I alone can command then to appear."
13.	"My Power is in the Sky"	None

Figure 3.B-iii, continued.

Duncan Strong's Transcription of the Cahuilla Creation Story

For a period of six months, in 1924-25, anthropologist Duncan Strong visited and

studied the culture of different Cahuilla, Cupeño, and Serrano bands. In 1929, Strong

published the results of his research, under the title of *Aboriginal Society in Southern*

California.[36] As part of his discussion of the Cahuilla, Strong included a text of the

Cahuilla creation story. In his discussion, Strong offered some comments that provide at

least some data regarding when, where, and how this story may have been told.

Strong had attended a Cahuilla biennial mourning ceremony, held in February,

1925, in Palm Springs, California. Upon the conclusion of the ceremony, Strong spoke

with the Cahuilla singer Alejo Potencio, who was also a ceremonial chief. With the help

of an interpreter, Jolian Nortes, Strong wrote down the creation story, using a kind of

clear, dramatic style that Underhill might have approved of. Strong's text consists of a

sequence of forty-one paragraphs of text, beginning thus:

> In the beginning there was nothing but darkness. At times it was light but with no
> moon or stars. One was called tūkmiatahat (female) the other tūkmiatelka (male).
> Sounds, humming or thunder, were heard at times. Red, white, blue, and brown
> colors came all twisting to one point in the darkness. These came together in one
> point to produce [sic]. This ball shook and whirled all together into one
> substance, which became two embryos wrapped in this placenta. This was
> formed in space and darkness. These were born prematurely, everything stopped
> for they were stillborn.

> Then again all the lights whirled together, joined and produced. This time the
> embryos grew fully—the children inside talked to one another. They asked each
> other, "What are we? We are eskwatkwatwitcem, and estanamwitum," for at that
> time they did not know themselves. While they were in this sack they rolled back
> and forth, they stretched their arms and knees to make a hole so they could get
> out. Then they named themselves Mūkat and Temaīyauit.

As can be seen, the above text contains no information about how the story was

---

[36] Duncan Strong, *Aboriginal Society in Southern California.* University of California
Publications in American Archaeology and Ethnology 26 (1929); republished by the
Malki Museum, Inc, Banning, California, 1987. See pages 130-131. Also see the
"Register to the Papers of William Duncan Strong," at the National Anthropological
Archives, Smithsonian Institution; online at http://www.nmnh.si.edu/naa/fa/strong.pdf
(accessed on June 2, 2010).

performed. However, Strong did include some brief remarks that offer at least some insights into how Potencio may have told this story. For one, Strong wrote that "this myth includes the greater number of songs sung at the mourning ceremony." With this remark alone, Strong indicates that a rendition of the story did include the singing of songs. Strong provided still more support for this notion, as he continued to discuss Potencio's recent performance. Referring to the text that he had just written down, Strong wrote that, "each sentence given here forms one verse." Again, this comment suggests that Potencio's narration did involve singing. His use of the word "verse" may further suggest that during his performance Potencio may have repeated each "sentence" a number of times before moving on to the next song. When Strong wrote, "the song takes three nights to sing completely," he provided still more fuel for the notion that Potencio's rendition involved singing.

Here is Strong's entire comment about Potencio's performance. As can be seen, his remarks fall short of answering many questions; nevertheless, when Strong's albeit brief observations about Potencio's performance are considered in relation to those that Kroeber, Halpern, and Densmore offered, it appears that Potencio's style of performance may have been similar in at least some respects to the styles of performance seen among the Mohave, the Quechan, and the Cocopa. As can be seen, Strong makes no mention of spoken narration, possibly suggesting that Potencio's performance involved singing but no spoken narration,

> This myth includes the greater number of songs sung at the mourning ceremony. Each sentence given here forms one verse, including much repetition, and the

song takes three nights to sing completely. It varies slightly from group to group,[37] and the versions of any two widely separated Cahuilla groups are different in detail though the general motifs are the same. It is a highly impressive and solemn chant, rising at times to rare beauty, but usually sung in a monotonous rising and falling cadence.[38]

---

[37] Strong is referring to the different Cahuilla bands which are located throughout the Anza Borrego Desert and in the surrounding mountains. Currently, there are nine different Cahuilla reservations: Aqua Caliente Band of Cauhilla Indians, Augustine Band of Mission Indians, Cabazon Band of Mission Indians, Cahuilla Band of Mission Indians, Los Coyotes Band of Mission Indians, Torrez-Martinez Desert Cahuilla Indians, Morongo Band of Cahuilla Indians, Ramona Band of Cahuilla Indians, Santa Rosa Band of Cahuilla Indians. See http://www.sci.sdsu.edu/salton/NativeAmericans SaltonBasin.htm

[38] See Strong's "Aboriginal Society," 130-131.

Constance DuBois's Transcriptions of

Kumeyaay and Luiseño Creation Stories

Constance Goddard DuBois who published a number of articles about the

Kumeyaay- and Luiseño- speaking tribes of San Diego county, between about 1898 to

1909.[39]   DuBois apparently traveled to southern California from the East coast each

summer. As I will show, DuBois's writings contain clues that suggest that the

performance of a creation story by singers from San Diego county involved both

speaking and singing. In some of her articles, DuBois addressed the poverty and

dislocation that tribal members were experiencing.[40]   In other articles, DuBois presented

the results of her studies of creation stories. She also took photographs of tribal

members, and made a number of audio recordings of singers. The Cornell University

Library holds a collection of DuBois's papers, containing some eighty-nine folders.[41]

Included are offprints of her published articles, typed manuscripts, and handwritten

fieldnotes and correspondence. Some of these letters are ones that were written to

DuBois. They show that DuBois corresponded with a variety of people, from Mary

Watkins, who was the school teacher at Mesa Grande, to Kroeber, who wanted to explore

---

[39] She also spoke with members of the Cupeño tribe and also possibly some Cahuilla
singers as well.
[40] For one example, see DuBois, *The Condition of the Mission Indians of Southern
California* (Philadelphia: Office of the Indian Rights Association, 1901); reprinted in
Laylander, *Listening*, 41-49.
[41] DuBois's papers are housed at the Division of Rare and Manuscript Collections
Cornell University Library. See http://rmc.library.cornell.edu/EAD/htmldocs/
RMM09167.html (Accessed on July 8, 2009.)

the similarities between the creation stories and songs of the Mohave and those of the tribes of San Diego county   Also in DuBois's papers are letters along with many other handwritten notes that appear to be in DuBois's distinctive hand.[42]   It seems possible that some of her handwritten notes may be the ones that DuBois wrote down as she listened to a singer tell a creation story. Whether handwritten or typed or offprint, any of these documents can prove helpful, for her handwritten notes sometimes contain information that is missing from her published articles, and vice versa.[43]   DuBois's published and unpublished manuscripts show that she spoke with singers from throughout San Diego county. Her numerous published articles along with her unpublished manuscripts provide a number of possibilities for considering how singers from Kumeyaay- and Luiseño-speaking tribes may have told their creation stories.[44]   When investigating this subject, it is however best to draw together data from a number of her writings, for no single article will suffice. Figure 3.C-i shows an excerpt of one of the Kumeyaay creations stories that DuBois wrote out by hand.

---

[42] I am not a handwriting expert. However, her collected papers contain letters signed by Constance DuBois, thus providing a sample of her writing. This same hand or at least what appears this hand can be seen throughout many of the other handwritten notes and drafts, in the collected papers of DuBois.

[43] Most of DuBois's papers are undated. This includes handwritten notes and typed manuscripts.

[44] Again, see note 1. For a partial list of the singers with whom Dubois worked, see Laylander, *Listening,* 17.

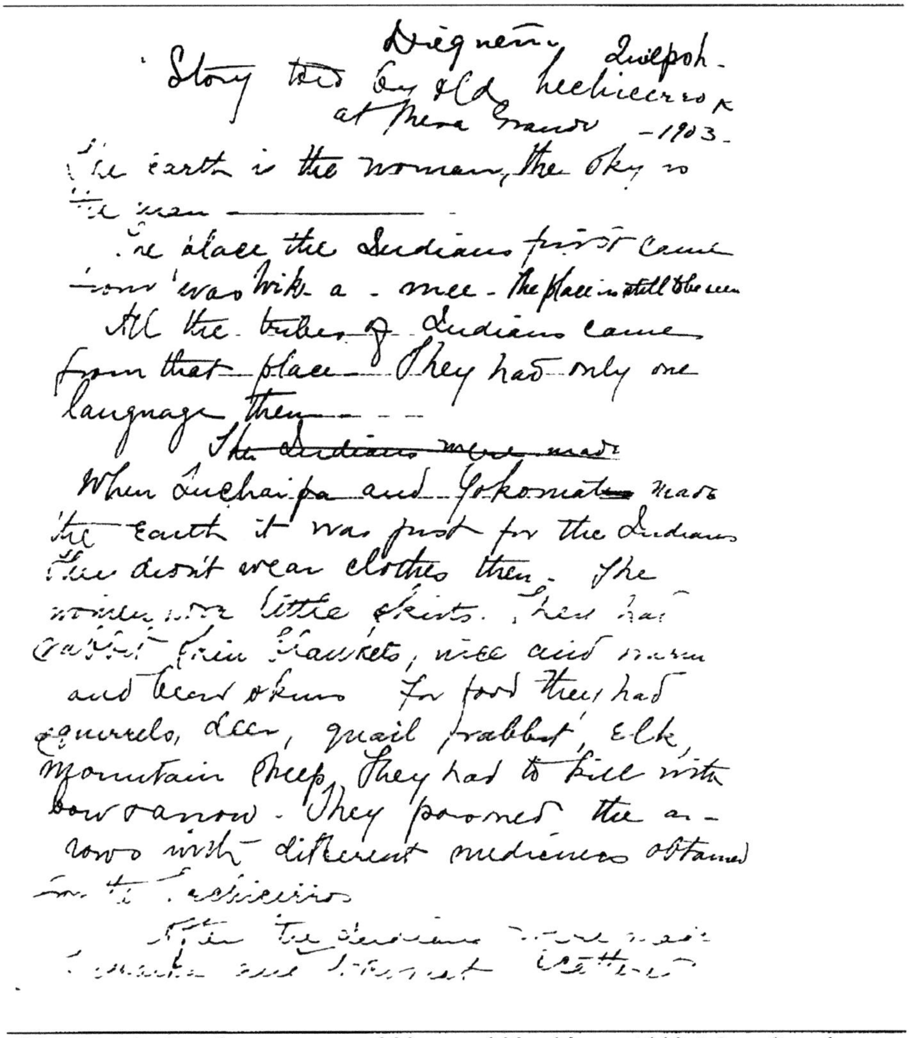

Diegueno Quilpoh.
Story told by old hechicerro at Mesa Grande -1903-
The earth is the woman, the sky is the man ——
The place the Indians first came from was Wiki-a-mee - The place is still there
All the tribes of Indians came from that place. They had only one language then - - -
~~The Indians were made~~
When Tuchaipa and Yokomat made the earth it was just for the Indians. They didn't wear clothes then. The women wore little skirts. They had rabbit skin blankets, nice and warm and bear skins. For food they had squirrels, deer, quail, rabbit, elk, mountain sheep. They had to kill with bow & arrow. They poisoned the arrows with different medicines obtained from the hechicerros

Figure 3.C-i. Creation story, as told by an old hechierro, 1903, Mesa Grande. Source: DuBois Papers. Folder 22. Also see footnote 41.
[Story told by old hechicerro [sic] (Diegueno Quilpol) at Mesa Grande, 1903. The earth is the woman, the sky is the man. The place the Indians first came from was Wiki-a-mee. The place in still there. All the tribes and Indians came from that place. They had only one language then. When Tuchaipa and Yokomat made the earth it was just for the Indians. We didn't wear clothes then. The women wore little skirts. They had rabbit skin blankets, nice and warm and bear skins. For food they had squirrels, deer, quail, rabbit, elk, mountain sheep. They had to kill with bow & arrow. They poisoned the arrows with different medicines obtained from the hechicerros]

Two Articles: **"The Mythology of the Dieguéños"** *and* **"The Story of the Chaup"**

One of DuBois's first publications of a creation story was her 1901 article "The Mythology of the Dieguéños" *(MOD),* as told to her by the elderly Kumeyaay singer Cinon Duro, from Mesa Grande.[45] DuBois writes that Cinon Duro was the eldest of four brothers, two of whom had already died. The other living brother was the Kumeyaay Antonio Duro. Cinon Duro explained that his father had taught each brother a different part of the Kumeyaay creation story; Cinon apparently knew the first part of the story. It can be summarized as follows: In the beginning, the sky and the earth were close together, not separate as they are today. Earth-Mother and Sky-Power worked together to create the brothers, Yokomatis and the more powerful Tuchaipa. At first, they sit together, both bearing the weight of the heavens on their shoulders. After issuing an incantation and rubbing tobacco between his fingers, Tuchaipa began blowing the heavens up and off their shoulders, into the position that they remain in today. Next, he will populate the earth and the heavens.

Figure 3.C-ii shows an excerpt from the start of DuBois's MOD. As can be seen, DuBois's text begins with the actions of Tuchaipai and Yokomatis as they sit bearing the weight of the heavens on their shoulders. In the excerpt, Tuchaipa causes the heavens to ascend. He chants, "We-hicht, we-hicht, we-hicht," three times. He then rubs tobacco in his hands and blows upon it. Of note here is the fact that the chant is not identified as a song per se; furthermore DuBois's MOD makes no mention of songs.

---

[45] See DuBois, "The Mythology of the Dieguéños," *Journal of American Folklore* 14 (1901): 181-5; for a reprint, see Laylander, *Listening,* 38-40.

When Tu-chai-pai made the world, the earth is the woman, the sky is the man. The sky came down upon the earth. The world in the beginning was pure lake covered with tules. Tu-chai-pai and Yo-ko-mat-is, the brother, sat together, stooping far over, bowed down under the weight of the sky. The Maker said to the brother, "What am I going to do?"

"I do not know," said Yo-ko-mat-is.

"Let us go a little farther," said the Maker.

Then they went a little farther and sat down again. "Now what am I going to do? said Tu-chai-pai.

"I do not know."

All this time Tu-chai-pai knew what he would do, but he was asking the brother.

Then he said, "We-hicht, we-hicht, we-hicht," three times, and he took tobacco in his hand, and rubbed it fine, and blew upon it three times, and every time he blew the heavens rose higher about their heads. Then the boy did the very same thing, because the Maker told him to do it. The heavens went high, and there was the sky.

Figure 3.C-ii. A excerpt from DuBois's "The Mythology of the Diegueños."[46]

DuBois published Antonio Duro's story in 1904, as the "The Story of the Chaup: A Myth of the Diegueños" (SOC).[47] Antonio Duro's story addresses the subjects of love and marriage. Thus, the events in his story occur after those that are included in Cinon Duro's narrative. Of note, however, is the fact that Antonio Duro's narrative, at least as presented by DuBois in SOC, is not obviously episodic. Some eighty songs are interwoven throughout the narrative, with specific songs being associated with specific parts of the story. Antonio's rendition of his story may have involved the recitation of a sequence of episodes; but, if this was the case, DuBois did not preserve this structure. In this sense, DuBois's SOC differs from Halpern's transcription of Lightning and all the

---

[46] See Listening, 38.

[47] See DuBois, "The Story of Chaup: A Myth of the Diegueños," Journal of American Folklore 17 (1904): 181-5; reprinted in Laylander, Listening, 66-78.

Mohave creation stories that Kroeber transcribed. Halpern's transcription and Kroeber's transcriptions are clearly episodic. Also different is the fact that DuBois, not only in SOC but also in most of her other creation story texts, did not translate or paraphrase the meaning of the songs (see Figure 3.C-v). In Halpern's transcription of *Lightning,* the structure of the narrative seems at least in part to be determined by the fact that a performance involved speaking and then singing, in alternation. This is made more obvious by the fact that the content of the songs differs from that which is delivered while speaking. DuBois's SOC does not allow for a direct comparison of what was conveyed in the narrative versus in the songs since DuBois does not translate or paraphrase the songs. At the same time, the idea that the songs were in some respects essential seems more evident in DuBois's handwritten version(s) of Antonio's story. Her handwritten drafts give the impression of DuBois almost struggling to write keep pace with a singer as the story was dictated, and not taking the time to puzzle out the meaning of each song.[48]

---

[48] For example, see Figure 3.C-iii for what may be the first page of the notes that DuBois took, possibly as she listened to the Kumeyaay singer Hatakek, from Manzanita, tell the story of Cuy-a-ho-marr. Hatakek used the name of Cuy-a-ho-marr in the place of Chaup. Hatakek's story is roughly equivalent of the story that A. Duro told. In Figure 3.C-iv, I have included the first four pages of DuBois's transcription of Hatakek's rendition. Hatakek's rendition formed the basis for DuBois's "Mythology of the Mission Indians," *Journal of American Folklore* 19 (1906): 145-164; for a reprint, see Don Laylander, *Listening,* 98-109

Hatakek's Story of Cuy-oh-lo-marr.

In the beginning the Sky was a man, the Earth was a woman. From their union a man and woman were born first and Sin-yo-hauch was their daughter. Sin-yo-hauch's father went up in the sky and she was left alone. She went towards the East crawling as a baby on hands and knees, and then later she walked back towards the West as far as the Mojave river. In the middle of the river is a solitary sharp pointed rock that may still be seen there, called Wei-ka-su-titt, and here she made her home, living in a cave on the west side of the river, a big house where she lived alone till she was grown.

Every morning she went to bathe in a pond near by and in a manner not explained she became by this

Figure 3.C-iii. Hatakek's "Story of Cuy-oh-lo-marr"[49]

---

[49] See Folder 22, also see footnote 41

Hatakek's Story of Cuy-oh-lo-marr

In the beginning the Sky was a man, the Earth was a woman. From their union a man and woman were born first and Sin-ya-hauch was their daughter. Sin-yo-hauch's father went up in the sky and she was left alone.

She went towards the East, crawling as a baby on hands and knees, and then--later she walked back towards the west as far as the Mojave river. In the middle of the river is a solitary sharp pointed rock that may still be seen there, called Wei-ka-ru-utt, and here she made her home, home in a cave on the west side of the river, a big house where she lived along till she was grown.

Every morning she went to bathe in a pond nearby and in a manner not explained she became by this bathing the mother of twin boys. (Song)

She left the babies hanging in their baskets outside the house[50] while she went to gather seeds for food. The babies were crying so the cricket came to tend them and sing to them, but when Sin-you-hauch came home he jumped down and ran into the brush and broke his legs. They have been crooked ever since and he can only go by hops.

The next morning when she went away again the babies came down from their baskets and played about and when she came home she saw their tracks and wondered how they could have gotten down by themselves. She determined to find this out. So next day instead of going far away she turns herself into a stump so that she could see what they would do in her absence.

As soon as she was gone, they boys jumped down from their baskets, and the elder called out, "See brother, there is something here that will do us harm. Come and look." What is it?" asked the younger. "It is something that will do us harm. But it is only a stump." "Still it was not there yesterday." "Let us go and get our bows and arrows." "Let us see what it is." "Shoot it, I say."

At this, Sin-yo-hauch called out. "My dear sons, do not kill you mother."

So they all came together to their home.

Then their mother told them that since they were grown so large they ought to have new large arrows and she would make them for them with eagle feathers. An arrow must have a white eagle feather and a black eagle feather, so they must get her two young eagles, one white and one black.

So they slept over night and in the morning she told them where to find the eagles and they agreed to go. They took the hard ball that boys still play with, starting it with the foot, running to where [it] falls and starting it again with a kick, and in a very short time they reached the place following the ball.

There was a great high rock there and the younger said, "I'll climb it first." The elder brother sat at the foot of the rock crying and singing about his brother. "He may fall and break his neck." (Song)

Figure 3.C-iv. Hatakek's "Story of Cuy-oh-lo-marr," transcribed, pages 1-4.

DuBois's transcription of Antonio Duro's story of Chaup begins with the appearance of two sisters. No attempt is made to link the appearance of these two sisters with the actions of Tuchaipai or Yokomatis. (Perhaps the details of their origin were told by another of the Duro brothers?) The younger sister becomes pregnant, but not as the

---

[50] Crossed out in the original. See Figure 3.C-iii.

result of her union with a man.[51]   She then gives birth to two boys, who under her care,

grow up and learn to hunt. When they are ready to meet girls, their mother asks them to

bring her the wood of a certain tree. She will use this wood to make each boy a flute.

This is one of the sections in DuBois's SOC in which the interplay between

singing and telling is obvious. As shown in Figure 3.C-v, the completion of almost every

significant action is in fact signaled by the singing of a song. The boys have brought

their mother a piece of wood that she will use to make their flutes. She begins to work

with the wood. When she touches the pieces together, they make "sweet music." At this

point a song is sung, beginning with the words, "Kwa-la-ha-le."   After she finishes

decorating the flutes, with "the colored feathers of woodpeckers and the topknots of

quails," another song is sung. This song begins with the words, "We-le-wa-cha-a-cha-a-

cha."   Facing north, the brothers play their flutes, now for the purpose of attracting

girls.   In fact girls do come, but the boys do not like them. Another song signals the end

of this moment. It is, "We-le-wah-cha-a-tal."   The brothers then face the opposite

direction:

> So they sat down facing the south, and played the same music so loud and so
> sweet that the girls from the south came to hear it, but they did not like them
> either, because they ate rats, snakes, and such animals as that, and their bodies did
> not smell good.

Another song heralds the completion of this step, "Ha-ma-ko-lu, Ha-ma-we-le."   At this

point, DuBois notes, that the audience clapped their hands along with Antonio as he sang

---

[51] The excerpt from Hatakek's story covers these events. See Figure 3.C-iii and Figure
3.C-iv.

this song. The boys then face to the west. Writes DuBois:

> So they sat down toward the west, and played the beautiful music again, until the girls from the west came to them, but they did not like them, because they ate all animals that live in the ocean.

This is followed by the song, "Ha-ka-so-lu, Ha-ma-we, Ha-ma-ko-lu, Ha-ma-we-le-we,

Ha-ma-cha." Finally, the boys face to the east. DuBois's text states,

> But when they played the sweet music facing the east, some girls came from there, the daughters of Ithchin, the buzzard, and they liked them because they lived on the fruit that grows in the east and they smelled sweet."

This last segment is not followed by a song.

Disappointed because the older brother did not greet them, the sisters go home. Soon, the brothers decide to follow the sisters. Once they arrive at the village of the sisters, the brothers become afraid, for the sisters' village is heavily populated. The world is still young, however; and the use of magic is not unusual. In the creation stories of the Yuman-speaking tribes within the ESCR, there is a recurrent theme of a young boy who is prescient. He is able to protect himself and others with magic. As a potential remedy to the barrier that the sisters' busy community presents, the younger brother uses magic. He assumes the shape of a chaup, meaning that he has either become a shining meteor or ball lightning. The older brother follows suit. Figure 3.C-vi contains still another excerpt from DuBois's SOC. Again, each significant action is also followed by the singing of a song. In this example, the same song, "Ha-mai-nau-e-chak-om-whi-i-i," is sung three times . The brothers are not invulnerable, however. Upon seeing two flying Chaups enter their village, the sisters' father and their clan respond with anger and hostility. Possibly as a sign that the value of intermarriage between clans has not been

discovered, the clan members respond with primitive hostility. They chop the two
Chaups (brothers) to pieces and eat them. One of the sister's, however, has already
become pregnant, and she gives birth to a son. It is this boy who is named Chaup, after
the last shape that his father assumed.[52]

When they brought it to their mother she was very glad, and she chopped the wood
up fine, and took the pieces and put them out in the sun to dry. And the pieces of
wood as she touched them made sweet music.
      Song: Kwa-la-ha-le, etc.

Then the old woman decorated the pieces with the colored feathers of woodpeckers
and the topknots of quails, and made them into flutes for her songs to play on.
      Song: We-le-wa-cha-a-cha-a-cha, etc.

So they the brothers sat down facing the north, and played on the flutes such sweet
music that the girls from the north came to them, attracted by the sound; but the boys
did not like girls from the north
      Song: We-le-wah-cha-a-tal, etc.

So they sat down facing the south, and played the same music so loud and so sweet
that the girls from the south came to hear it, but they did not like them either, because
they ate rats, snakes, and such animals as that, and their bodies did not smell good.
      Song: Ha-ma-ko-lu, Ha-ma-we-le
      (Singer and Indian audience clapped hands in time.)

So they sat down toward the west, and played the beautiful music again, until the
girls from the west came to them, but they did not like them, because they ate all
animals that live in the ocean.
      Song: Ha-ka-so-lu, Ha-ma-we, Ha-ma-ko-lu, Ha-ma-we-le-we, Ha-ma-cha.

But when they played the sweet music facing the east, some girls came from there,
the daughters of Ithchin, the buzzard, and they liked them because they lived on the
fruit that grows in the east and they smelled sweet.

Figure 3.C-v. The boys play their flutes, excerpt from SOC.[53]

---

[52] After Chaup grows older, he is given the name Cuyahomar, by his mother. See SOC,
in Laylander, *Listening,* 77. Also see the rendition by the Kumeyaay singer Hatakek,
from Manzanita, in DuBois, "Mythology of the Mission Indians," *Journal of American
Folklore* 19, no. 72 (1906): 52-60; and reprinted in Laylander, *Listening,* 98-109.

[53] See *Listening,* 72

"Look at all those people," said the older. "How are we going to be able to get to the place in safety?"

So the younger brother stood up and held up his hands to the sky, and got a lot of stars and put them all over his body. And his brother did the same, and they sat down and were watching the people. They were shining like stars.

Song: Ha-mai-nau-e-chak-om-whi-i-i, etc.

They rose as if they had wings, and flew over to where they wanted to go.

Song: Ha-che-nau-e-cha-kom-whi-i--i- etc.

"I am going to fly to the girls' house," said the younger. :Watch me very closely and you will see where I go in among the crowds of people."

"We will die for the sake of the girls," said the older. "We shall never see our home again."

The older brother watched his brother and saw him fly towards the houses in the midst of all the people. Among all the houses he did not know where to go; but he came to one of the houses where there was a crowd of people about it, and the roof opened and he went in shining like a star. As he flew over their heads the people looked up and saw the Chaup. The wanted to catch him, but they could not. The father of the girls was there, and he told the people not to catch him, and that was not a start by a person. When the roof opened he went into the house, and there found his wife.

Song: Ha-che-nau-e-cha-kom-whi-i--, etc.

The older brother, left on the mountain, and flew after his brother shining like Chaup. People tried to catch him in the same way, but the girls; father warned them again, and he too went into the house, where he found his wife.[54]

Figure 3.C-vi. The brothers become Chaups, from SOC.[55]

A parlor talk: "Mission Indian Myth and Song"

As just shown, DuBois's SOC does contain clues that suggest that a rendition of A. Duro's story involved both spoken narrative and singing. Because DuBois does not translate the songs or paraphrase their meanings, it is difficult to understand what the songs contribute to the story. In others of her writings, DuBois seems to offer more

[54] Ibid., 25-26.
[55] See *SOC*, 75.

specific comments regarding how the story of Chaup may have been told. In her

manuscript "Myth and Folklore of Mission Indians," for instance, DuBois does clearly

state that the songs were integral to the story. In this manuscript, DuBois refers to an

elderly singer named Diego.[56] Concerning Diego, DuBois writes that he is "very old and

is the only survivor of four brothers each of whom had his own story with its

accompanying songs." She also adds that Diego "knew the whole story of chaup."[57]

Speaking about Diego's story, DuBois seemed to come very close to saying that it

involved the narration of a sequence of episodes. She wrote that the story was "not one

story but a series of connected adventures." She then went on to say that the structure of

the narrative might be likened to "a string of beads." Explained DuBois, each of these

"beads" was set off from each other by "intervals" of varying lengths, during which

songs were apparently sung. Here is the entire quotation in question. With it, DuBois

certainly seems to say that the story involved singing as well as spoken narration,

> Diego knew the whole story of chaup which is not one story but a series of
> connected adventures beginning with his parents and grandparents; and the course
> of the tale is accented and illustrated with songs, as a string of beads may be
> marked at intervals, with those of varying size; story and song running together to
> form an inseparable whole. This proves the primitive perfectionism of the
> narrative for Indian stories as they become modernized lose all trace of musical
> form, which must depend on the carefully educated memory of the reciter.[58]

A chance to learn still more about how the stories that DuBois studied and

documented may have been performed can be found in her "Mission Indian Myth and

---

[56] "Myth and Folklore of Mission Indians" is another of DuBois's undated and
unpublished manuscripts; see DuBois's papers, folder 28.
[57] Could Diego be another name for Antonio Duro, possibly a pseudonym?
[58] Folder 28, p. 6, see note 58.

Song" (MIMS), an undated and unpublished manuscript that is typewritten, double-spaced, and twenty pages in length.[59]   MIMS appears to be a prepared text, one that DuBois planned to read at one or more "parlor talks."   Possibly because she was speaking to a live audience, DuBois did not attempt to reach her audience by presenting them with a rendition of a creation story, the approach she had employed in her *Mythology of Diegueños* (MOD), where she presented a text of Cinon Duro's story, and in her *Story of Chaup* (SOC), which contains a text of Antonio Duro's story; but in MIMS, DuBois would use another strategy.   She would play recordings from Cinon Duro's rendition of the first moments of the Kumeyaay creation story, from Antonio Duro's story of Chaup, and from the Luiseño singer Maria Luisa's "Story of the Footprint."   Each of the songs that DuBois planned to play were ones that these singers apparently sang as they told their stories.   As the text of MIMS shows, as she addressed her audience, she planned to speak about the meaning of these songs, making it clear that they were not simply ornamental.   Because she would be talking about these three singer-storytellers, DuBois included still more clues regarding how they might have narrated

---

[59] And numbered by hand. For DuBois's "Mission Indian Myth and Song," see Folder 27, of her collected papers.

their stories.[60]

Included in DuBois's collected papers are nine typewritten sheets, each of which contains the text of one or more songs;[61] in the discussion I will refer to these as "song sheets." Some songs are in Kumeyaay, others are in Luiseño.[62] Each song sheet contains both a title and a brief paraphrase of the meaning of a song. In addition, each song sheet contains a number of lines for the same song (not just the first few words). Figure 3.C-vii shows the first eighteen lines of text for the "The flute is making music to call the girls."

DuBois's papers also include her musical transcriptions for sixteen songs. Again, some of words are in Kumeyaay, others are in Luiseño. The first page of this set contains DuBois's musical transcriptions for three songs. In the discussion that follows, I will refer to this collection of song sheets and musical transcriptions as being "DuBois's

---

[60] While it is not clear that DuBois actually gave this talk, other unpublished and undated documents included in her collected papers support the idea that she did give talks or that she helped to organize them. It seems possible that DuBois might have brought some of these documents with her to her talks. One document, for instance, contains the heading "Lecture Course Tickets," and shows the names of sixty-six parties who had purchased a total of eighty-four tickets. Figure 3.C-xiii, p. 235, shows the first page of this list. Other documents show lists of expenses. One includes a list of the following items and each of their costs: telegram, $.25; ad, $2.50; printing, $2,50; chairs, $2.50; phonograph, $.50; janitor, $.50; and $35, for an unidentified Mr. Curtis. (See Figure 3.C-xiv, p. 236). This list of expenses also includes a notation for the dates, "March 29, April 5 and 12, 1905," possibly suggesting that DuBois spoke on these three occasions. Still another document shows a list of seven people who had apparently agreed to loan blankets. At the very least, these documents appear to suggest that DuBois was involved in organizing talks. See Folder 22, also see note 41.

[61] Folder 20, "Chaup songs."

[62] Folder 48, "Music."

packet of songs" or simply as the "packet." Figure 3.C-viii brings together the

information

	No. 1, 1st Chaup song. "The flute is making music to call the girls."	
1	Ich́-tá-há	*Even emphasis but some*
2	Kwa-tá-há	*extra stress on last.**
3	Ich-tá-há	
4	Kwa-tá-há	
5	To-lé ot-to-lé ko-te-lé	*Accent on "le" but "o"*
6	To-lé ot-to-lé ko-te-lé	*and "ko" long drawn and almost double.**
7	Ich́-tá-há	
8	Kwa-tá-há	
9	Ich-tá-há	
10	Kwa-tá-há	
11	To-lé ot-to-lé ko-te-lé	
12	To-lé ot-to-lé ko-te-lé	
13	Ich́-tá-há	
14	Kwa-tá-há	
15	Ich-tá-há	
16	Kwa-tá-há	
17	To-lé ot-to-lé ko-te-lé	
18	etc repeated	
	English spelling, but "a" as in "ah".	

Figure 3.C-vii. "The flute is calling the girls," a song sheet.
*This is a semi-diplomatic transcripion. In the original the lines are not numbered and the sections marked with * are in cursive writing.

the information from her song sheets and her musical transcriptions, but only those that

pertain to either Antonio Duro's or Maria Luisa's songs. The left column of Figure

3.C-viii contains the titles of the story and the songs. The right column contains

DuBois's paraphrase for the meaning of each song. Although these are taken from

Dubois's song sheets, some of this information can also be found in her musical

transcriptions. As can be seen, in her packet of songs, DuBois had the words and the

music for five songs from Antonio Duro's "Story of Chaup" and four songs from Maria

Luisa's "Story of the Footprint." It seems possible that DuBois may have brought both

song sheets and musical transcriptions to her talks.

As the text to MIMS shows, DuBois began her parlor talk by first referring to the

advertising that had preceded the talk. Next, she began to prepare her audience for the

kind of talk that they would be hearing. DuBois explained that she would be playing

unedited recordings to them rather than arrangements or harmonizations,

> In advertising this parlor talk, I have used the word Song advisedly, for what you
> will hear has little resemblance to our conception of music. We speak of the song
> of a bird, the song of a brook, and of the wind in the pine trees, and these things
> cannot be harmonized according to our rules of musical composition. It is, in
> fact, a great mistake to attempt, as so many composers are now doing, to give the
> white man's musical form to Indian songs. In all cases where this work is at all
> genuine, the musician takes a graphophone record directly from the Indians, as I
> have done in those you will hear; he transcribes this into piano notes, and then
> with that theme builds up any sort of harmonization he chooses upon it.[63]

Next DuBois began to talk about Cinon Duro's creation story. Here she explained why

her 1901 text of Cinon Duro's creation story had contained no songs. When Duro first

---

[63] MIMS, 1.

Songs from Antonio Duro's *Chaup*	
Flute song	
first:	The flute is making music to call the girls
second:	The mother of Chaup calls the girls from the East to come and marry her sons.
Girls' farewell:	(no explanation given.)
Elder brother's song:	We shall die for the sake of the girls. I shall never see my home again.
Grandmother's song:	The younger Chaup returning to his blind old grandmother, sits on her lap, and she puts her arms around him and they both cry. Antonio feels like crying when he sings it.
Songs from Maria Luisa's *Footprint on the Rock*	
First:	The departing god stood and looked about him to see the condition of his people.
Second: a & b	Mukut, the god, set up a rock to mark the place. His heart was sad at parting.
Third:	Mukut steps from the rock to the mountain, from the mountain to the Pacific Ocean, before he sings as follows, "Ocean come nearer."

Figure 3.C-viii. Songs by Antonio Duro and Maria Luisa, in the packet of songs.

spoke with DuBois, he did not identify Tuchaipai's incantation as being a song (see Figure 3.C-ii). He apparently also did not speak about any of the other songs that where part of his story. By the time DuBois had written MIMS, Cinon Duro had changed his mind and decided to share his songs with DuBois. As DuBois explained,

> When Cinon told me the story of Creation he omitted the introduction and the songs that went with it; and the reason he did this was by no means that he forgot to give it, but that it was too sacred to be said or sung to the uninitiated, to one of an alien race. But two years later he sang these songs to me; and they are the ones which I can reproduce for you upon the phonograph.[64]

---

[64] Ibid. 4.

Thus C. Duro's story did in fact contain songs as well as spoken narration, even though no songs had been included in 1901 in MOD.[65] The idea that both the songs and the spoken narrative were integral is a point that DuBois stressed in MIMS; but how would she convey this to her audience? In her 1904 article "Diegueño Mythology and Religion: The Story of Creation, " DuBois had included the Kumeyaay words for two of Cinon Duro's songs, both about the first moments of creation (see Figure 3.C-ix). But as can be seen, without an accompanying translation or an explanation of the meaning of the songs, this approach does not explain how or in what way the song contributes to the narration of the story.[66]

The Sky-Power sings:----"Yo-haw-ma-ya-ha-ee. Yo-haw-ma-ya-ha-ee." These words are repeated six times. Then a long-drawn sigh is repeated.

Ich-a-pa-wha-che-ho Yo-o-o
Ich-a-pa-wha-che-yo Yo-o-o

Ma-to Tu-chai-pa   Mai-i-i Yo-ko-mat

Ich-a-pa-wha-chi-yo

The Earth-Mother, Sin-yo-hauch, brings forth the two gods.

Chu-pa-chu-wha   Wi-i-i
Chu-pa-chu-wha   Wi-i-i
Tu-chai-pa   Chu-pa-chu-wha I-i-i
Yo-ko-mat-is   Chu-pa-chu-wha
Wa   Wi-i-I   Wi-i-i.

Figure 3.C-ix. Songs of Sky-Power and Earth-Mother.[67]

---

[65] See note 45.

[66] See DuBois, "Diegueño Mythology and Religion: The Story of Creation," *Southern Workman* 33 (1904): 100-2; for a reprint, see Laylander, *Listening*, 79-80.

[67] Ibid., 80.

It seems possible that as she played some of her audio recordings DuBois may have

looked at the corresponding song sheets and musical transcriptions for her own reference.

In MIMS, DuBois did not present the Kumeyaay words to the songs; instead, she

proceeded in another fashion. On one hand, she included comments such as the

following that clearly state that the songs complemented the narrated stories. Referring

to Cinon Duro, DuBois wrote,

> The song emphasizes the narrative, adding to it and elucidating it. It is not
> intended at all as a musical accompaniment, but is like the shading in a picture,
> without which there would be no distinctiveness in the work.[68]

Before playing the first recording, DuBois again spoke about the meaning that these

songs had to Cinon,

> The value of things is altogether relative, and depends not only their rarity, but on
> popular estimation or interest. To me these reproductions of sacred song never
> heard by a white person before, and never to be secured again, for old Cinon is
> nearing his end, seem more valuable than the great diamond recently discovered
> in Africa; but I can not expect the public, in general, to agree with me; after my
> placing this estimate upon them even half in jest, you are likely to be much
> disappointed when you hear them, unless you can sympathetically transport
> yourself back in time and place, and realize what they meant to the old man who
> sang them with bent head and reverent gestures; his voice lowered to express the
> sacredness of the theme, and his whole being filled with the consciousness that he
> alone was the hereditary repository of these ancient traditions, and that with him
> they would forever perish unless the white man's magic or diabolic instrument,
> the talking machine, would preserve them, as his friend, La Constancia, promised.
> I will give you now the first of these songs.[69]

DuBois then played her recording of C. Duro singing the song about Sky-Power, and then

immediately explained its meaning. Regarding the first song, DuBois wrote,

> In the beginning, all was shapeless, dark, inert, a chaos full of untried potencies.

---

[68] MIMS, 4.
[69] Ibid., 5.

The Sky-Power, brooding mystery, rested upon the receptive earth. Out of chaos came a voice, a song, ending in a long-drawn sigh, signifying accomplishment, rest at the end of achievement.

Dubois then played her recording of the next song. Again, she immediately spoke about its meaning.

Again, voice, song, and sigh; and with each act of the First cause, an effect. The Earth-Mother, Sin-yo-hauch, the mysterious name, brought forth to the Sky-Power a god, Tu-chai-pa, the greatest, the first-born; and then Yokomatis, the lesser, his brother.

These comments clearly indicate the importance of the songs. See Figure 3.C-x for an excerpt that contains the above quotation. "Graphophone I" refers to the song of Sky-Power, and "Graphophone II" refers to the song of Earth-Mother.[70]

Having given her audience an introduction to Cinon Duro's story and two of his songs, DuBois next spoke about the Luiseño singer Maria Luisa. In her short description of Luisa, DuBois makes it clear that Luisa both sang and told, as she narrated her story:

Old Maria Luisa, the Indian woman who sang these songs and told the story, also showed intense religious feeling and reverence for the past.[71]

The songs and the story that Luisa told had to do with the god Mukut, more commonly spelled "Mukat" and sometimes referred to as Ouiot.[72] Apparently poisoned by the bitter

---

[70] Ibid., 6. I have not been able to locate DuBois's audio recordings of these two songs by Cinon Duro. DuBois does, however, list these two recordings along with others in her *The Religion of the Luiseno Indians of Southern California*; reprinted in *Listening,* p. 120-165. Some of her audio recordings are at U.C. Berkeley and are listed in Keeling's *Guide.* Also see, for instance, the collections of the Library of Congress and of the Indiana University Archives of Traditional Music.

[71] Ibid, 8.

[72] DuBois spells this name Mu-kut but here I use Bean's spelling. See note 73.

thoughts of frog, Mukat gradually sickens and dies.[73] Luisa's story describes the giant steps that Mukat took before eventually disappearing into the ocean. Luisa's story documented Mukat's progress, step by step. DuBois's packet of songs includes a song for three of Mukat's steps (see Figure 3.C-xi) .[74]

--- Graphophone Record I ---

This is the song of Sky-Power or First cause who begot Tuchaipa, the God who created the World.

To give the story in brief form I will read an extract from an article I printed in *Southern Workman*.[75]

The Diegueño, this is the tribe to which Cinon belongs, the Diegueño has no surmise concerning the creation of the earth. To him it is a primeval fact. Earth and Sky existed in the beginning of things; but not as illumined by sun, moon, and stars, informed with purpose and active with life. In the beginning, all was shapeless, dark, inert, a chaos full of untried potencies. The Sky-Power, brooding mystery, rested upon the receptive earth. Out of chaos came a voice, a song, ending in a long-drawn sigh, signifying accomplishment, rest at the end of achievement. Again, voice, song, and sigh; and with each act of the First cause, an effect. The Earth-Mother, Sin-yo-hauch, the mysterious name, brought forth to the Sky-Power a god, Tu-chai-pa, the greatest, the first-born; and then Yokomatis, the lesser, his brother. Then did Tu-chai-pa, with the assistance of his brother, create man to inhabit the earth, and the sun, moon, and stars to give light; first of all uprearing from primal prostrate position, the sky to be the arch of the heavens as we see it now above our heads.

--- Graphophone Record II ---

This is the song which describes the bringing forth of the Creator Gods Tuchaipa and Yokomatis by the Earth-Mother. You will hear these names if you notice them, in the songs, or chant. [76]

Figure 3.C-x. Excerpt from DuBois's MIMS

---

[73] Mukut also spelled Mukat, as in Lowell Bean, *Mukat's People; The Cahuilla Indians of Southern California* (Berkeley: University of California Press, 1972.) Regarding Ouiot and Wahawut, the frog, see, for instance, DuBois's "The Religion of the Luiseno Indians of Southern California," published in 1908, in Laylander, *Listening*. See p.150 for Salvador Cuevas's account. See p. 156 for the account of Lucario Cuevish. Also see Richard Applegate, "The Red, the Black, and the White: Duality and Unity in the Luiseño Cosmos." *Journal of California and Great Basin Anthropology* 1 (1979): 71-88.

[74] I was not able to find the audio recordings. See note 70.

[75] What follows, starting with, "the Diegueño has no surmise," can be found in DuBois's "Diegueño Mythology and Religion: The Story of Creation," *Southern Workman* 33 (1904): 100-2; reprinted in Laylander, *Listening,* 79-80.

[76] MIMS, 4-6.

1	The departing god stood and looked about him to see the condition of his people
2	Mukut, the god, set up a rock to mark the place. His was sad at parting.
3	Mukut steps from the rock to the mountain, from the mountain to the Pacific ocean. Before he does this he sings as follows, "Ocean come nearer."

Figure 3.C-xi. Three songs from Luisa's "Story of the Footprints."

Luisa's "Story of the Footprint" begins by identifying the place where Mukut came from, namely "Dark Wood." Like Wonderboy, in Halpern's transcription of *Lightning,* Mukut is concerned about his people. He pauses at certain places, to "look about and see the condition of my people." Like Wonderboy, Mukut also pauses to name certain places and to sing songs. With the first song, Mukut pauses to consider the condition of his people. At this point, the narrator sings a song, and Dubois paraphrases its meaning, as follows,

Song 1   The departing god stood and looked about him to see the condition of his people.

Next Mukut pauses to create a geographical mark of some sort, one that he will be remembered by. The second song is as follows,

Song 2   Mukut, the god, set up a rock to mark the place. His heart was sad at parting.

Figure 3.C-xii includes an excerpt from the start of Luisa's narrative along with the descriptive titles for two songs, taken from DuBois's song sheet. As can be seen in this excerpt, DuBois equates the two gods Mukat and Tuchaipa. She writes, "In the beginning Mu-kut (the San Luiseño name for Tu-chai-pa)," suggesting that Mukat and Tuchaipa are two different names for god.

As she discussed Antonio Duro's creation story, Dubois offered some of her most convincing comments regarding the idea both the songs and the story were essential. On one hand, DuBois explained that people used to invite Antonio Duro to sing and tell his

story. As he told his story, DuBois writes that "he would tell his tales and sing his

songs." Here is the quotation,

> In the old days, Antonio Duro, brother of Cinon, used to be much in request as a
> story teller. Like the old Welsh bards he would tell his tales and sing his songs
> and the people listened about the bonfire or festival or [on] social occasions. All
> night long he would sit and sing.[77]

In addition, DuBois also explained in concrete terms the number of songs that were

included in Antonio Duro's story and how much time it took to record and or document

them,

> To secure this myth, and the songs, nearly a hundred in number which accompany
> it, I sat down with him[78] and an educated Indian interpreter one morning at nine
> o'clock. I took down the story word for word as he related it and transcribed
> some of the words of the songs. We worked from nine till two, without a pause,
> and again from seven till eleven the same night. The following year I had him
> repeat some of these hundred songs, and I secured them upon graphophone. I
> wish I had time to tell you the complete story of this unique and perfect myth. I
> will give you a very brief outline of a part of it; and a few of the songs connected
> with it.[79]

The above quotation indicates that there were approximately one hundred songs

associated with Antonio Duro's story. Dubois included approximately eighty of these in

her *SOC*, indicating that she did not include all his songs. In MIMS, DuBois included

another comment that provides still more information about what it was like to hear

Antonio perform his Chaup songs. DuBois explained that each song was relatively short.

It seems possible that her song sheets may contain all the words that Antonio, for each

---

[77] Ibid, 15-16.
[78] Refers to A. Duro.
[79] Ibid., 11. I have not been able to find these songs in DuBois, either in the form of song
sheets or musical transcriptions or the associated audio recordings.

song (see Figure 3.C-vii) Dubois further reported that Antonio Duro used a soft voice as

he sang these songs. She also noted that the melodies contained a number of repeated

notes.[80]   Referring to the first of Antonio's songs, which she was about to play, DuBois

wrote,

> The first song in the Chaup series which I will give you means that the flutes are
> making music to call the girls. You will notice that it consists of a monotonous
> repetition of recurrent sounds as most of them do. The fact is the songs are very
> brief, perhaps not more than half a dozen lines; but to fill out my record the singer
> would go on repeating it until it seemed that he had given all I desired. They are
> not very loud and any who cannot hear are at liberty to come nearer for the
> purpose.[81]

---

[80] For a more detailed analysis of these songs, see "Evidence from DuBois's Song
Sheets," Appendix 2.
[81] MIMS, 17.

In the beginning Mu-kut (the San Luiseño name for Tuchaipa) came from a place called Dark Wood. He started and came, naming all the places as he passed by. A place on one side of the mountain he named Ke-chich-che, and in that place he stood and from it he looked around him, and said, "I will look about and see the condition of my people." [82]

First song: The departing god stood and looked about him to see the condition of his people[83]

He then moved forward looking for a place for his feet. "I shall leave the marks of my going," he said, "that in time to come my children can never be deceived, but may know the truth of the matter. And from that place I shall start. I am sad at heart to be going like this.

He sang another song and was going on, he set up a rock[84] in a place called Ke-lich-le.

Second song: Mu-kut, the god, set up a tock to mark the place. His heart was sad at parting.[85]

From there he went to a place named Water.[86]

Figure 3.C-xii. Excerpt from "Story of the Footprints," with two songs.[87]

---

[82] Here, I have changed the text slightly. In DuBois's text, instead of writing (first song), she wrote, "he sang the song that I have already given to you," meaning that prior to reading this synopsis of Luisa's story, DuBois had already play an audio recording of this song.

[83] "The departing god stood." This is song sheet no. 2, from DuBois's packet of songs.

[84] By this, DuBois meant that Mukut established a rock marker, one that would clearly indicate the physical location of this place.

[85] "Mu-kut, the god, set up a rock..." This is song sheet no. 3, from DuBois's packet of song.

[86] Ibid., 12-13.

[87] See note 86.

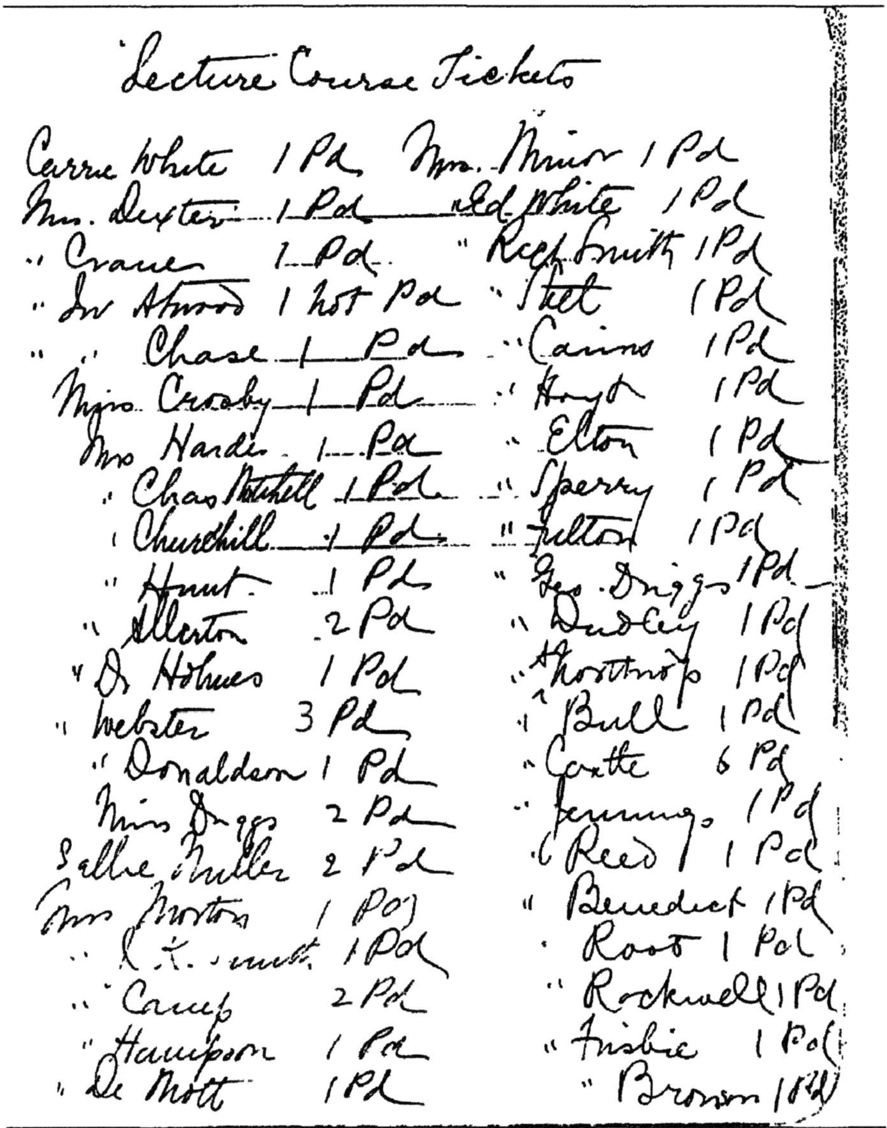

Lecture Course Tickets

Carrie White 1 Pd   Mrs. Minor 1 Pd
Mrs. Dexter 1 Pd   Id. White 1 Pd
" Crane 1 Pd   " Keep Smith 1 Pd
" Dr Atwood 1 hot Pd   " Stett 1 Pd
" " Chase 1 Pd   " Cairns 1 Pd
Miss Crosby 1 Pd   " Hoyt 1 Pd
Mrs Harde 1 Pd   " Elton 1 Pd
" Chas Mitchell 1 Pd   " Sperry 1 Pd
" Churchill 1 Pd   " Fulton 1 Pd
" Hunt 1 Pd   " Geo. Driggs 1 Pd
" Allerton 2 Pd   " Dudley 1 Pd
" Dr Holmes 1 Pd   " Northrop 1 Pd
" Webster 3 Pd   " Bull 1 Pd
" Donaldson 1 Pd   " Cratte 6 Pd
Miss Driggs 2 Pd   " Jennings 1 Pd
Sallie Miller 2 Pd   " Reed 1 Pd
Mrs Morton 1 Pd   " Benedict 1 Pd
" K. Smith 1 Pd   " Root 1 Pd
" Camp 2 Pd   " Rockwell 1 Pd
" Hampson 1 Pd   " Frisbie 1 Pd
" De Mott 1 Pd   " Bronson 1 Pd

Figure 3.C-xiii. List of Attendees.[88]

[88] See Folder 22, also see footnote 41

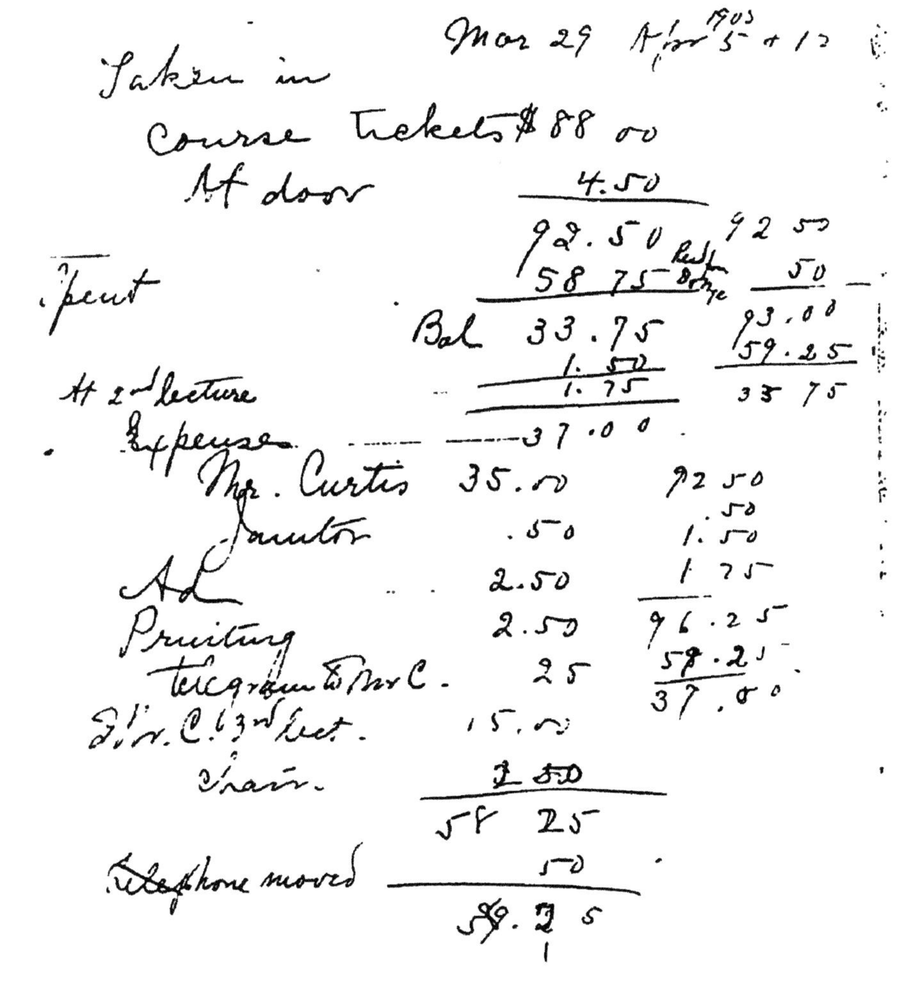
Mar 29 Apr 5 + 12 1903
Taken in
Course tickets $88 00
At door 4.50
92.50
Spent 58 75
Bal 33.75
At 2nd lecture 1.50
1.75
Expense 37.00
Mr. Curtis 35.00
Janitor .50
Ad 2.50
Printing 2.50
telegram to Mr C. 25
To Mr. C. 3rd lect. 15.00
Train 2.50
58 25
Telephone moved 50
58.75

Figure 3.C-xiv. Amounts spent for a lecture.[89]

[89] See Folder 22, also see note 41

CONCLUSION

Working in the first half of the twentieth century, but in different parts of the Extended Southern California Region (ESCR), Kroeber, DuBois, Densmore, Strong, and other scholars had the opportunity to speak with singers who not only knew a creation story or stories but probably also how to tell them. Confronted with the task of writing down the complex and detailed oral narrative of one or more these stories, scholars generally avoided the additional challenge of documenting how these stories were told. Each of the creation stories texts that I have considered contains, however, at least some clues regarding how that story was told. Kroeber's transcriptions of Mohave creation stories, for example, consist of a sequence of episodes. In many of the stories that he transcribed, most episodes are associated with a song or songs. In addition to writing down the texts of these stories, Kroeber also recorded hundreds of the associated songs, thus giving the impression that he initially recognized that the songs were significant; yet he seems to have changed his mind. In his *Handbook* (1917), and also in his detailed transcriptions of Mohave creation stories (the first of which appeared in 1948), Kroeber makes does not attempt to discuss the dynamic relationship between each episodes and its associated songs. In fact his word-for-word translations (of songs) seem designed to drive home the notion that the information contained in the songs was not needed, clearly eclipsed by lengthy oral narratives that he studied and wrote down. When he does refer to the songs or to how the stories were told, it is generally only to argue that there was no reason to include performance-related data in his transcriptions. While he included a list of the audio recordings that he had made of Mohave creation story songs, in MMM, he does not supplement this discussion with any thoughts about the relationships between the oral narratives and their songs;[1] nevertheless, this list offers a valuable resource for future study. Underhill also seems to have believed that a transcription of a Mohave creation story need not take into account the songs. DuBois, on the other hand, working in the first decade of the 1900's, seems to have concluded that the songs were an integral part of each story. This is suggested by the fact that she included many songs in her published transcriptions of the creation stories of the Kumeyaay. As an example, her transcription of Antonio Duro's creation story includes numerous songs. However, because DuBois did not include translations of the songs, it is difficult for readers to understand precisely how or in what ways the songs may have complemented the stories. Strong, in his remarks about his transcription of the Cahuilla creation story, seems to imply that a performance of the story may have involved the singing of a long sequence of songs. He suggests this when he writes that each sentence in his transcription corresponded to a song. However, he adds no further information about what a performance may have been like, meaning that a precise description of how the Cahuilla told their creation story remains out of reach. Halpern, possibly because he had both the opportunity to see the transcriptions of other scholars and to observe Quechan singers telling their creation stories, may have realized that it was a mistake to leave out the songs. His transcription of *Lighting* not only includes songs but sets of songs, both in Quechan and English. As a result, his transcription makes it possible for readers to begin

---

[1] Included in *More Mohave Myths,* published in 1960.

to see, or, at least, to begin to imagine, that an ESCR singer/storyteller may have complemented his spoken narration with a set of songs and vice versa. Other than the briefest of remarks, Halpern did not describe how *Lighting* was told; nevertheless, his brief comment, "In the narration, the singer as a rule first described the actions of the protagonist and then sang a series of songs relating to the same actions," is suggestive. It seems to imply that both singing and spoken narration were involved. By itself, this single comment also falls short of resolving the question of how *Lighting* was performed, in the 1930's, when Halpern hear it first.

Songs

As explained in Chapters 2 and 3, some scholars such as DuBois, Kroeber, and Underhill devoted a significant portion of their careers to the study of the culture of ESCR tribes. Still, they apparently lacked the more inclusive perspective that Halpern seems to have developed, namely that some significant portion of each creation story was conveyed through songs. The problem may have been that ESCR creation stories were considerably more complex and sophisticated than many scholars expected or imagined. It seems possible that a similar problem may have also hampered the efforts of the musicians who studied ESCR music. While detailed analyses of the melodies of songs are helpful, they can be misleading if other aspects of the music are not taken into account. An inclusive approach is needed, one that takes into account the fact that ESCR music is not only vocal music but also dance music. In his article "The Yuman Musical Style," Herzog did explain that ESCR musicians performed song cycles (he referred to these as "song-series"). He also mentioned that most song cycles were associated with a creation story ("myth"). However, with his analyses of songs, he focused primarily on the melody and its rhythm. He found that each song contained sections that were repeated during a performance. Based on his interviews with singers, Herzog found out the melody of most songs ascended at a certain point. He then identified the "rise" in his musical transcriptions. Without a knowledge of the dance steps, Herzog could not, however, accurately identify the metric changes in fancy songs. Without an analysis of the words and the dance steps, Herzog was also unable to understand how each section grew out of a subtle variation of the words, the dance steps, and the associated metric changes, as well as the melody.

Part of the skill of ESCR singers lies in their ability to generate a seamless fusion that brings together the elements of dance, the words, the melody and its rhythm, and the rhythm of the percussion instruments, and even as they work within certain known or predictable limits. The melodic range of the songs is relatively narrow. Each song generally contains relatively few words, perhaps six or fewer. Also the songs are relatively short in duration, perhaps no more than three to six minutes. Each song is divided into sections that are repeated during a performance. Despite these seemingly stark limitations, outright is in fact rare, with subtle variation one of the hallmarks of ESCR music.

The words provide an important starting point, when attempting to understand the form of each song. It appears that singers carry over into their songs the patterns of stressed and non-stressed syllables that are found in everyday speech. At the same time, singers sometimes use words in ways that go against the patterns of everyday speech.

The "fancy" song *Huyawa kwena,* one of the Mohave Bird songs that Herzog recorded and transcribed, provides a useful review.[2] In this song, the shift between duple and triple meters seems to be triggered by a lengthening or a shortening of the duration of certain syllables. In this instance, the syllables in question are ones that follow the patterns of the accents used in speech. The text is based on two words: *uunyáw kenáp,* probably meaning something on the order of, "you know it, therefore you can tell it." In everyday speech, the last syllable of each word is accented, as in *uun-yáw* and *ke-náp.* In the song, the word *uun-yáw* is transformed by the insertions of two vocables, with *uun-yáw* becoming *hu-ya-wa-a.* The second word, *ke-náp,* hardly changes, appearing as *kwe-ná.*

As he sings this song, the Mohave singer Sitcomai uses the word, *kwe-ná* as a pivot point, as he shifts between duple and triple meters. Figure 4-i provides an example, taken from the second line of the song. As can be seen, the first and third syllables of the first words, *hu-ya-wa-a,* each receive the downbeat. On the other hand, each time Sitcomai sings *kwe-ná,* and mimicking the patterns of stress heard during speech, the first syllable, *kwe,* takes the upbeat. The second syllable, *ná,* receives the downbeat. The first time that Sitcomai sings *kwe-ná,* the second syllable *ná,* is held for a single eighth note. The meter is still duple. In measure 8, Sitcomai repeats *kwe-ná.* Again, *ná* receives the downbeat. This time, however, Sitcomai holds *ná* for two eighth notes, setting the stage for a shift to a triple meter. In measure 9, he repeats the word *kwe-ná,* for a third time. *Kwe* again takes the upbeat. *Ná* takes the following downbeat,

---

[2] See *Huyawa kwena,* in Section 2.A.

this time becoming *ná-a-a*. *Ná-a-a* is now held for three eighth notes. By extending *na-a-a* over three eight notes, Sitcomai reaffirms that the meter has shifted from to triple. This is example of another of the kinds of subtle variation that are part characteristic of ESCR music.

The variation in these measures involves changes in the dance steps as well as the melody. In Figure 4-i, "L" indicates that the weight is placed on the left foot, "R" that the weight is on the right foot. The song begins with a shifting of weight from one foot to the other, every two eighth notes. In measure 9, this pattern is interrupted. In measure 9, where the meter has shifted to triple, the singers and dancers shift their weight to one foot, for two eighths, and then to the other foot, but for only one eighth. It seems likely that the finely honed integration of the dance steps, the melody, the words, and the rhythm of the percussion instruments is one of the features that singers and dancers rely on, as they sing and dance for long periods of time, an issue that is significant since a performance of a song cycle can last from dawn to dusk.

Figure 4-i. The second line of the song *Huyawa kwena*.

Sets of Songs

With a set of songs, it would appear that singers are able to move beyond the limitation of individual songs, most of which contain relatively few words. With a set of songs, singers have the additional flexibility of working with a collection of songs, each of which is unique in some fashion. The songs in a set may be similar because they all use similar words and melodies. Each song in a set may also address a similar subject. Singers distinguish the songs in a set and by various means. Some songs are "single steps," that is, they use the same meter (or "step") from start to finish. Other songs might be "fancy," they contain metric shifts between duple and triple meters.

With his transcriptions of Mohave creation stories, Kroeber had only hinted at the idea that most episodes were associated with a set of songs; but he failed to realize that singers used sets of songs to complement their spoken narrative. In contrast with his transcription of *Lighting*, Halpern demonstrated that a set of songs could convincingly complement the spoken narrative, for instance, expanding upon a singer's description of the motion of the stars in the skies.

As seen in my review of a select number of ESCR creation stories, each creation-story text contains at least some information about how a creation stories may have been performed. It appears that there may have been some variation in the way that singers combined the arts of singing and spoken oration. Based on Kroeber's transcriptions, it is difficult to know whether a performer first spoke and then sang and a set of songs, or whether the reverse may have been true. Dock clarified this issue, however, with her report that Mohave singers first sang and then told. Linking the technique of singing and telling to the dynamics of group participation, Dock further explained that everyone stood up and danced and also sang, as each set of songs was sung. They then sat down and listened, as the lead singer told the section of the story associated with the songs that had just been sung. Halpern's transcription of *Lightning* also consists of a sequence of episodes, most of which contain a set of songs along with a section of spoken narration. In Halpern's transcription, it seems clear that the singer first narrated a section of the story, by speaking, then sang a set of songs. From Densmore's transcription of *Lightning,* it is not clear whether a rendition involved singing alone or singing along with spoken narration. She does offer comments that suggest that a rendition involved both singing and spoken narration; but the issue is far from clear. From Strong's remarks, it is also difficult to know whether a performance of the Cahuilla creation story involved singing alone or singing in combination with telling.

DuBois's text of Antonio Duro's Chaup, on the other hand, does provide clues regarding how Antonio may have told his story. Based on what DuBois wrote, it seems likely that Duro's narration did involve singing along with spoken narration. On the other hand, in DuBois's "Story of Chaup," the story is not clearly divided into separate episodes. What is clear from DuBois's transcription, is that the songs were interspersed throughout the narrative; but the episodes are not obviously divided into sections of speaking, each of which is followed by a set of songs, as is the case in Halpern's transcription of *Lightning.* Instead, in DuBois's "Story of Chaup," there are sections where no songs are sung. In other sections, songs are built into the narrative. The episode in which the boys first acquire their flutes provides an example. Having received their newly fashioned flutes, the boys immediately put them to use. Facing to the north, they play their flutes; girls do in fact respond, but the boys do not find them desirable. Next, the boys turn around, facing to the south. Again they play their flutes. Again, girls respond with interest, and again Antonio pauses to sing a song. Each time the boys play they flutes, girls respond. Each time, Duro pauses to sing a song. This is but one

example of the way that Antonio Duro appears to have integrated the singing of songs

with his spoken narration of the story.[3]

In conclusion, out of this analysis one idea in particular emerges, one that can affect

our perception and reception both of creation-story texts and of today's song cycles.

Both may in fact be one and the same. In both cases story and song seem to illuminate

---

[3] There are a number of questions that I have not explored. Based on Kroeber's transcriptions of Mohave creation stories and Ione Dock's description of how they were told, it appears that Mohave creation stories and the ESCR song cycles of Yuman-speaking tribes may be quite similar. Both appear to involve the narration of a long sequence of episodes most of which are associated with a set of songs. Musical instruments were/are used and people danced as they sang the songs. (In the performance of a song cycle, it seems likely that the singers think about the story even though they generally do not stop to narrate it.) With her discussion of the Kumeyaay creation stories that she wrote down, DuBois's emphasizes the idea that their narration involved both telling and singing. It seems likely, however, that songs were interspersed throughout the story, but it is not clear that the song cycle form or structure was utilized. Thus there may have been more than one style of narration that ESCR singer/storytellers used as they told a creation story. If scholars were to take into account still more data and/or possibly even a larger geographical area, then they could explore this and other questions further. One useful source would be Leanne Hinton's *Havasupai Songs: A Linguistic Perspective* that includes Hinton's discussion and transcriptions of a number of different types of Havasupai songs. *Cante fables,* one of the kinds of Havasupai songs that Hinton studied, contain songs that are interspersed throughout each story. In addition, *cante fable* songs do not contain a "rise" section. It seems noteworthy that at least at least one of the creation stories songs that DuBois transcribed (see Figure 5.B iii. The First *Chaup* song) also does not contain the rise. This raises the question: Might there have been a style of storytelling that involved spoken narration, with inclusions of occasional songs, ones that lacked a rise section, and ones that were delivered with a soft voice, that was used not only throughout the ESCR but in the surrounding regions? Regarding this latter style, might it also have been the case that musical instruments were not used and that the songs were not danced to? The presence or absence of the rise may be just one that factor that future researchers might want to consider. In of itself, it is not a determining factor. For instance, whereas most of the songs in ESCR Yuman song cycles apparently do contain the rise, most of the songs in ESCR Uto-Aztecan song cycles apparently do not. Then there is the question of what type of style of narration did Uto-Aztecan singer/storytellers employ as they told a creation story?

each other, creating a larger whole. In order to understand this, scholars need to approach the music and the stories with a more holistic or inclusive approach, and at every level. When examining the songs, if we focus primarily on their melodies, we are likely to miss the larger picture, for ESCR musicians finely mesh together the elements of melody, with the words, the rhythm of the percussion instruments, and the dance steps. Similarly if listeners make the mistake of only analyzing individual songs, then they may not think to examine the ways in which ESCR singers used sets of songs during a rendition of a creation story, or how singers employ brother songs while singing a song cycle. I have considered two examples of song sets. As demonstrated in my analysis of a set of songs from Halpern's transcription of *Lighting*, the singer is able to convey an almost transcendent quality as he variously describes the appearance and the movement of the stars in the sky. I also attempted to reconstruct what may be a set of songs from Kroeber's transcription of *Deer*. Here a set of songs is used to describe a series of actions, as they unfold, step by step, thereby depicting the actions of a lion as it moves closer and closer to his prey. Thus it certainly appears that ESCR singer/storytellers were able to complement a story with sets of songs. It seems likely that further explorations of the interplay between the spoken segments and the songs will lead to a greater understanding of the art form that ESCR singers developed and continue to develop.

APPENDICES

Appendix 1: Pronunciation Guides.

The following Alphabets, one for 'Iipay and Tiipay, and the following one for Quechan, were created by Amy Miller. The 'Iipay and Tiipay alphabet and pronunciation guide have been extracted from "Dictionary Notes" in Amy Miller's and Margaret Langdon's *Barona Inter-Tribal Dictionary: 'Iipay Aa Tiipay Aa Umall* (Lakeside: Barona Museum Press. 2008). The Quechan Alphabet was extracted from Miller's introduction to the forthcoming book *Xiipúktan (First of All): Three Views of the Origins of the Quechan People, Told or Retold in the Quechan language by George Bryant*, by George Bryant, edited by Amy Miller.

'Iipay and Tiipay Alphabet

'Iipay and Tiipay[1] have slightly different sound systems. The sound *q* is distinctive in 'Iipay but not in Tiipay; *r* is found in native words in 'Iipay but not in Tiipay, and *o, oo,* and *v* are found in native words in 'Iipay, but occur only in borrowed words in Tiipay. A unified writing system is used here to represent both languages (with differences in distribution and pronunciation noted below), but one orthographic difference has been maintained: in 'Iipay words, the voiceless velar fricative /x/ is written *h* and its labialized counterpart /x/ is written *hw*, while in Tiipay words the same sounds are written *x* and *xw*.

a	As in Spanish *mañana*. For southern speakers, *a* may be influenced by neighboring sounds; for instance, when followed by *y* or *ny* it becomes more like the *a* in *say*.
aa	Like the *aa* in *father*, but held for a longer time.
b	Like the *b* in *about*. This sound is found primarily in borrowed words but also in one native word, *nyimbi* 'anyhow, anyway'.
ch	This sound is typically pronounced like the *ch* in *mischief*. In southern languages, a *ch* at the end of a word may be pronounced with a *ty* sound like that found the British pronunciation of *tune*, while a *ch* which occurs in a suffix may be softened until it is somewhere between the *ch* in *mischief* and the *dy* sound in *would you*.
d	Like Spanish *d*, this sound is somewhere between the *d* in *door* and the *th* in *them*. This sound is found in borrowed words.
e	This sound is known as "schwa". It is usually pronounced like the *e* in *government*, but its pronunciation may be influenced by neighboring sounds; for instance, before *y* or *ny* it could be pronounced like *i*, and before *hw* or *xw* it could be pronounced like *u*. Variable pronunciation is one thing that makes this sound

---

[1] See Miller's comment in footnote 4, chapter 1.

special; another is the fact that it may disappear when the word is prefixed or, in some cases, even in variants of the unprefixed form.

é *or* **è** Like the *e* in *pet*. This sound is found only in borrowed words. In accented syllables it is written *é* and in unaccented syllables it is written *è*.

ée *or* **èe** Like the *e* in *bed* but held for a longer time. This sound is found only in borrowed words. It is written *ée* in accented syllables and *èe* in unaccented syllables.

f As in *five*. This sound is found in borrowed words.

g As in *again*. This sound is found in borrowed words.

h Like the *j* in Spanish *frijoles*. This spelling is found in 'Iipay and Los Conejos speech.

hw The same as *h* but made with rounded lips. The resulting sound is similar to the *ju* in Spanish *Tijuana*. This spelling is found in 'Iipay and Los Conejos speech.

i Like the *i* in *spit*.

ii This sound is usually pronounced like the *i* in *petite* but held for a longer time. When *ii* is followed by *y* or *ch*, some northern speakers pronounce it like the *ai* in *pair*.

k Like the *k* in *skip*. In southern speech, when a suffix begins with *k*, that *k* may be softened until it is similar to *g*.

kw Like the *qu* in *square*.

l Like the *l* in *light*. This sound is made with the tongue near the upper teeth.

ll This sound is not found in English. Put your tongue in position to say *l*, and blow air out without vibrating your vocal cords.

lly This is another sound not found in English. Put your tongue in position to say *ly*, and blow air out without vibrating your vocal cords.

ly Like the *lli* in *million*. This sound is made with the tongue against the lower teeth.

m As in *mother*.

n Like Spanish *n*, as in *Tijuana*. The tip of the tongue touches the upper teeth.

ng Like the *ng* in *sing*. This sound is found in borrowed words.

nn This sound is like *n* but made with the tip of the tongue against the ridge behind the upper teeth. This sound is found in native words but it is rare.

ny Like Spanish *ñ*, as in *mañana*.

o Like Spanish *o*, as in *bonito*. This sound is found in both native and borrowed words in the northern languages; in southern languages it is found only in borrowed words.

oo Like the *aw* in *law*, but held for a longer time. In northern languages, this sound is found in both native and borrowed words; in southern languages it is found only in borrowed words.

p As in *spin*. In Tiipay and Los Conejos, when a suffix begins with *p*, that *p* may be softened until it is somewhere between the *p* in *spin* and the *b* in *about*.

q This sound is similar to *k* but pronounced farther back in the mouth. This sound is found in 'Iipay.

r Like English *r*, as in *rare*. This sound is found in 'Iipay and in Los Conejos.

rr	Like Spanish *r*. At the beginning of the word is like *r* as in *rojo* and elsewhere it varies between *r* as in *rojo* and *r* as in *cara*.
s	This sound, similar to English *s*, is made with the tip of the tongue against the upper teeth.
sh	This is a whistling sound made with the tip of the tongue against the ridge behind the upper teeth.
t	Like Spanish *t*, as in *tío*. The tip of the tongue touches the upper teeth.
tt	Like English *t* as in *stay*. The tip of the tongue touches the ridge behind the upper teeth.
u	Somewhere between the *u* in *put* and the *u* in *flute*.
uu	Usually pronounced like the *u* in *Susan* but held for a longer time. In southern languages, when it occurs between a non-palatal consonant and *y* (in either order), accented *uu* is pronounced like the *o* in *boy* but held for a longer time.
v	In the 1970s at Barona, this sound was pronounced "somewhat between the sounds of English *v* and *b*" and was found in suffixes, borrowed words, and the native word *nyímvey* 'anyhow, anyway'. Today, *v* is pronounced like the *v* in *every*. 'Iipay speakers still use *v* in suffixes and in a few native words. Speakers from all areas use *v* in borrowed words.
w	As in *war* or *now*.
x	Like the *j* in the Spanish word *frijoles*. This spelling is found in Tiipay.
xw	The same as *x* but made with rounded lips. The resulting sound is something like The *ju* in the Spanish word *Tijuana*. This spelling is found in Tiipay.
y	as in *yes*.
'	This represents a brief silence, such as the one that separates the syllables of the English negative word *uh-uh*. It is made by closing the vocal cords.

Each of the symbols above – regardless of whether it is composed of one letter, two letters, or three letters – represents a single sound. When a sequence of symbols might otherwise be confused with a multi-letter symbol, we use a hyphen to separate the sequential symbols. For instance, if a word contains the sound *s* followed by the sound *h*; we write a hyphen between the *s* and the *h* so that the *s-h* sequence will not be confused with the symbol *sh*. Thus 'I scratch' is written *'es-hwall*. Likewise, a hyphen is used to separate a sequence of *tt* followed by *t* in the word *matt-taay* 'tree squirrel'; a hyphen is used to separate a sequence of similar vowels such as that in *aa-ap* 'he puts or sets something down; he throws it; he drops it'.

Pronunciation tips: (1) Most words are accented on the final syllable. There are a few exceptions, and in these cases an acute accent (the symbol ´ written over a vowel) is used to indicate the accented syllable. (2) When a vowel is followed by *y* or *w*, pronounce the two sounds in sequence; do not combine them as we do in English. (3) When *t* is followed by *h*, pronounce the two sounds separately, do not combine them as we do in English.

Quechan Alphabet

á, à	Like the *a* in *about*
aa	A longer sound, like the *a* in *father*
a	This *a*, written without an accent, represents "schwa," a special vowel whose pronunciation depends upon the sounds which surround it, as discussed below, and which may disappear when prefixes are added to the word
Æ	This vowel represents schwa in post-stress position, where it sounds like the *e* in *government*
e	Like the *e* in *pet*
ee	The same sound, only held for a longer time. In certain contexts (for example, following *th*, *sh*, or *ny*), *ee* is lowered and sounds almost like the *a* in *cat*.
i	Like the *i* in *pit*
ii	Like the *i* in *machine*, only held for a longer time
k	Like the *k* in *sky*
kw	The same sound, but made with rounded lips. It sounds like the *kw* in *backward*
ky	Like the *ky* in *backyard*
l	Like the *l* in *light*
lly	To make this sound, put your tongue in position to say *ly*, then blow air out so that it goes around the sides of your tongue.
ly	Like the *lli* in *million*. This sound is made with the tip of the tongue touching the lower teeth
m	Like the *m* in *mom*
n	Like Spanish *n*, as in *bonito*
ng	Like the *ng* in *sing*. This sound is found in few spoken words but many song words.
ny	Like the *ny* in *canyon*
o	Like the *o* in *pot*
oo	The same sound, only held for a longer time
p	Like the *p* in *spin*
q	A sound similar to *k* but pronounced farther back in the mouth
qw	The same sound, but made with rounded lips.
r	A slightly trilled *r*, similar to the *r* in the Spanish pronunciation of *Maria*.
s	Like Spanish *s*, as in *peso*
sh	This is not like English *sh*; instead, it is a whistling sound made with the tip of the tongue at the roots of the teeth and slightly curled back.
t	Like Spanish *t*, as in *bonito*. Made with the tongue touching the upper front teeth, or even between the front teeth.
th	Like the *th* in *this*
ts	Like the *ts* in *lots*
tt	Like English *t*, as in *stun*. Made with the tongue touching the roots of the upper front teeth.
ty	Like the *ty* in the expression *got ya!*.
u	Like the *u* in *put*

uu	Like the *u* in *rule*, only held for a longer time
v	Like the *v* in *very*
w	Like the *w* in *wet*
x	Like the *ch* in German *ach*, or like Spanish *j* as in *jota*
xw	The same sound, but made with rounded lips
y	Like the *y* in *yes*
'	This sound, known as "glottal stop", is actually a brief period of silence made by closing the vocal cords. It is found in the English expressions *uh-uh* and *uh-oh*.

Abbreviations:

K – suffix that follows predicates, exact meaning in this context is uncertain

SJ– subject case marker

SS – same subject

Appendix 2: Evidence from DuBois's Song Sheets

The observations that DuBois offered in the above quotation[2] can be further explored by considering her packet of song sheets and musical transcriptions. Based on what DuBois wrote, it appears each of Antonio's songs were brief and possibly consisted of the repetition of only a few words. DuBois's songs sheets, on the other hand, may contain all or many of the repetitions of the words that Antonio Duro sang for each song. Consider, for example, DuBois's song sheet for "The flute is making music to call the girls" (in Figure 5.B-i). The song sheet contains seventeen lines of text. However the songs consists of relatively few words, but there is what appears to be a certain amount of systematic variation (see Figure 5.B-ii). The text is based on two phrases. One phrase consists of the words *ich-ta-ha,* which is restated but in variation, as *kwa-ta-ha.* Here, *kwa* has been substituted for the initial syllable *ich.* To represent the difference between these two words, I label them as *ich-ta-ha (A)* and *kwa-ta-ha (B).* A second phrase is based on the words, *To-le, o-to-le, ko-te-le,* labeled as *C.* As shown in DuBois's song

---

[2] See the quotation, at the end of Chapter 3.

sheet (Figure 5.B-i), the song opens with two repetitions of *Ich-ta-ha, kwa-ta-ha (A + B)*. This is followed by the introduction of *To-le, o-to-le, ko-te-le (C)*. I have arranged the lines differently, to show that the song has three lines. Each of lines contains *(A + B^x) +* *(A + B)* and *C + C* (Figure 5.B-ii). The variation in these lines occurs in *B^x*. DuBois writes the first iteration as *kwa-ta-ha (B)*. In line 2, *B^x* appears in variation, now as *ko-to-ho (B)'*. In the third line, *B^x* is varied again, now as *ko-lo-ho (B'')*.

```
   No. 1, 1st Chaup song. "The flute is making music
   to call the girls."

 1    Ich-tá-há                    Even emphasis but some
 2  Kwa-tá-há                      extra stress on last.
 3    Ich-tá-há
 4  Kwa-tá-há

 5  To-lé ot-to-lé ko-te-lé        Accent on "le" but "o"
 6    To-lé ot-to-lé ko-te-lé      and "ko" long drawn and
                                   almost double.
 7    Ich-tá-há
 8  Kwa-tá-há
 9    Ich-tá-há
10  Kwa-tá-há

11  To-lé ot-to-lé ko-te-lé
12  to-lé ot-to-lé ko-te-lé

13    Ich-tá-há
14  Kwa-tá-há
15    Ich-tá-há
16  Kwa-tá-há

17  To-lé ot-to-lé ko-te-lé
18                             etc repeated
```

English spelling, but "a" as in "ah".

Figure 5.B-i. "The flute is calling the girls," a song sheet.
*This is a semi-diplomatic transcripion. In the original, the lines are not numbered and the sections in italics are in cursive writing.

Figure 5.B-ii. "The flute is making music to call the girls."

1.	Ich-ta-ha,	kwa-ta-ha,	ich-ta-ha,	kwa-ta-ha,	to-le, o-to-le, ko-te-le,	to-le, o-to-le, ko-te-le.
	A +	*B*	*A* +	*B*	*C*	*C*
2.	*ich-ta-ha*	*ko-to-ho,*	*ich-ta-ha,*	*kwa-ta-ha,*	*to-le, o-to-le, ko-te-le,*	*to-le, o-to-le, ko-te-le.*
	A +	*B'*	*A* +	*B*	*C*	*C*
3.	*ich-ta-ha*	*ko-lo-ho,*	*ich-ta-ha,*	*kwa-ta-ha,*	*to-le, o-to-le, ko-te-le,*	*to-le, o-to-le, ko-te-le.*
	A +	*B''*	*A* +	*B*	*C*	*C*

The flute is making music to call the girls.

DuBois also made a musical transcription of this song, but in her transcription she did not follow the order of the text shown in her song sheet, possibly suggesting that she had made her musical transcription at a different time. In her musical transcription, DuBois also spelled some of the words differently. I copied out and rearranged it to show the repetition of the words: *Ich-ta-ha, kwa-ta-ha (A + B)* and of *To-le, o-to-le, ko-te-le (C)* (in Figure 5.B-iii). The systematic variation of B^x, as seen in her song sheet, is not present. The words in each line are the same, except for one minor variation. Her musical transcription begins with two repetitions of *To-le, o-to-le, ko-te-le (C)*. This is followed by two repetitions of *A + B, Ich-ta-la, kwa-ta-ha.* (When this is repeated, instead of *Ich-ta-la*, the first word is *Ich-ta-wa*.) Thus, her musical transcription shows this song as involving no systematic variation; instead, a performance consisted of an initial line that was repeated twice.

The question remains, however, whether the information contained in the packet can enrich our understanding of any of the creation story texts that DuBois published, such as her *Story of Chaup?* Figure 5.B-iv shows the five Chaup songs contained in the packet and the corresponding passages for each in SOC.

Most of the songs in the packet can be matched to some point in the story, as elucidated in SOC. The first song from the packet contains the descriptive title, "The flute is making music to call the girls." This song is based on the words, *Ich-ta-ha, kwa-ta-ha* and *To-le o-to-le, ko-te-le.* Figure 5.B-v shows the corresponding episode, in SOC. As can be seen, in SOC DuBois has included three songs in which the boys play their flutes, hoping to attract the attention of girls. First, they turn to the north; the corresponding song is *We-le-wah-cha-a-tal*, etc. Next, they turn to the south. The song is *Ha-ma-ko-lu, ha-ma-we-le*; and DuBois notes that Antonio Duro and his audience clapped their hands along with the song. Then, the boys turned and faced to the west. After speaking, Duro sang this song, *Ha-ka-so-lu, ha-ma-we, ha-ma-ko-lu, ha-ma-we-le-we, ha-ma-cha*. Lastly, the boys faced to the east. DuBois does not provide the words for the song that presumably followed. The texts for the preceding three songs (when the boys faced to the north and sang, then the south, and then the east) do not match the flute song from the packet, namely *Ich-ta-ha, kwa-ta-ha* and *To-le o-to-le, ko-te-le*. Based on its text, the flute song shown in Figure 5.B-iii was not included in SOC.

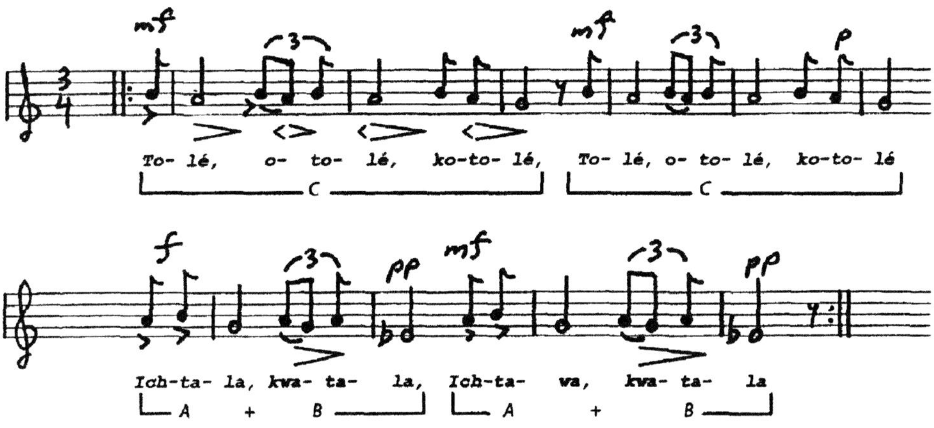

Figure 5.B-iii. The First *Chaup* song. The flute is making music to call the girls.[3]

---

[3] DuBois's transcription is difficult to read, so I have re-notated it. Her tempo marking is *allegretto*.

	From DuBois's packet	In SOC[4]
1. Flute song, rst:	The flute is making music to call the girls	For the flute songs, see p. 72. Also, see Figure 3.D-vi.
2. Girls' farewell:[5]	(no explanation given.)	So they went away one day towards where the boys lived, and from far away they looked back and saw their old home and sang a song of farewell, p. 72
3. Flute song, second:	The mother of Chaup calls the girls from the East to come and marry her songs.	Not in SOC, closest is on p. 73-4
4. Elder brother's song:	We shall die for the sake of the girls. I shall never see my home again.	"We will die for the sake of the girls," said the older ..." p. 75
5. Grandmother's song:	The younger Chaup returning to his blind old grandmother, sits on her lap, and she puts her arms around him and they both cry. Antonio feels like crying when he sings it.	...He came to her but she could not see him. She was blind. He sat on her lap, and she put her arms around him, and they both cried..." SOC, p. 78.

Figure 5.B-iv. Songs by Antonio Duro, in the packet of songs.

Even though *Ich-ta-ha, kwa-ta-ha* is not contained in SOC, DuBois's paraphrase

for its meaning, "The flute is making music to call the girls," suggests that there is a

straightforward connection between the meaning of each song and the corresponding

place in the story. At the same time, since each of the other flute songs has unique

words, it seems likely that each of their meanings differed, at least somewhat. Still, each

song probably refers to flute music, in some fashion. Based on the English translation

that DuBois gives for each song, it seems possible that these flute songs belonged to a set.

---

[4] The page numbers in this column are from SOC, in Laylander's *Listening*.
[5] This is the title that DuBois gave to one of her musical transcriptions. There is no corresponding song sheet.

When they brought it to their mother she was very glad, and she chopped the wood up fine, and took the pieces and put them out in the sung to dry. And the pieces of wood as she touched them made sweet music.

Song: Kwa-la-ha-le, etc.

Then the old woman decorated the pieces with the colored feathers of woodpeckers and the topknots of quails, and made them into flutes for her songs to play on.
Song: We-le-wa-cha-a-cha-a-cha, etc.

So they the brothers sat down facing the north, and played on the flutes such sweet music that the girls from the north came to them, attracted by the sound; but the boys did not like girls from the north
Song: We-le-wah-cha-a-tal, etc.

So they sat down facing the south, and played the same music so loud and so sweet that the girls from the south came to hear it, but they did not like them either, because they ate rats, snakes, and such animals as that, and their bodies did not smell good.
Song: Ha-ma-ko-lu, Ha-ma-we-le
(Singer and Indian audience clapped hands in time.)

So they sat down toward the west, and played the beautiful music again, until the girls from the west came to them, but they did not like them, because they ate all animals that live in the ocean.
Song: Ha-ka-so-lu, Ha-ma-we, Ha-ma-ko-lu, Ha-ma-we-le-we, Ha-ma-cha.

But when they played the sweet music facing the east, some girls came from there, the daughters of Ithchin, the buzzard, and they liked them because they lived on the fruit that grows in the east and they smelled sweet.

Figure 5.B-v. The boys play their flutes, excerpt from SOC.[6]

The "Girls' Farewell song" (song 2, Figure 5.B-iv) appears to be associated with an episode one that occurs after the boys play their flutes to attract girls. After the girls meet the boys, the girls are suddenly back at home. Eventually they decide to go and live with the boys.[7] It is at this point that they sing a farewell song, probably addressed to their father. As shown in SOC, they sing, Kai-o-ñe, Ma-ha-qui-po-ke, etc. No translation

---

[6] See *Listening,* 72.
[7] Ibid., 72.

is given.[8] In her packet, DuBois did <u>not</u> include a song sheet, but she did include a musical transcription that includes a song titled "Girls' song of Farewell." Again, the content of the song matches that of the story. In the packet, there is still another flute song, this one entitled "2nd song of flute. The mother of Chaup calls the girls from the East to come and marry her songs." This appears to be an instance where the song sheet contains a reference to a portion of the story that is not contained in SOC. In SOC, the mother does not welcome the girls; but seems to challenge them. In addition, she has instructed the boys to "not allow themselves to care for" the girls. The older brother behaves accordingly. It is therefore not surprising that the girls return home after only one night. At this point, DuBois shows Antonio Duro as having sung two songs; but she does not provide the words.

After the girls leave, the boys eventually decide to travel to the home of the girls. Upon their arrival, the younger brother transforms himself into a Chaup. He then soars through the air, in order to reach the home of the girls. Frightened , the elder brother's sings, "We will die for the sake of the girls." An excerpt taken from the corresponding passage in SOC, is shown in Figure 5.B-vi. The excerpt contains three songs, with words in Kumeyaay. As shown, the second and the third songs have the very similar words. They differ in that the second syllable of song 1 is *mai*. In contrast, in songs 2-3, the second syllable is *che* (see Figure 5.B-vii). The packet contains a single song that corresponds to this part of the story (Figure 5.B-viii). In the packet, the descriptive title to this song is, "Elder brother's songs. 'We shall died for the sake of the girls. I shall

---

[8] See SOC, in Laylander, *Listening,* 72.

never see my home again." The words to this song are very similar to the second and

third songs contained in SOC, for this passage. In the packet, each line of the

corresponding song ends with the syllables, *kom-whe-e-e,* corresponding with the last

syllables *kom-whi-i-i* in the three SOC songs, suggesting a match. There are more

similarities, as shown in Figure 5.B-ix, wherein the syllables of song 2, from SOC, are

compared with the corresponding one from the packet.

From there they travelled till they came to the top of a high mountain, and the elder came first to the top and sat down, and then the younger came, and they watched the people in the valley. [There] a large crowd was playing a game of ball.

"Look at all those people," said the older. "How are we going to be able to get to the place in safety?"

So the younger stood up and held up his hands to the sky, and got a lot of stars and put them all over his body. And his brother did the same, and they sat down and were watching the people. They were shining like stars.
Song: Ha-mai-nau-e-chak-om-whi-i-i, etc.

They rose as if they had wings, and flew over to where they wanted to go.
Song: Ha-che-nau-e-cha-kom-whi-i-i, etc.

"I am going to fly to the girls house," said the younger. "Watch me very closely and you will see where I go in among the crowds of people."

"We will die for the sake of the girls," said the older. "And we shall never see out home again."

The older watched his brother and saw him fly towards the houses in the midst of all the people. Among all the houses he did not know where to go; but he came to one of the houses where there was a crowd of people about it, and the rook opened and he went in shining like a star. As he flew over their head the people looked up and saw the Chaup. They wanted to catch him, but they could not. The father of the girls was there, and he told the people not to catch him, and that was wa not a start but a person. When the roof opened he went into the house, and there he found his wife.

Song: Ha-che-nau-e-cha-kom-whi-i-i, etc.

Figure 5.B-vi. The brother are transformed into Chaups, in SOC.

1. Ha-<u>mai</u>-nau-e-cha-kom-whi-i-i, etc.
2. Ha-<u>che</u>-nau-e-cha-kom-whi-i-i, etc.
3. Ha-<u>che</u>-nau-e-cha-kom-whi-i-i, etc.

Figure 5.B-vii. Flying songs, in SOC.

Ce-nan-can-kom-whe-e-e
Ce-nan-can-kom-whe-e-e
   (Words repeat indefinitely but time varies at times.)

Mi-na-cha-kom-whe-e-e
Ka-mi-na-kom-whe-e-e
   (Words repeat, tune varies)

Figure 5.B-viii. Elder brother song, in the packet.

In SOC	*Ha-*	*che-*	*-nau-*	*e-*	*cha-*	*kom-*	*whi-*	*i-*	*i*
	↓	↓		↓	↓	↓	↓	↓	↓
In the packet	*Ce-*	*nan-*	-	*can-*	*kom-*	*whe-*	*e-*	*e*	

Figure 5.B-ix. The elder brother song.

BIBLIOGRAPHY

Archival Sources

Ruth Fulton Benedict Papers. Vassar College Library.

The Edward Harvey Davis Papers. San Diego Historical Society.

Constance Goddard DuBois Papers, 1897-1909. Division of Rare and Manuscript Collections, Cornell University Library. http://rmc.library.cornell.edu/ EAD/htmldocs/RMM09167.html (accessed on July 8, 2009).

George Herzog Papers. Archives of Traditional Music, Indiana University.

Lorraine Miller Sherer Papers, ca. 1860-1980. Special Collections. Young Research Library. University of California, Los Angeles.

Underhill Papers. Bailey Library and Archives, Denver Museum of Nature and Science.

Audio and Video Recordings

Golding, Daniel, director, videography, and film editor. *Journey from Spirit Mountain.* DVD. Produced by the Ah-Mut Foundation in association with the Hokan Media Productions, 2007.

Densmore, Francis. *Songs of the Yuma, Yaqui, Cocopa: From the Archive of Folk Song.* Long Playing Vinyl Disc. Folk Music of the United States (Washington, D.C. : Library of Congress, Division of Music, Recording Laboratory, 1951).

DuBois, Constance. "United States, California, Diegueño Indians, ca. 1905." Performers: José Trinidad, Laguna Jim, Ha-ta-kek, and other unidentified musicians. Archives of Traditional Music, Indiana University. Accession number, 54-113-F. Audio recordings.

⸺. "United States, California, Luiseño Indians, 1906." Performers: José Luis Albañez, Salvador Cuevas, Juan de Dios, Margarita Subish, Ha-ta-kek [sic], and Laguna Jim. Archives of Traditional Music, Indiana University. Accession number, 54-123-F. Audio recordings.

Herzog, George. "United States, Arizona and California, Campo Diegueño Indians, 1927." Performer: Kate Coleman. Archives of Traditional Music, Indiana University. Accession number, 54-114-F. Fieldnotes and audio recordings.

⸺. "United States, Arizona and California, Mohave Indians, 1927." Performers: Sitc'o'm'ai [sic] and John Carter, vocals with gourd rattle or basket drum accompaniment Archives of Traditional Music, Indiana University. Fieldnotes and audio recordings. Accession number, 54-124-F.

———. "United States, Arizona, Yuma Indians, 1927." Performer: Frank Hills. Archives of Traditional Music, Indiana University. Accession number, 54-142-F. Fieldnotes and audio recordings. Fieldnotes and audio recordings.

———. "United States, New York, ca. 1937-1938." Performer: Abe Halpern, singing *Lighting.* Archives of Traditional Music, Indiana University. Accession number, 87-043-F. Audio recordings.

Mahone, Keith. *Bird songs of the Hualapai.* CD (Phoenix, Arizona: Canyon Records, 1996).

Siva, Ernest. *Voices of the Flute: Songs of Three Southern California Indian Nations.* CD and booklet. (Banning, California: Ushkana Press, 2004).

Print Sources

Allen, Paula Gunn. "Special Problems in Teaching Leslie Marmon Silko's *Ceremony.*" *American Indian Quarterly* 14, no. 4 (1990): 379-386.

Apodaca, Paul. "Tradition, Myth, and Performance of Cahuilla Bird Songs" (PhD diss., University of California, Los Angeles, 1999).

Applegate, Richard. "The Red, the Black, and the White: Duality and Unity in the Luiseño Cosmos." *Journal of California and Great Basin Anthropology* 1 (1979): 71-88.

Anderson, Kat. "An Ecological Critique," in *Forgotten Fires: Native Americans and the Transient Wilderness,* Henry T. Lewis and Kat Anderson, eds. (Norman: University of Oklahoma Press, 2002).

———. *Tending the Wild: Native American Knowledge and the Management of California's Natural Resources* (Berkeley, California: University of California Press, 2005).

Arom, Simha. *African Polyphony and Polyrhythm: Musical Structure and Methodology* (Cambridge: Cambridge University Press, 1991).

Arrowweed, Preston Jefferson. *Whirlwind Warrior* (Imperial, California: Imperial Valley College Desert Museum Society, 2001).

Aunger, Robert. "On Ethnography: Storytelling or Science?" *Current Anthropology* 36, no. 1 (1995): 97.

Bean, Lowell. *Mukat's People: The Cahuilla Indians of Southern California* (Berkeley, California: University of California Press, 1972).

Beaudry, Nicole. "Toward Transcription and Analysis of Inuit Throat-Games: Macro-Structure." *Ethnomusicology* 22, no.2 (1978): 261-274.

Bettinger, Robert. "Aboriginal Occupation at High Altitude: Alpine Villages in the White Mountains of Eastern California." *American Anthropologist*, New Series, 93, no. 3 (September, 1991): 656-679.

————. "Native Land Use: Archaeology and Anthropology," *Natural History of the White-Inyo Range: Eastern California,* Clarence A. Hall, Jr., ed. (Berkeley, California: The Regents of the University of California, 1991), 463-487.

Bettinger, Robert and Martin A. Baumhoff. "The Numic Spread: Great Basin Cultures in Competition." *American Antiquity* 47, no. 3 (July, 1982): 485-503.

Briggs, C. L. *Learning How to Ask : A Sociolinquistic Appraisal of the Role of the Interview in Social Science Research.* (Cambridge: Cambridge University Press, 1986).

Bryant, George. *Xiipúktan (First of All): Three Views of the Origins of the Quechan People, Told or Retold in the Quechan language by George Bryant.* Amy Miller, ed. Forthcoming.

Clifford, James. *The Predicament of Culture, Twentieth-Century Ethnography, Literature, and Art* (Cambridge: Harvard University Press, 1988).

Clifford, James, and George E. Marcus. *Writing Culture: The Poetics and Politics of Ethnography.* A School of American Research Advanced Seminar. (Berkeley: University of California Press, 1986).

Couro, Ted and Margaret Langdon. *Let's Talk 'Iipay Aa: An Introduction to the Mesa Grande Diegueño Language* (Banning, California: Malki Museum Press, 1975).

Couro, Ted, Leanne Hinton, Christina Hutcheson, and Margaret Langdon. *Dictionary of Mesa Grande Diegueño: Iipay Aa-English, English-Iipay Aa* (Banning, California: Malki Museum, Morongo Indian Reservation, 1973).

Crosby, Harry. *Antigua California: Mission and Colony on the Peninsular Frontier, 1697-1768* (Albuquerque, New Mexico: University of New Mexico Press, 1994).

Cuero, Delfina and Florence Shipek. *Delfina Cuero: Her Autobiography, an Account of Her Last Years, and Her Ethnobotanic Contributions* (Menlo Park, California: Ballena Press, 1991).

D'Azevedo, Warren L., volume editor. *Great Basin.* Handbook of North American Indians, Vol. 11, Sturtevant, William C., series editor. (Washington: Smithsonian Institution, 1986).

DeMallie, Raymond J. " 'These Have No Ears:' Narrative and the Ethnohistorical Method." *Ethnohistory* 40, no. 4 (1993): 516-538.

Densmore, Frances. *Yuman and Yaqui Music*. Smithsonian Institution Bureau of American Ethnology 110 (Washington, D.C.: Government Printing Office, 1932).

―――. "The Words of Indian Songs as Unwritten Literature." *The Journal of American Folklore*, 63, no. 250 (October-December,1950): 450-458.

―――. "Music of the Indians in Our Western States." *The Journal of American Folklore* 70, no. 276 (April-June,1957): 176-178.

Devereux, George. "Mohave Soul Concepts." *American Anthropologist* 39, no. 3, part 1 (July-September, 1937): 417-422.

―――. "Mohave Beliefs Concerning Twins." *American Anthropologist* 43, no. 4, part 1 (October- December,1941): 573 -592.

―――. "Mohave Coyote Tales," *The Journal of American Folklore* 61, no. 241 (July-September, 1948): 233-255.

―――. *Mohave Ethnopsychiatry and Suicide: the Psychiatric Knowledge and the Psychic Disturbances of an Indian Tribe* (Washington, D.C.: U.S. Government Printing Office, 1961).

Dowd, Gregory Evans. *A Spirited Resistance: The North American Indian Struggle for Unity, 1745-1815*. The Johns Hopkins University Studies in Historical and Political Science (Baltimore, Maryland: Johns Hopkins University Press, 1992).

DuBois, Constance. *The Condition of the Mission Indians of Southern California* (Philadelphia: Office of the Indian Rights Association, 1901); reprinted in Laylander, *Listening*, 41-49.

―――."The Mythology of the Diegueños." *Journal of American Folklore* 14 (1901): 181-185; reprinted in Laylander, *Listening*, 38-40.

―――."Diegueño Mythology and Religion: The Story of Creation." *Southern Workman* 33 (1904): 100-102; reprinted in Laylander, *Listening*, 79-80.

―――."The Story of Chaup: A Myth of the Diegueños." *Journal of American Folklore* 17 (1904): 181-185; reprinted in Laylander, *Listening*, 66-78.

―――. "Mythology of the Mission Indians." *Journal of American Folklore* 19, no. 72 (1906): 52-60; reprinted in Laylander, *Listening*, 98-109.

————.*The Religion of the Luiseno Indians of Southern California.* University of California Publications in American Archaeology and Ethnology 8 (1908): 69-166; reprinted in Laylander, *Listening,* 120-165.

Elster, Steven. "A Harmonic and Serial Analysis of Ben Johnston's String Quartet No. 6." *Perspectives of New Music* 29, no. 2 (Summer, 1991): 138–165.

Erlmann, Veit. *African Stars: Studies in Black South African Performance.* (Chicago Studies in Ethnomusicology (Chicago, Illinois: University of Chicago Press, 1991).

Fogelson, Raymond D. "The Ethnohistory of Events and Non-events." *Ethnohistory* 36 no. (1989): 133-147

Frank, Ross. "The Changing Pueblo Indian Pottery Tradition: The Underside of Economic Development in Late Colonial New Mexico, 1750-1820." *Journal of the Southwest* 33, no. 3 (Autumn, 1991): 282-321.

————. *From Settler to Citizen: New Mexican Economic Development and the Creation of Vecino Society, 1750-1820.* (Berkeley, California: University of California Press, 2000).

Frisbie, Charlotte. "Vocables in Navajo Ceremonial Music." *Ethnomusicology* 24, no. 3 (September, 1980): 347-392.

Geertz, Clifford. "Deep Play: Notes on the Balinese Cockfight." *Daedalus* 101 (1972): 1-37.

Gifford, Edward and A. L. Kroeber. *Karok Myths,* Grace Buzaljko, ed. (Berkeley: University of California Press, 1980).

Halpern, Abraham M., Amy Miller, and Margaret Langdon. *Kar'uk: Native Accounts of the Quechan Mourning Ceremony.* University of California Publications in Linguistics 128 (Berkeley, California: University of California Press, 1997).

Harrington, J. P. Review of *The Religious Practices of the Diegueño,* by T. T. Waterman. *American Anthropologist* 12 (1910): 329-335

Heidsiek, Ralph. "Music of the Luiseño Indians of Southern California: A Study of Music in Indian culture with Relation to a Program in Music Education." (PhD diss., University of California, Los Angeles, 1966).

Heizer, Robert, volume editor. *California.* Handbook of North American Indians Vol. 8 Sturtevant, William C., series editor. (Washington: Smithsonian Institution, 1978).

Henley, Paul. "Narrative: The Guilty Secret of Ethnographic Documentary?" in *Reflecting Visual Ethnography: Using the Camera in Anthropological Research* 145 (Leiden: CNWS Publications, 2006).

Herzog, George. "The Yuman Musical Style." *Journal of American Folklore* 41, no. 160 (1928): 183-231.

———. review of *Form in Primitive Music. An Analytical and Comparative Study of the Melodic Form of Some Ancient Southern California Indian Songs*, by Helen H. Roberts. In *American Anthropologist* 36, no. 3 (July-September, 1934): 476-478.

———. "A Comparison of Pueblo and Pima Musical Styles." *The Journal of American Folklore* 49, no. 194 (October-December, 1936): 283-417.

Hinton, Leanne. "Vocables in Havasupai Songs," in *Southwestern Indian Ritual Drama*, Charlotte Frisbie, ed. (Albuquerque: University of New Mexico Press, 1980), 275-305.

———. "When Sounds Go Wild: Phonological Change and Syntactic Re-Analysis in Havasupai." *Language* 56, no. 2 (1980): 320-44.

———. "Havasupai Songs: A Linguistic Perspective." (PhD diss. University of California, San Diego, 1977); also published as *Havasupai Songs: A Linguistic Perspective*. Ars Linguistica 6 (Tuebingen: G. Narr, 1984).

———. "Songs Without Words," in *Flutes of Fire: Essays on California Indian Languages* (Berkeley: Heyday Books, 1994), 145-151.

Leanne Hinton and Lucille Watahomigie, eds. *Spirit Mountain: An Anthology of Yuman Story and Song* (Tucson: University of Arizona Press, 1984).

Hoffman, Harlan Lanas, "In the Shadow of the Mountain: The Cahuilla, Serrano, and Cupeño People of the Morongo Indian Reservation, 1885–1934. " (PhD. Diss., University of California, Riverside, 2006).

Hofmann, Charles. "Frances Densmore and the Music of the American Indian." *The Journal of American Folklore* 59, no. 231 (January-March,1946): 45-50.

Howard, James Henri, and Victoria Lindsay Levine. *Choctaw Music and Dance* (Norman: University of Oklahoma Press, 1990).

Jacknis, Ira. "Margaret Mead and Gregory Bateson in Bali: Their Use of Photography and Film." *Cultural Anthropology* 3 (1988): 160-177.

———. "Alfred Kroeber and the Photographic Representations of California Indians." *American Indian Culture and Research Journal* 20, no. 3 (1996).

————. "The First Boasian: Alfred Kroeber and Franz Boas, 1896-1905."*American Anthropologist* 104, no. 2 (June 2002): 520-532.

Jackson, Robert. *Indian Population Decline: The Mission of Northwestern New Spain, 1687-1840* (Albuquerque: University of New Mexico Press, 1993).

Jackson, Robert and Edward Castillo. *Indians, Franciscan, and Spanish Colonization: The Impact of the Mission System on California Indians* (Albuquerque: University of New Mexico Press, 1995).

Jacobson, David. *Reading Ethnography* (Albany: State University of New York Press, 1991).

Keeling, Richard. *Women in North American Indian Music: Six Essays* (Bloomington, Indiana: Society for Ethnomusicology, 1989).

————. *A Guide to Early Field Recordings (1900-1949) at the Lowie Museum of Anthropology.* University of California Publications 6 (Berkeley: University of California Press, 1991).

————. *Cry for Luck: Sacred Song and Speech Among the Yurok, Hupa, and Karok Indians of Northwestern California* (Berkeley: University of California Press, 1992).

————. *North American Indian Music: A Guide to Published Sources and Selected Recordings.* Garland Reference Library of the Humanities 1440 (New York: Garland Publications, 1997).

Koegel, John. *Music in German Immigrant Theater: New York City, 1840-1940* (Rochester, New York: University of Rochester Press, 2009).

Kroeber, Alfred Louis. *Handbook of the Indians of California.* Bureau of the American Ethnology at the Smithsonian Institution. Bulletin 78 (Washington: Government Printing Office, 1925; reprinted by New York: Dover Publications, Inc., 1976).

————. review of *Growing up in New Guinea*, by Margaret Mead. *American Anthropologist* 33, no. 2 (1931): 248-250.

————. "A Karok Orpheus Myth." *Journal of American Folklore* 59, no. 231 (1946): 13-19.

————. "A Yurok War Reminiscence: The Use of Autobiographical Evidence." *Southwestern Journal of Anthropology* 1, no. 3 (1946): 318-332;

————. *Seven Mohave Myths.* Anthropological Records 11, no. 1. (Berkeley, California: University of California Press, 1948).

————. *A Mohave Historical Epic.* Anthropological Records 11, no. 2 (Berkeley, California: University of California Press, 1951).

————. *More Mohave Myths.* Anthropological Records 27 (Berkeley, California: University of California Press, 1972).

————. *Yurok Myths*, Grace Buzaljko, ed. (Berkeley: University of California Press, 1976).

Kroeber, Theodora. *Alfred Kroeber, A Personal Configuration* (Berkeley: University of California Press, 1970).

————. "Foreword," in Gifford and A.L. Kroeber, *Karok Myths*, xv-xxx.

————. "Preface," in A.L. Kroeber, *More Mohave Myths.*

Kurath, Gertrude. "Native Choreographic Areas of North America." *American Anthropologist* 55, no. 1 (January-March,1953): 60-73.

————. "A Basic Vocabulary for Ethnic Dance Descriptions." *American Anthropologist* 56, no. 6, part 1 (December, 1954): 1102-1103.

Kwiatkowska, Barbara. "The Present State of Musical Culture Among the Diegueño Indians from San Diego County." (PhD diss., University of California at Los Angeles, 1981).

Laylander, Don. *Listening to the Raven: The Southern California Ethnography of Constance Goddard DuBois.* Archives of California Prehistory. no. 51 (Salinas, California: Coyote Press, 2004).

Langness, L. L., and Gelya Frank. *Lives: An Anthropological Approach to Biography.* (Novato, Calif: Chandler & Sharp, 1981).

Leap, William. *American Indian English* (Salt Lake City, Utah: University of Utah Press, 1993).

Lévi-Strauss, Claude. *The Savage Mind* (Chicago: University of Chicago Press, 1966).

————. *The Raw and the Cooked.* (New York: Harper & Row, 1969).

Levine, Victoria Lindsay. "Choctaw Indian Musical Cultures in the Twentieth Century." (PhD diss., University of Illinois, Urbana-Champaign, 1990).

————. "Musical Revitalization Among the Choctaw." *American Music* 11, no. 4 (1993): 391-411.

———. "Arzelie Langley and a Lost Pantribal Tradition." *Ethnomusicology and Modern Music History* (1993): 190-206.

———. *Writing American Indian Music: Historic Transcriptions, Notations, and Arrangements.* (Middleton, Wisconsin: Published for the American Musicological Society by A-R Editions, 2002).

Long, Frederick Alexander. " 'The Kingdom Must Come Soon': The Role of A. L. Kroeber and the Hearst Survey in Shaping California Anthropology, 1901-1920" (master's thesis, Simon Frazer University, 1998).

Mead, Margaret. *Growing Up in New Guinea, A Comparative Study of Primitive Education* (New York, William Morrow, 1930).

———. "Visual Anthropology in a Discipline of Words." in *Principles of Visual Anthropology.* World Anthropology (The Hague: Mouton, 1975).

Merrell, James H. *The Indians' New World: Catawbas and Their Neighbors from European Contact Through the Era of Removal* (New York: W.W. Norton and Company, 1991).

Michelsen, Ralph. "Peon: A North American Indian Game of Strategy." (PhD diss., University of California, Irvine, 1981).

Miller, Amy. *A Grammar of Jamul Tiipay.* Mouton Grammar Library 23 (Hawthorne, New York: Mouton de Gruyter, 2001).

———. "Dictionary Notes," in *Barona Inter-Tribal Dictionary: 'Iipay Aa Tiipay Aa Umall,* Amy and Margaret Langdon, eds. (Lakeside: Barona Museum Press, 2008).

Miskwish, Michael Connolly. *Kumeyaay: A History Book.* (El Cajon, California: Sycuan Press, 2007).

Munro, Pamela, Nellie Brown, and Judith G. Crawford. *A Mojave Dictionary.* UCLA Occasional Papers in Linguistics. no. 10 (Los Angeles: Department of Linguistics, University of California, 1992).

Nettl, Bruno. "Stylistic Variety in North American Indian Music." *Journal of the American Musicological Society* 6, no. 2 (Summer, 1953): 160-168.

———. "North American Indian Musical Styles." *The Journal of American Folklore* 67, no. 266 (October-December, 1954): 351-368.

———. "Notes on Musical Areas." *Acta Musicologica,* 30, Fasc. 3 (1958): 170-177.

————. "Polyphony in North American Indian Music." *The Musical Quarterly* 47, no. 3 (July, 1961): 354-362.

————. "Speculations on Musical Style and Musical Content in Acculturation." Acta Musicologica 35, Fasc. 1 (January-March, 1963): 35-37.

————. "Comparison and Comparative Method in Ethnomusicology." *Anuario Interamericano de Investigacion Musical* 9 (1973): 148-161.

Ortiz, Alfonso, volume editor. Southwest. Handbook of North American Indians, Vol. 9 Sturtevant, William C., series editor. (Washington: Smithsonian Institution, 1979).

Parezo, Nancy J. *Hidden Scholars Women Anthropologists and the Native American Southwest.* (Albuquerque: University of New Mexico Press, 1993).

Phillips, G. H. *Chiefs and Challengers: Indian Resistance and Cooperation in Southern California* (Berkeley, California: University of California Press, 1975).

————. *Indians and Intruders in Central California, 1769-1849* (Norman: University of Oklahoma Press, 1993).

————. *Indians and Indian Agents: The Origins of the Reservation System in California, 1849-1852* (Norman, University of Oklahoma Press, 1997).

Randall, Frederika. "Why Scholars Become Storytelllers," The New York Times, January 29, 1984. http://query.nytimes.com/gst/fullpage.html?res= 9D0CE6DB163 BF93AA15752C0A962948260 (accessed on March 6, 2010).

Roberts, Helen H. *Form in Primitive Music An Analytical and Comparative Study of the Melodic Form of Some Ancient Southern California Indian Songs* (New York: American Library of Musicology, 1933).

————. "Musical Styles in Aboriginal North America." *Bulletin of the American Musicological Society* no. 2 (June, 1937): 2-3.

Rodriguez, Sylvia. "Art, Tourism, and Race Relations in Taos: Toward a Sociology of the Art Colony." *Journal of Anthropological Research* 45, no. 1 (1989): 77-99.

Rodriguez, Sylvia. "The Taos Pueblo Matachines: Ritual Symbolism and Interethnic Relations." *American Ethnologist* 18, no. 2 (1991): 234-256.

Sangren, Steven P. "Rhetoric and the Authority of Ethnography: 'Postmodernism' and the Social Reproduction of Texts." Current Anthropology 29, no. 3 (June,1988): 405-435.

―――. "Anthropology of Anthropology? Further Reflections on Reflexivity." Anthropology Today 23, no. 4 (August 2007): 13-16.

Sapir, Edward. "Song Recitative in Paiute Mythology." *The Journal of American Folklore* 23, no. 90 (October-December,1910): 455-472.

―――. *Southern Paiute and Ute Linguistics and Ethnography,* William Bright, ed. The Collected Works of Edward Sapir. Vol. 10 (Hawthorne, New York: Mouton de Gruyter, 1992).

―――. "Kaibab Paiute and Northern Ute Ethnographic Field Notes." Reprinted in Sapir, *Southern Paiute and Ute Linguistics and Ethnography.* The Collected Works of Edward Sapir. Vol. 10.

―――. *Culture.* Darnell, Regna, Judith Irvine, and Richard Handler, eds. The Collected Works of Edward Sapir. Vol. 3 (Berlin: Mouton de Gruyter, 1999).

―――. "The Mourning Ceremony of the Southern Paiutes." Reprinted in Sapir, *Culture.* The Collected Works of Edward Sapir. Vol. 3.

Seeger, Charles. "Prescriptive and Descriptive Music-Writing." *The Musical Quarterly* 44, no.2 (1958): 184-195.

Silko, Leslie Marmon. "Language and Literature from a Pueblo Indian Perspective.," in *Critical Fictions: The Politics of Imaginative Writing.* Philomena Mariani, ed. (Seattle: Bay Press, 1991) 83-93.

Sherer, Lorraine. *The Clan System of the Fort Mojave Indians* (Los Angeles: Historical Society of Southern California, 1965).

Shipek, Florence. "A Native American Adaptation to Drought: The Kumeyaay as Seen in the San Diego Mission Records 1770-1798." *Ethnohistory* 28, no. 4 (Autumn, 1981): 295-312

―――. *Pushed into the Rocks: Southern California Indian Land Tenure, 1769-1986* (Lincoln: University of Nebraska Press, 1988)

Smith, Kalim. *Language Ideology and Hegemony in the Kumeyaay Nation: Returning the Linguistic Gaze* (master's thesis, University of California, San Diego, 2005).

Smith, Sherry L. *Reimagining Indians: Native Americans Through Anglo Eyes, 1880-1940* (Oxford: Oxford University, 2000).

Spier, Leslie. *Yuman Tribes of the Gila River* (Chicago: University of Chicago Press, 1933).

Spott, Robert and A. L. Kroeber. *Yurok Narratives.* University of California Publications in American Archeology 35, no. 9 (1942): 143-256

Staub, Michael E. "(Re)Collecting the Past: Writing Native American Speech." *American Quarterly* 43, no. 3 (1991): 425-456.

Stocking, George W. *Observers Observed: Essays on Ethnographic Fieldwork.* History of Anthropology 1 (Madison, Wisconsin: University of Wisconsin Press, 1983).

Strong, Duncan. *Aboriginal Society in Southern California.* University of California Publications in American Archaeology and Ethnology 26 (Berkeley, University of California Press, 1929; Reprinted by Banning, California: Malki Museum, Inc, 1987).

Swann, Brian, ed. *On the Translation of Native American Literatures.* (Washington: Smithsonian Institution Press, 1992).

Sweet, Jill D. *Dances of the Tewa Pueblo Indians: Expressions of New Life* (Santa Fe, New Mexico: School of American Research Press, 1985).

Taylor, William B. *Magistrates of the Sacred: Priests and Parishioners in Eighteenth-Century Mexico* (Stanford, Calif: Stanford University Press, 1996).

Thorensen, Timothy. "A.L. Kroeber's The Theory of Culture: The Early Years." (PhD diss., University of Iowa, 1971).

———. "Kroeber and the Yurok, 1900-1908," in A. L. Kroeber, *Yurok Myths,* xix-xxvii.

Tisdale, Shelby Jo-Anne. "Cocopah Identity and Cultural Survival: Indian Gaming and the Political Ecology of the Lower Colorado River Delta, 1850-1996." (Ph.D. diss., University of Arizona, 1997).

Underhill, Ruth. *The Autobiography of a Papago Woman.* American Anthropological Association, Memoirs. No. 46 (Menasha, Wisconsin: The American Anthropological Association ,1936).

———. *Singing for Power. The Song Magic of the Papago Indians of Southern Arizona.* (Berkeley, California: University of California Press, 1938).

Vigouroux, Cécile B. "Trans-scription as a Social Activity." *Ethnography* 8, no.1 (2007): 61-97.

———. " 'The Smuggling of La Francophonie': Francophone Africans in Anglophone Cape Town." *Language in Society* 37 (2008): 415–434.

———. "The Making of a Scription: A Case Study on Authority and Authorship." *Text & Talk* 29, no. 5 (2009): 615–637.

Waterman, T.T. "Analysis of the Mission Indian Creation Story." *American Anthropologist* 11, no. 1 (January-March, 1909): 41-55.

―――. *The Religious Practices of the Diegueño.* University of California Publications in American Archaeology and Ethnology 8, no.6 (Berkeley, University of California Press, 1910). Reprinted in *The Early Ethnography of the Kumeyaay.* Classics in California Anthropology, Steven Shackley, ed. (Berkeley: Phoebe Hearst Museum of Anthropology, University of California, Berkeley, 2004)

White, Phillip M., and Stephen D. Fitt. *Bibliography of the Indians of San Diego County: The Kumeyaay, Diegueño, Luiseño, and Cupeno.* Native American Bibliography Series. No. 21 (Lanham, Maryland: Scarecrow Press, 1998).

White, Richard. *The Middle Ground: Indians, Empires, and Republics in the Great Lakes Region, 1650-1815* (Cambridge: Cambridge University Press, 1991).

―――. *The Roots of Dependency Subsistence, Environment, and Social Change Among the Choctaws, Pawnees, and Navajos* (Lincoln, Nebraska: University of Nebraska Press, 1998).

9 781243 799555